FALLEN LEAVES

Major Henry Livermore Abbott (1842–1864). *Courtesy Harvard Law Art Collection.*

FALLEN LEAVES

The Civil War Letters of

Major Henry Livermore Abbott

edited by

Robert Garth Scott

THE KENT STATE UNIVERSITY PRESS
Kent, Ohio, and London, England

© 1991 by The Kent State University Press, Kent, Ohio 44242
All rights reserved
Library of Congress Catalog Card Number 91–8019
ISBN 0–87338–440–7
Manufactured in the United States of America

Second printing, 1992

Library of Congress Cataloging–in–Publication Data

Fallen leaves : the Civil War letters of Major Henry Livermore Abbott
/ edited by Robert Garth Scott.
    p.   cm.
Includes bibliographical references and index.
ISBN 0–87338–440–7 (alk.)∞
1. Abbott, Henry Livermore, 1842–1864—Correspondence. 2. United
States. Army. Massachusetts Infantry Regiment, 20th (1861–1865)—
Biography. 3. United States—History—Civil War, 1861–1865—
Regimental histories. 4. Massachusetts—History—Civil War,
1861–1865—Regimental histories. 5. Soldiers—Massachusetts—
Correspondence. I. Scott, Robert Garth, 1957–
E513.5 20th.F35   1991
973.7'444—dc20
                                                        91–8019

British Library Cataloging-in-Publication data are available.

To my wife, Karen, for her undying support

Those fallen leaves that keep their green,
The noble letters of the dead . . .
                    —Henry Livermore Abbott

CONTENTS

ILLUSTRATIONS

ILLUSTRATIONS

22 Maj. Gen. Ambrose Burnside 153
23 George N. Macy 157
24 Maj. Gen. Joseph Hooker 171
25 Maj. Gen. John Sedgwick 177
26 Col. Paul J. Revere 180
27 First page of Abbott's letter on the Battle
of Gettysburg 185
28 Lt. Henry Ropes 187
29 Maj. Gen. George G. Meade 190
30 Capt. Oliver Wendell Holmes, Jr. 195
31 Capt. Herbert Mason and Capt. Henry
L. Patten 200
32 Surgeon Nathan Hayward 204
33 Lt. Fletcher Abbott, 2d Mass. 214
34 Henry L. Abbott 222
35 Grave of Maj. Henry L. Abbott, Lowell, Mass. 256

ACKNOWLEDGMENTS

Throughout the six years I spent working on *Fallen Leaves*, I was assisted by numerous people and institutions, without whose help this book would not have been possible. First and foremost, I must thank the Houghton Library of Harvard University, which graciously granted me permission to edit and publish Abbott's letters in their entirety. Ms. Elizabeth Ann Falsey and the staff of the manuscripts department at Houghton kindly photocopied the letters, enabling me to do the majority of my work at home. The Harvard University Archives and the Harvard Law School Library also rendered valuable assistance.

No lesser amount of thanks is due my wife, Karen, and my daughters, Kristen and Rachel, for providing me with the time to work on the book. They, along with my wife's parents, Ron and Carol Carlson, accompanied me on a trip to Lowell, Massachusetts, where Ron was able to take the photo of Abbott's gravesite that appears in this book. Ron, with an artist's eye and an engineer's skill, also offered valuable technical assistance in preparing the map for the book. Ron, Karen, and my parents, Robert P. and Gail Scott, were helpful in reading and commenting on the manuscript. To each of them I am eternally grateful.

Mr. Thomas Rice of the University of Illinois was of immense help in directing me toward some important sources, as well as providing me with photocopies of information he had obtained while doing research for his article "The Bright and Particular Star," which appeared in the May 1987 issue of *Civil War Times Illustrated*. I must also acknowledge the services of Mr. James E. Fahey, curator of the Massachusetts Military Historical Society Archives in Natick, Massachusetts. Any historian doing work even remotely connected to Massachusetts's role in the Civil War would do well to contact Mr. Fahey.

Of course, I would be remiss if I did not thank Dr. John T. Hubbell, director of the Kent State University Press, for agreeing to publish my book. Senior editor Julia J. Morton, Linda Cuckovich, and the rest of the staff at Kent State were also of immense help, as was my copy-editor, Joanna Hildebrand, who did a marvelous job of polishing the text.

The following organizations also rendered invaluable help: The Library of Congress; the National Archives; the United States Military History Institute; the Massachusetts State Archives; the Massachusetts Historical Society; the Boston Public Library; the Nantucket Historical Association; the Bostonian Society; the Samuel S. Pollard Memorial Library of Lowell, Massachusetts; the Boston Athenaeum Library; the Commonwealth of Massachusetts Office of the Secretary of State; the State Library of Michigan; the Flint Public Library; and finally, the McFarlen Public Library in my hometown of Grand Blanc, Michigan. To all of the above I am forever indebted.

INTRODUCTION

A PORTRAIT OF GALLANTRY

> He steered unquestioning nor turning back,
> Into the darkness and the unknown sea;
> He vanished in the starless night, and we
> Saw but the shining of his luminous wake.
> —Oliver Wendell Holmes, Jr.

He was, without question, the most widely known, most highly respected officer of his rank ever to serve in the Army of the Potomac. To private soldiers and general officers alike, Henry Livermore Abbott, or "Little" Abbott as he was known to his friends, was the epitome of courage. General John Sedgwick, who had taken a particular liking to Abbott, declared him "a wonderfully good soldier," and thought him to be "a bright, particular star." In a like manner, the superb General Winfield Scott Hancock wrote that "his reputation was built upon a solid foundation, and the closest scrutiny could not diminish it."[1] But it was Abbott's closest friend, Oliver Wendell Holmes, Jr., a fellow officer in the 20th Massachusetts and a future associate justice of the U.S. Supreme Court, who best summed up his soldierly abilities: "In action he was sublime."[2]

Born January 21, 1842, in Lowell, Massachusetts, Henry was third among the eleven children born to Josiah Gardner Abbott and his wife Caroline. The Abbotts were a rather wealthy, politically minded family. Henry's father, a graduate of Harvard University and one of the state's most successful attorneys, had devoted much of his life to public service and was a prominent figure in the Northern Democratic party. At various times throughout his political career, Josiah had been elected to the offices of county judge, state representative, state senator, and finally, in 1876, he won a seat in the U.S. House of Representatives. Henry's mother, the former Caroline Livermore of Boston, also hailed from a political background, as her

[1]Thomas H. Wentworth, ed., *Harvard Memorial Biographies* (Cambridge: Sever and Francis, 1866), 2:106–7; Lt. Col. George A. Bruce, *The Twentieth Regiment of Massachusetts Volunteer Infantry 1861–1865* (Boston: Houghton, Mifflin and Co., 1906), 357.

[2]Mark De Wolfe Howe, ed., *Touched with Fire: Civil War Letters and Diary of Oliver Wendell Holmes, Jr.* (Cambridge, Mass: Harvard University Press, 1946), 40–41 n. 5.

father was Congressman Edward St. Loe Livermore. Moreover, both Josiah and Caroline were directly descended from officers who served in the Continental Army during the Revolutionary War. Clearly, the Abbotts belonged to that portion of society known as the "Boston Aristocracy," though they did not actually reside in that city until 1861.[3]

Henry was a studious boy who excelled in scholastics and enjoyed reading adventure novels in his spare time. In the fall of 1856, at the unusually early age of fourteen, he, along with his older brother Edward, enrolled in the freshman class at Harvard. There, Henry and Ned (as Edward was known to his family) roomed together at a private boardinghouse near campus. The accommodations were "by general consent, the most handsomely furnished and best situated rooms in Cambridge." Nineteenth-century Harvard was a rather formal, puritanical institution whose goal was not merely to educate its students but to make "gentlemen" of them as well. For example, apart from their usual studies and recitations, students were required to attend morning chapel throughout the week and regular worship services on Sunday. Simply stated, Henry found life at Harvard to be "irksome."

Many students rebelled under this oppressive atmosphere, and Henry was no exception. During his four years at Harvard, he was repeatedly admonished for "neglect at mathematics," "indecorum at prayers," and "tardiness at recitations." He was twice suspended: once for "visiting sundry freshmen at a late hour . . . for the purpose of annoying them," and again for "throwing articles from a window of a college building."[4] In spite of his failure to always abide by college rules, Henry nevertheless managed to keep his head above water scholastically; in 1860 he and Ned graduated in the middle of their class. That summer found them back in Lowell studying law in their father's office. But as the crisis between North and South rapidly came to a head, they were forced to contemplate the course they would take in the impending conflict.

[3]Much of the biographical information on Henry Abbott that is used in this sketch is from Francis Winthrop Palfrey, In Memoriam: Henry L. Abbott (Boston: Privately printed, 1864). For information on Josiah Gardner Abbott, see Illustrated History of Lowell and Vicinity (Lowell, Mass.: Courier-Citizen Co., 1897), 741–43, and Charles Cowley, LL.D., Memoir of the Hon. Josiah Gardner Abbott, LL.D. (Boston: Little, Brown & Co., 1892), 21.

[4]Henry L. Abbott to his aunt, November 1856, Henry Livermore Abbott Letters, Houghton Library Collection, Harvard University; Harvard Faculty Records, 1855–1860 15:135, 169, 470.

Soon after the bombardment of Fort Sumter in April 1861 and President Abraham Lincoln's subsequent call for troops, it seemed as if all the young men of Lowell were enlisting. Edward immediately dropped his studies and, with the aid of his father, obtained a captaincy in the 2d Massachusetts Infantry. In a like manner, Henry's younger brother, Fletcher, was commissioned second lieutenant in the same regiment.

Henry, however, was not swept up by the patriotic fervor that had consumed Ned, Fletcher, and the rest of Lowell. Indeed, he seems to have questioned his own courage and confessed to being "constitutionally timid."[5] Nevertheless, in spite of his fears, and feeling somewhat intimidated by Ned and Fletch, Henry decided that he must also do something to show his support for the Union. Therefore, in early May 1861 he and his friend Holmes decided to sample military life by enlisting for a month's service in the Fourth Battalion, Massachusetts Volunteer Militia, then serving at Fort Independence in Boston Harbor.

Holmes, however, soon left the militia to accept a lieutenancy in the 20th Massachusetts. After several more of Abbott's companions left camp to become officers in the army, Henry decided that he too must try for a commission. "My tastes are not warlike like Ned and Fletcher's, but literary & domestic," he wrote his father. "I can think of nothing more odious than the thought of leaving home & profession for the camp. . . . But now that I have once begun, the prospect of backing out without doing any thing is still more odious. I can't stand it. I should be ashamed of myself forever if I didn't do something now."[6]

Judge Abbott was at first opposed to Henry's idea of entering the service, feeling that "two are enough to be shot out of one family."[7] Henry, however, remained adamant and soon convinced his father to help him out. Finally, on July 10, 1861, Abbott was commissioned second lieutenant in Company I of the 20th Massachusetts, then forming at Readville.[8]

The 20th—also known as the "Harvard Regiment" because so many of its officers were graduates of the college—differed from most

[5]Henry L. Abbott to his father, May 1861.
[6]Ibid.
[7]William Greene Roelker, "The Abbotts of Lowell, Massachusetts in the Civil War" (Lowell, Mass.: Lowell Historical Society, 1941), 4.
[8]Bruce, Twentieth Massachusetts, 1–2. Other information concerning Abbott's dates of commission, etc., was obtained from his service record at the National Archives.

other regiments in that most of its troops had not been recruited from any particular county or region of the state. The only exception was Abbott's Company I, which was largely composed of sailors and fishermen from Nantucket Island. The 20th was also fortunate to have as its commander Colonel William Raymond Lee, a professional soldier who had attended the U.S. Military Academy at West Point. Unlike most other regiments which, at this early stage of the war, were led by inexperienced businessmen and politicians, the 20th would benefit immensely from Lee's military experience and organizational abilities as it strove to get itself into fighting trim.

While in camp at Readville, Henry first attracted the attention of his superiors by his rapid progress in learning his duties and the diligent manner in which he carried them out. In early September the regiment was sent to Washington, and on the twelfth of that month it at last took the field, marching to Poolesville, Maryland, where it joined other units in General Charles P. Stone's Corps of Observation encamped on the Potomac River. The day following its arrival at Poolesville, much to Henry's surprise, the 20th was visited by the 2d Massachusetts, which was encamped just outside of town. This, of course, gave Henry and his brothers an opportunity for a lengthy chat, during which Edward made some rather critical observations of the 20th. "The officers," he wrote, "are all green and appear as I have no doubt we appeared when we first came on thinking a fight was going to take place every five minutes. They actually believed that they were going to march to meet 30,000 men that very night."[9]

Indeed, the 20th was eager for a fight, Henry included. "I have always wanted to have a speedy engagement in order to try myself," he confessed, adding that "we shall be awfully indignant if they get through a battle without us."[10] As it happened, Abbott's wish was soon granted. On October 21, 1861, the 20th, along with other elements of Stone's command, was ordered to cross the Potomac for the purpose of making a "slight demonstration" toward the town of Leesburg. The resulting engagement, commonly referred to as the Battle of Ball's Bluff, was a relatively minor action of the Civil War, but it cut the 20th to pieces.

Crossing the river in pontoon boats near Edward's Ferry, elements of the 20th, including Abbott's Company I, scaled the steep bluff on the opposite shore and, upon reaching the crest, cautiously advanced

[9]Mark De Wolfe Howe, *Justice Oliver Wendell Holmes, Vol. 1: The Shaping Years, 1841–1870* (Cambridge: Belknap Press of Harvard University, 1957), 91.
[10]H. L. Abbott to his father, Sept. 11, 1861.

through the woods to the edge of a large clearing. There, subjected to a murderous fire from Confederates concealed in the woods at the opposite end of the field, the 20th rapidly formed a line of battle alongside other Federal regiments which were already engaged. The casualties began to mount quickly, and Abbott's friend Holmes was one of the first to fall, critically wounded with a bullet in the chest.

With the river and the bluff at their backs, it was evident that the Union troops were in a rather precarious situation. Moreover, the Confederates whom they faced were veterans of a sort, having previously fought at Bull Run, whereas the Yankee troops, many of whom had just been issued their muskets, were green, almost to a man. To make matters worse, the lack of an adequate number of boats meant that reinforcement would be slow in coming, and a rapid and orderly retreat was almost an impossibility.

In spite of these handicaps, the men of the 20th put up a valiant defense and held their ground as best they could. The Rebels, however, fired low and accurately, and the men of Company I were ordered to lie down in order to escape the shower of lead. Little Abbott, however, seemed oblivious to the hail of bullets as he and his former classmate and company commander, Captain William F. Bartlett, remained erect, walking calmly among their men in an effort to keep them more "self-possessed." Bartlett wrote in a letter to his mother four days after the battle: "I kept speaking to Little [Abbott], surprised that he was not hit amongst the rain of bullets. . . . I said two or three times, 'Why Lit., aren't you hit yet?' I remember [First Lieutenant George] Macy was lying where the grass was turned up, and I 'roughed' him for getting his coat so awfully dirty. Lit. was as cool and brave as I knew he would be."[11]

Bravery alone, of course, could not keep the Johnnies at bay for very long, and as the gray-clad line surged forward through the battle smoke, it steadily forced the Federals back toward the edge of the bluff. Finally, with no more ground to give, and with Confederates converging on both front and flanks, the Union line snapped.

By this time all sense of order had vanished, and with it went the last bit of Federal resistance. Hundreds of panic-stricken Yankees were either shot or captured as they huddled near the edge of the bluff, while many others leaped and tumbled over the brink to the jutting rocks below. Those who managed to survive the fall then made a wild rush for the Potomac striving to reach the safety of the opposite bank. Many of these men drowned while attempting to swim the

[11]Howe, *Justice Holmes* 1:96.

river. Others met a similar fate when they crowded into the few available pontoon boats, capsizing the overloaded boats in midstream. And there were also those men who fell victim to enemy bullets as Rebel troops perched atop the bluff continued to pour volley after volley into the mass of helpless Yankees crowding the muddy bank below.

Even in the midst of this stampede, however, there was a handful of Union officers who managed to keep their wits, and Abbott and Bartlett were among them. Quietly slipping away from the battleground through the wooded Virginia twilight, the two young officers led the remnants of their command down the bluff and cautiously made their way upriver to the vicinity of Smart's Mill. There, with darkness enveloping them and expecting to be taken prisoner at any moment, they managed to resurrect a small, moss-covered rowboat from the bottom of the mill's pond. Fortunately the craft was still seaworthy, and the men proceeded to cross the river in groups of five until the entire command was safely in Federal territory.[12]

Two days after the battle, the wounded were transferred by canal boat to hospitals in Washington, where Henry's brother Edward was on leave. Distressed over rumors regarding the destruction of the 20th, and uncertain about his brother's fate, Edward hastily penned a letter to his father expressing his fears and his affection for Henry:

> I am fearfully worried about Henry and the Twentieth. The papers said to-night that the wounded would be brought in by canal-boat, and for the last half-hour I have been riding in a hack vainly endeavoring to find whether they have come or not. . . . What if anything should have happened to Henry! The thought drives me almost crazy. He may be here in the city and I not looking after him. I could never forgive myself if he were. He ought not to have gone to the war. If he did go, he should have gone with me. . . . I never felt so nervous before in my life.[13]

Henry, of course, was safe, as Ned would soon find out, but the rumors about the 20th were only slightly exaggerated. Out of nearly 300 men engaged in the fight, 87 had either been killed or wounded, while 111 men—including Colonel Lee—had been captured.[14]

Naturally, these losses, particularly that of Colonel Lee, severely dampened the regiment's morale. Not only had it been defeated in

[12]Kim Bernard Holien, *Battle at Ball's Bluff* (Alexandria, Va.: Moss Publications, 1985), 75–76.
[13]Edward G. Abbott to his father, Oct. 24, 1861.
[14]Bruce, *Twentieth Massachusetts*, 59–61.

its first encounter with the enemy, but it had felt for the first time the stinging pain of combat casualties. Indeed, nearly every member of the regiment had lost either a tentmate or a boyhood friend. Nevertheless, the 20th had at last seen action and had performed its part well. Even while other commands dissolved all around them, the 20th faced the enemy and was one of the last units to abandon the field.

Abbott, too, took pride in the accomplishments of his men. Moreover, the battle gave him a fair opportunity to learn something about himself. "You know I told you that I didn't believe I was physically brave," he wrote his father. "In fact I was pretty sure I should be frightened on the field of battle. . . . The fact is, however, that . . . I was very much surprised to find that I wasn't frightened at all."[15]

For the next four and a half months, the regiment remained in its camp near Poolesville to recover from its wounds and patrol the muddy banks of the Potomac. Here, amidst the drudgery of drills and inspections, new recruits arrived almost daily to fill the 20th's decimated ranks. A number of officers received promotions in order to fill the vacancies created by the casualties of Ball's Bluff. Accordingly, on November 25, 1861, Abbott was mustered in as first lieutenant and made acting commander of Company I, a move which pleased both Abbott and his men immensely.

In late March 1862, the monotony of camp life finally came to an end as the 20th was ordered to break camp and report to Washington, D.C. Shortly after arriving in the nation's capital, the regiment was formally incorporated into the newly formed Second Corps of Major General George B. McClellan's Army of the Potomac, and on March 28 it boarded a transport ship bound for Fortress Monroe, Virginia.

There, at the tip of the peninsula between the York and James rivers, McClellan concentrated his army of one-hundred-thousand-plus men in hopes of taking the Confederate capital of Richmond by the backdoor. Unfortunately, the enterprising Confederate general John B. Magruder had supervised the construction of an immense line of earthworks stretching from Yorktown to the James River; although he had barely twelve thousand troops to man these entrenchments, Magruder nevertheless managed to halt the Union advance long enough for Confederate reinforcements to arrive.

McClellan had been duped. A bit of showmanship on Magruder's part had convinced the Federal commander that he faced the bulk of the Confederate army, "probably not less than one hundred thousand

[15]H. L. Abbott to his father, Nov. 7, 1861.

7

men, and possibly more."[16] Consequently, McClellan decided that the only way out was to take Yorktown by siege. Thus, for the next four weeks the men of the 20th Massachusetts waited patiently in camp—occasionally skirmishing with rebel pickets in the surrounding woods—while McClellan brought up the heavy artillery.

The weather was frightful. The April showers came down almost incessantly; when Abbott and his men were not on picket duty, they could be found huddling around their campfires trying to keep dry. Worse yet was the fact that, through some oversight by the brigade quartermaster, the regiment had not been issued its shelter tents and, for nearly a week, the men were "sleeping & living in mud puddles."[17] Yet even amidst these hardships morale remained high. The men had a boundless faith in McClellan, as well as in their regimental officers, and they expected to emerge from the campaign victorious. Moreover, the spirit of the 20th soared even higher when the beloved Colonel Lee rejoined the regiment after being released from Libby Prison in an exchange of prisoners.

In the end, the long-awaited siege of Yorktown never came off. The Confederates evacuated the town just one day before the big Yankee guns were scheduled to begin their bombardment. When the Federals entered the town on the morning of May 4, there was not a Rebel in sight. The victory had been a hollow one.

After the fall of Yorktown, the 20th, together with the rest of McClellan's army, advanced up the neck of the Peninsula pursuing the Confederate rear guard to the gates of Richmond. Upon reaching the Confederate capital, General Joseph E. Johnston, commanding the Rebel forces, moved his army into the safety of the city's outer defenses while McClellan, once again, made preparations for a siege. Johnston, however, was not about to sit idly by and watch McClellan move his siege guns into place. Therefore, on May 31, the Confederates came out of their entrenchments and struck that portion of the Federal forces which were encamped near the village of Fair Oaks. It was here that Abbott fought his first major action of the campaign.

After crossing the rain-swollen Chickahominy River, which divided the Union forces, Abbott and the 20th proceeded to cut their way through the marshy thickets eagerly and steadily pressing toward

[16]*Military Historical Society of Massachusetts Papers*, vol. 1, *The Peninsular Campaign of 1862* (Boston: James R. Osgood and Co., 1881), 36. See also Stephen W. Sears, *George B. McClellan: The Young Napoleon* (New York: Ticknor & Fields, 1988), 177–78.

[17]H. L. Abbott to his mother, Apr. 9, 1862.

the scene of action. Having finally reached the smoke-enshrouded field, the regiment was rushed into line along the crest of a commanding hill, where it then unleashed a staggering volley into a screaming pack of Rebels charging up the slope. The long hours spent drilling and instructing his men had at last paid off; Henry Abbott proudly recorded that the men of Company I "stood up straight in their places, firing low & the most tremendous volleys, no man dodging or kneeling. Our men showed wonderful discipline, firing & ceasing to fire just as they were ordered."[18]

That night the men of the 20th bivouacked where the fighting had ended, sleeping "on marshy ground, without blankets . . . every body wet through to his feet and trousers." They were bone tired but happy with the performance they had given during the day's engagement. The next day, however, as the battle drew to a close, the 20th remained out of action while occupying an unengaged portion of the Union line. Abbott later expressed his disappointment at being left out of the conflict, confessing, "I had much rather fight all day, any time."[19]

The 20th suffered relatively few casualties at the Battle of Fair Oaks (about 28 killed and wounded out of approximately 350 engaged), although a few other Federal regiments were not so fortunate. Nevertheless, the Yankee troops managed to keep the Rebels at bay, finally forcing them to return to the Richmond defenses. But the ten days immediately following the Battle of Fair Oaks were nearly as hard on the regiment as the actual fighting had been. Soaked with rain and provided with little food and no shelter, Abbott and his men skirmished with the Rebels by day and slept in the mud at night. After finally being relieved of outpost duty on June 11, the 20th went into camp on higher ground about a mile to the rear. For the first time in nearly two weeks, the men were able to take a bath and wash their clothes, and the regiment settled into what Abbott termed "an awful life of inglorious ease & inaction."[20]

The regiment's two-week rest period abruptly ended on June 25 with the engagement at King's School House on the outskirts of Richmond. Although the 20th did not take an active part in that battle, the action nevertheless marked the beginning of a series of engagements known collectively as the Seven Days. For the first time

[18]H. L. Abbott to his father, June 6, 1862.
[19]Ibid.
[20]Ibid.; Bruce, *Twentieth Massachusetts*, 100–101; H. L. Abbott to his mother, June 24, 1862.

during the war, the men of McClellan's army were to be subjected to the skill and daring of General Robert E. Lee, who had been commanding the Army of Northern Virginia since the wounding of Johnston at Fair Oaks. The association was to become a familiar one.

After leaving a token force to guard the approaches to Richmond, General Lee marched with the bulk of his forces to the north side of the Chickahominy and, on June 26, drove in a line of Union outposts stationed near Mechanicsville. The following day, at the Battle of Gaines' Mill, the Confederates smashed the exposed right flank of McClellan's army forcing it to withdraw to the south side of the river. This event compelled the Federal commander to abandon his position in front of Richmond. On June 28 McClellan began to withdraw his forces to the James River and the protection of Union gunboats.

Abbott and the 20th took part in nearly every rear-guard action during the retreat to the James, and they fought admirably. On June 29, the regiment participated in what amounted to heavy skirmishing at Allen's Farm and Savage's Station incurring negligible casualties. At the Battle of Glendale on the following day, however, their losses were staggering. It was during this engagement, as the 20th advanced under a galling fire across an open field, that Abbott was severely wounded when a bullet tore into his right arm just above the elbow. Although the pain was intense, Abbott refused to leave the field and remained with his command until after the Battle of Malvern Hill on July 1.[21]

After recuperating for a month at his family's new home in Boston, Henry rejoined the army at its encampment on the James River. His stay there, however, was destined to be a short one; for while McClellan regrouped his army and wasted time on the banks of the James, Lee promptly seized the initiative by dispatching nearly half his force into northern Virginia preparatory to a general movement by the rest of the army. The objective of this detachment, commanded by General Thomas J. "Stonewall" Jackson, was to threaten Washington and to harass the Union forces under General John Pope, then gathering near Warrenton, Virginia. Lee could hardly have realized how completely Jackson would fulfill those goals.

In order to check the advance of the Confederate army, President Lincoln ordered McClellan to abandon the Peninsula and report at

[21]Palfrey, In Memoriam, 11.

once to Washington. Thus, by August 16 the Army of the Potomac had struck its tents and was marching for Newport News on the Virginia coast. There the men would board transports and sail back up the Potomac to Alexandria. Spirits sagged as the troops plodded along the dusty roads back to the point where the campaign had originated. They were abandoning the territory that many of their comrades had fought and died for and were returning to the North, just as if the battles on the Peninsula had never been fought. Much had been sacrificed, but nothing had been gained.

For Abbott in particular, the march had been a trying one. The ranks had been swept by rumors that Jackson had soundly defeated General Nathaniel P. Banks's forces at Cedar Mountain on August 9, and the 2d Massachusetts was said to have suffered heavily. Henry, quite naturally, was anxious about the fate of his brothers; but he heard nothing until August 20, when he received a distressing letter from home. Captain Edward Gardner Abbott, Henry's beloved brother Ned, had been killed in action at the head of his command. His body, which had been stripped by Confederate soldiers in search of clothing, had been recovered after the battle and shipped home.[22]

The news hit Henry "with terrible force." He later wrote in an emotional letter to his father, "I could hardly believe it. . . . I thought Ned would surely come through all right. I wish to God I could have seen him on the battlefield." There was little time for mourning, however; although he found it difficult to "keep up appearances at first," Henry deemed it necessary "to force cheerfulness before the men."[23] The regiment had some rough days ahead of it, and Abbott realized that every officer must do his utmost to instill confidence in his command.

On August 25, after spending three leisurely days on the Virginia coast, the regiment embarked on the crowded transport steamer *Collins* and arrived in Alexandria early the next morning. For the next nine days, Abbott and his men were continually on the move as they patrolled the vicinity of Fairfax Court House. During one stretch the men marched a total of sixty miles in forty-eight hours "with scanty rations & no sleep."[24] Yet the 20th's most arduous duty during this period came on September 2 when it covered the retreat of Pope's dejected army, recently defeated at the Second Battle of

[22]Roelker, "The Abbotts of Lowell," 9.
[23]H. L. Abbott to his father, Aug. 24[?], 1862, Sept. 3, 1862.
[24]H. L. Abbott to his father, Sept. 3, 1862.

Bull Run. All throughout the day, the regiment waited behind muddy breastworks fending off the enemy's pursuing cavalry, while the remnants of Pope's demoralized forces trudged back to the Washington defenses in the pouring rain. When the 20th finally marched back to Alexandria, being the last Federal unit to leave the field, it was greeted by none other than McClellan himself, who praised the manner in which the regiment had guarded the Union rear.

As a result of Pope's disastrous defeat at Second Bull Run, the Federal forces were in a state of disarray. Pope had been fired, and his troops were to be merged with those of the Army of the Potomac—a reorganization that would take some time to complete. Conversely, the mood in the Confederate camps had reached a new height. That fact, combined with the confusion that permeated the Federal capital, convinced Lee that it was an opportune time to launch an invasion of the North. By September 3 the Confederates were on the road to Maryland.

Upon learning of Lee's intention to cross the Potomac, McClellan moved promptly to check the Rebel invasion. By September 7, the bulk of the Union army was snaking its way northward from Washington, and the Maryland campaign had thus begun. Although the 20th was destined to take an active role in the campaign, Abbott was not. Weeks of hard duty and exposure, combined with deep grief over his brother's death and the fact that he had not yet fully recovered from his Glendale wound, had taken their toll on the young soldier. Shortly after the regiment joined the army in pursuit of Lee, Henry was stricken with typhoid fever and was left in the care of the Union hospital at Frederick, Maryland. While Abbott was considerably displeased at having missed the battle of Antietam, he was nonetheless fortunate. The 20th had suffered fearfully in the battle. Lieutenant Colonel Francis Palfrey was so seriously wounded that he was never able to rejoin the regiment, and Wendell Holmes was wounded again when a minié ball struck him in the neck.

Immediately following the Federal victory at Antietam, Henry was joined at the hospital by his brother Fletcher, who was suffering from dysentery. Their stay in Frederick was a relatively short one, however, for as soon as Caroline Abbott learned of their condition she promptly set out for Maryland and took her boys home to recover. But by mid-November 1862, Abbott had completely recovered from his bout with typhoid and was anxious to return to duty. From Boston, Abbott, accompanied by Holmes, traveled by rail to Warrenton, Virginia, where the pair set out on foot in search of the Army of the Potomac. After a perilous march of nearly thirty-five miles, the two young officers finally found the Union forces en-camped near Falmouth, on the Rappahannock River just opposite the town of Fredericksburg.

Upon his return, Abbott, now a captain, was immediately struck by the sullen mood that hung over the army. Abbott learned that just twelve days before, General McClellan—having failed to launch an aggressive pursuit of the Confederates after the Battle of Antietam—had been relieved as commanding general of the army. The troops would sorely miss him. Succeeding McClellan was General Ambrose E. Burnside, a West Point-trained soldier who, unfortunately, knew noth-ing about commanding an army, as he openly admitted. Unwilling to undertake the somewhat complicated strategy that McClellan had devised for pursuing Lee, Burnside chose instead to move the army to Falmouth where he would cross the Rappahannock, capture Fredericksburg, and move south on the road to Richmond before Lee fully realized what was happening. Incredibly, Burnside's plan went remarkably well in its initial stages. The Federals had reached Falmouth well ahead of the enemy, the nearest Confederates being a full two days' march away at Culpeper Court House.

It was at this point, however, that things began to go wrong for the hapless Burnside. Because his pontoon trains had not yet arrived, the Federal commander postponed the river crossing, although he could have easily crossed at any one of a number of shallow fords upstream. The Confederates, of course, were not long in discovering their pre-dicament, and by November 21 they had begun to occupy Marye's Heights, just west of Fredericksburg, and the line of hills that extended to the south. Rather than alter his plan, Burnside insisted on cross-ing the Rappahannock at Falmouth and attacking the Confederates—now firmly entrenched on the heights—head-on. The resulting battle was the most disheartening defeat the Union forces would experience, and it was one in which the 20th Massachusetts suffered a higher percentage of casualties than any other regiment in the army.[25]

The predawn twilight of December 11, 1862, revealed a dense fog slowly rising from the Rappahannock and enshrouding the town of Fredericksburg. Under cover of this dank mist, Federal engineers labored vigorously along the overgrown bank in an attempt to bridge the river. Their efforts, however, were stiffly resisted. Rebel

[25]Lt. Col. William F. Fox, *Regimental Losses in the American Civil War, 1861–1865* (Albany: Albany Publishing Co., 1889), 154. Of the nearly two thousand regiments that served in the Civil War, the 20th Mass. was fifth among those units which suffered the most in killed and wounded.

sharpshooters stationed in Fredericksburg had been alerted by the sound of hammering and immediately began to fire into the fog. Considering the fact that the Confederates could not quite see their targets, the effect of their fire was remarkable. Four times the un-armed engineers were driven from their work, and fifty of them were killed. Yankee artillery opened on the town in an effort to dislodge the Rebels, but it was to no avail.

By noon the fog had lifted, giving the Confederates a clear target, and with the bridges only half finished it was obvious that another means would have to be found to cross the river. After some delib-eration, it was determined that the only chance the Federals had of capturing the town was to send a detachment of infantry over in pontoon boats under cover of a heavy and sustained artillery bar-rage. Colonel Norman J. Hall, then commanding the brigade to which the 20th belonged, was present when that decision was made and wasted no time in offering his men for the hazardous assignment.

Throughout most of the day, the 20th had been waiting in a field near the Lacy house, with the officers lounging on a pile of wood watching a nearby battery lob shells into the town. At about 4:00 P.M., Hall rode up and gave the regiment its orders, explaining that it was to follow the 7th Michigan and the 19th Massachusetts across in the pon-toons. A few moments later the sound of sharp firing mixed with wild cheering swept up the bank to announce that the crossing had begun. With that, the 20th filed out onto the road and marched down to the river. Due to the absence of Colonel Lee, whose age would soon oblige him to retire from active service, Captain Macy would serve as acting colonel during the battle, with Abbott acting as major.[26]

The scene that greeted the 20th at the riverbank was one of dev-astation. Dead and wounded soldiers lined the bank, having been struck down before they could climb into the boats. Nevertheless, the 7th Michigan had completed its crossing and had established a foothold on the south side of Fauquier Street, which led westward from the Rappahannock. The 19th Massachusetts then stormed ashore and seized some houses on the north side of the street.

Then it was the 20th's turn. Jumping into the boats, the Bay Staters grabbed the oars, pulled in earnest for the opposite shore, and glided across the water within easy range of Rebel muskets. Bul-

[26]The Lacy house, on Stafford Heights opposite Fredericksburg, served as head-quarters for Gen. Edwin Sumner (commanding the Right Grand Division in Burnside's army) during the battle; Henry Ropes to John Codman Ropes, Dec. 18, 1862, Henry Ropes Letters, Boston Public Library. Ropes's letter offers the most detailed account of the 20th's action of Dec. 11. See also Bruce, *Twentieth Massachusetts*, 182–222.

lets plopped into the water like huge raindrops; despite the heavy fire, only a few men had been hit by the time the boats reached the other side of the river. After wading ashore, the 20th re-formed along the water's edge and exchanged shots with the Confederates, who were soon obliged to fall back to Caroline Street. Their withdrawal allowed the Federal engineers to complete the bridges. When that task was finished, the 20th was ordered to advance up the street following the skirmishers of the 7th Michigan.

As the men swung into column, with Abbott's company taking the lead, the regiment advanced a short distance up the street until it was alongside the 7th, who occupied a house and an alleyway on the left. In compliance with his orders, Macy called over to them and signaled the men to go ahead; but, as Lieutenant Henry Ropes remembered it, the Michigan regiment would not budge:

> Capt. Hunt, their commanding officer, was there and he hesitated and refused. Macy was obliged to halt and urged him to go forward. Capt. Hunt still refused, saying he had no orders, and Macy, much irritated, told him his orders, which were very plain, to go forward and follow the 7th. Orders came from the rear to press on, Hunt still hanging back, saying the Rebels were there in force and "no man could live beyond that corner" or some such words. Macy was of course terribly angry and turned off, saying "go to hell with your regiment then," or something like that, and gave the order to advance.[27]

Though angered at Hunt's refusal to obey orders, Captain Macy quickly regained his composure, turned to Abbott, and quietly said, "Mr. Abbott, you will take the first platoon forward." At that, Abbott drew his sword, turned to face his men, and shouted, "1st platoon, forward—March!"[28]

As the thirty-man unit neared the intersection of Caroline Street, it was caught in murderous crossfire from Confederates who, as one of Abbott's men recalled, "were concealed in every house and behind every fence."[29] A flurry of musketry rang out, echoing off the surrounding buildings; ten men—one-third of the platoon—dropped dead at Abbott's side.

[27]Henry Ropes to John Codman Ropes, Dec. 18, 1862. Excerpt published courtesy of the Trustees of the Boston Public Library.

[28]Howe, *Touched with Fire*, 90.

[29]Josiah F. Murphey, "Sketch of My Life in the Army During the Late War of the Rebellion, 1861–1865," unpublished manuscript in the collections of the Boston Public Library.

Although his first platoon had virtually vanished during the first few minutes of combat, Abbott himself remained unruffled. Quietly turning back to where the remainder of his company was waiting, he gave the order, "Second platoon, forward!" and once again led his men up the bullet-swept street. "The end was distant only a few seconds," Holmes later recounted, "but if you had seen him with his indifferent carriage, and sword swinging from his finger like a cane, you never would have suspected that he was doing more than conducting a company drill on the camp parade ground."[30] While Company I battled its way up Fauquier Street, the remainder of the regiment moved to its support, wheeling to the left and right down Caroline Street, taking heavy casualties but slowly forcing the Rebels back. Finally, as night drew on, other Union regiments arrived on the scene, and the Confederates were at last forced to abandon the town.

Covering the Rebel retreat that evening was a detachment of the 21st of Mississippi, which, oddly enough, was commanded by Abbott's friend and Harvard classmate, Lieutenant Lane Brandon. In some manner, Brandon had discovered during the course of the battle that the regiment he faced was the 20th Massachusetts and that its leading company was commanded by his old chum Henry Abbott. It was no longer just a question of states' rights vs. Union; the war, for this Confederate, had become personal. Brandon was not going to willingly yield ground to Abbott and his Yankees, and he determined to fight it out then and there. Thus, when orders came for his detachment to retire from the town, Brandon refused and instead launched a counterattack that temporarily repulsed Abbott's men. Urgent orders were again issued for Brandon to break off the fight, but the young lieutenant, angered at the prospect of abandoning the town to Abbott, still refused and eventually had to be placed under arrest before the Rebel withdrawal could be completed.[31]

With the street fighting finally at an end, Abbott led what was left of his exhausted command back through the body-strewn town to bivouac for the night near the riverbank. Of the sixty men Abbott had taken into combat, thirty had been killed or wounded. The remainder of the regiment suffered equally appalling losses with a total

[30]Howe, *Touched with Fire*, 40–41 n. 5.
[31]Douglas Southall Freeman, *Lee's Lieutenants* (New York: Charles Scribner's Sons, 1943), 2:338.

of 113 men either killed or wounded of the 335 who marched into battle.[32] But the Battle of Fredericksburg had just begun.

Two days following the capture of Fredericksburg, Burnside launched his main assault against Lee's army, which was firmly entrenched along a winding range of hills stretching roughly from Marye's Heights to Hamilton's Crossing, some seven miles to the southeast. It was the imposing earthworks along Marye's Heights, however, that would prove the most difficult obstacle for Burnside's forces to overcome. Rebel artillery lined the crest of the heights, and as each succeeding wave of Yankees surged forward, the booming guns virtually swept them from the field. Most of those who did manage to survive the murderous cannonade were quickly brought down by a raking fire of musketry unleashed by a line of Confederates safely ensconced behind a stone wall. Thus, when the battle smoke cleared, all that was visible was a field of Union soldiers, writhing and moaning in agony on the frozen ground.

As usual, Henry and the 20th found themselves in the thickest of the fight—occupying the extreme right flank of the Union line. Advancing over the brow of a hill, the 20th was immediately subjected to a horrifying enfilade of shot and shell, and the men began to drop. One bullet pierced the left eye of Abbott's second lieutenant and tentmate, Leander Alley, killing him instantly. Another struck Henry's scabbard, although Abbott himself escaped injury. During the few minutes the regiment was engaged, sixty men and three officers had been killed or wounded. These figures, combined with the casualties of December 11, brought the regiment's total losses to 168 men and eight officers out of the 335 officers and men who went into battle.[33] The Army of the Potomac as a whole numbered about 13,000 killed, missing, and wounded. This staggering waste of life, combined with the loss of the battle, brought troop morale to an all-time low. "The whole army is demoralized," wrote Abbott. "I firmly believe that . . . the men who ordered the crossing of the river are responsible to God for murder. I believe that Alley was just as much murdered as if he had been deliberately thrown into the river with a stone tied round his neck. . . . McClellan alone can save the army."[34]

[32]Howe, *Touched with Fire*, 90. The figures for the regiment's losses on Dec. 11 were obtained by deducting the figures for the regiment's losses on Dec. 13 (listed in Abbott's letter to his father, Dec. 14, 1862) from the unit's combined loss of 176 (as stated by Henry Ropes in his letter to John Codman Ropes, Dec. 20, 1862).

[33]Henry Ropes to John Codman Ropes, Dec. 20, 1862.

[34]H. L. Abbott to George Perry, Dec. 17, 1862; Abbott to his sister Carry, Dec. 21, 1862.

As a Democrat, however, Abbott did not think the generals were solely to blame for the Army's woes. The radical Republicans, he believed, had prompted Lincoln to cashier McClellan because of the general's political views, and they were also directing the war toward the abolition of slavery rather than toward the preservation of the Union. Although Abbott personally regarded slavery as an abhorrent institution and opposed its extension into the western territories, he nonetheless believed that the North's war effort should only be aimed at reestablishing the "Union as it was." Slavery was a doomed institution that would be extinguished soon enough without a war. Moreover, many other soldiers in the Army of the Potomac held similar views, as Henry indicated in a letter to his aunt shortly after the Emancipation Proclamation took effect in January 1863: "The president's proclamation is of course received with universal disgust, particularly the part which enjoins officers to see that it is carried out. You may be sure that we shan't see to any thing of the kind."[35]

Even as the men griped and complained and prayed for McClellan to return, President Lincoln was contemplating a change in the army's high command. After the infamous Mud March of January 1863, the ax finally fell. Burnside was relieved of command and the army was given to the hard-fighting, hard-drinking General Joe Hooker. Although the men had hoped that their beloved McClellan would resume command, Hooker was nevertheless regarded as an improvement over Burnside. During the early months of 1863, the Army of the Potomac, still in its camps opposite Fredericksburg, was reorganized and reoutfitted in preparation for the spring offensive. Tighter discipline, fresh fruits and vegetables in the camp kitchen, and a generous system of furloughs all served to substantially improve troop morale.

Henry's spirits also seemed to lift with the change in command and the overall improvement in the army.

In late March, however, Henry was dealt a crushing blow: Arthur Abbott, Henry's nine-year-old brother, died, succumbing to what was diagnosed as "the croup."[36] It was the second death in the Abbott family within eight months. Although Henry had been granted an immediate leave of absence, he was unable to make it home in time to see his brother laid to rest. After barely two weeks in Boston, Henry reluctantly, but dutifully, bid his family farewell and set out

[35]H. L. Abbott to his Aunt Lizzie, Jan. 10, 1863.
[36]Vital Records (1841–1890), Vol. 167, p. 139, in the Massachusetts Archives at Columbia Point.

once again for the front. John Perry, the 20th's new assistant surgeon, accompanied Abbott back to the regiment and later recalled the mood aboard ship:

> On the Sound boat I gave way, and I confess to behaving as I did when a child for the first time away from home. I cried as I did then,—all night long. I thought Harry Abbott in the berth above me was fast asleep, when suddenly he rolled over and looked down upon me. I felt for the moment thoroughly ashamed of myself, but he said nothing and settled back into his place, and then I heard him crying also. We had talked things over a bit, and I knew the poor fellow felt that he had seen his home for the last time, and that he had passed safely through so many battles he could hardly escape unscathed again.[37]

While Henry was understandably anxious about his chances of surviving another battle, he did not have to wait long in anticipation. On May 3, just over two weeks after his return, Abbott and the 20th, along with the rest of General John Sedgwick's left wing of the Federal army, took part in what has frequently been referred to as the Second Battle of Fredericksburg. While Hooker, with nearly eighty thousand men, was pinned down by the bulk of Lee's much smaller army near Chancellorsville (nine miles west of Fredericksburg), Sedgwick, with but a quarter of the total Union forces, was instructed to carry Marye's Heights and march at once to Hooker's relief.

Though bogged down initially, the sheer weight and momentum of Sedgwick's assault eventually carried the Heights, driving the Rebel defenders down the opposite slope. The 20th, on the far right of the line, suffered relatively few casualties in the attack with just two killed and thirteen wounded, a stark contrast to the butchering it received on the same ground the previous December.[38] And among the wounded, once again, was the indomitable Captain Holmes, who had been struck in the heel by a shell fragment. This was Holmes's third wound of the war and, while not a life-threatening one, it would nonetheless keep him out of action for the next eight months.

Immediately following the capture of Marye's Heights, and in compliance with Hooker's orders, Sedgwick marched with the bulk of his command to rescue "Fighting Joe" Hooker. The 20th, however, took no part in that expedition. Instead the regiment and the rest of General John Gibbon's division remained in Fredericksburg to

[37]Martha Derby Perry, comp. *Letters from a Surgeon of the Civil War* (Boston: Little, Brown and Co., 1906), 22.
[38]Bruce, *Twentieth Massachusetts*, 258.

guard Sedgwick's line of retreat. As it turned out, however, Sedgwick was soon compelled to find another point at which to recross the river. Late in the afternoon of May 3, his troops ran into a strong line of Rebels at Salem Church, four miles west of Fredericksburg. Outnumbered, and with the enemy converging on three sides, Sedgwick's troops battled desperately, barely escaping disaster by crossing the river at Banks' Ford on the night of May 4. Shortly after Sedgwick's withdrawal, Hooker too began to retire across the river, thus bringing the battle to an end.

The Yankees who marched back into the camps at Falmouth were about as dejected as men can get. Neither Burnside nor Hooker had been able to achieve any amount of success over Lee, and cries for McClellan once again began to rise from the ranks. "I am afraid we shall never lift our heads out of this terrible infamy," Abbott wrote his father, summing up the feelings of the entire army. "Whatever you think at home, papa, remember that our feeling here is only to call back McClellan, recruit, & *wipe out this disgrace.*"[39]

On June 3, 1863, elated by his recent success over Hooker, Robert E. Lee launched his second invasion of the North, withdrawing from his Fredericksburg entrenchments and heading for the river crossings on the upper Potomac. It was nearly two days later, however, before Hooker got wind of the Rebel movement; thus, the Army of the Potomac did not begin its pursuit of Lee until June 5. Yet even as the Union army began its northward trek, Hooker remained uncertain as to how he should go about intercepting Lee—or, for that matter, if he should even attempt to intercept him. At one point the Federal commander entertained thoughts of making an about-face and taking his army to Richmond, leaving Lee free to move on the Federal capital. This strategy, known as "swapping queens," was one which President Lincoln swiftly nixed. Moreover, convinced that Hooker was dragging his heels, newspapers throughout the North began calling for his removal. Indeed, Lincoln himself was becoming increasingly agitated and encouraged Fighting Joe to strike a blow—and to do it soon.

Finally, on June 27, feeling restrained by orders to keep his army on the inside track to cover both Washington and Harpers Ferry, Hooker offered to resign. With the Rebel host moving ever northward, and with the fate of the Union hanging in the balance, Lincoln was in no mood to argue. He promptly accepted Hooker's resignation and appointed General George Gordon Meade in his stead. Meade, how-

[39] H. L. Abbott to his father, May 5, 1863.

ever, had little time to familiarize himself with the intricacies of leading such an immense force into combat. On July 1, 1863, just three days after Meade assumed command, advance elements of the Army of the Potomac and the Army of Northern Virginia stumbled into one another on the outskirts of a sleepy little Pennsylvania village called Gettysburg, and the largest battle of the war had begun.

For the Federals, the first day of battle nearly ended in disaster. After seven hours of obstinate fighting, Union troops posted north and west of Gettysburg were driven back to the southern edge of town, where they established a new defensive position along the crest of a commanding line of hills. This new Federal line (shaped much like a huge inverted fishhook) faced westward and ran in a generally north-south direction.

Like most of Meade's army, the 20th Massachusetts did not reach the field until well after the first day's fighting had ended. On the morning of July 2, the regiment arose from its bivouac two miles south of town along the Taneytown Road, prepared a hearty breakfast, and marched to its assigned position on Cemetery Ridge, smack in the center of the Union position. There, under the direction of its newly appointed colonel, Paul J. Revere (grandson and namesake of the famous patriot), the regiment was deployed in the second line of defenses, just one hundred yards to the left of a soon-to-be-famous clump of trees.

Although not engaged in the fighting of July 2, the 20th was nevertheless exposed to the enemy's fire when, at about 6:30 P.M., the advanced portion of Gibbon's line was attacked by the Rebel division of General Richard H. Anderson. The Confederate batteries supporting Anderson's attack aimed too high, overshooting the main Union line and pelting the 20th with shot and shell. By the time the action ended, eleven Bay Staters were either dead or gravely injured, and Colonel Revere was lying on the ground mortally wounded.[40] Late that night the regiment was moved into the Union front line, where the men settled down to get some rest and await the events of the coming day.

The morning of July 3 saw the sun rising into a cloudless sky, promising that the day would be hot. Although the early morning hours witnessed an intense battle of musketry on the far right of the

[40]Report of Capt. Henry L. Abbott, Twentieth Massachusetts Infantry, *The War of the Rebellion: A Compilation of the Official Records of the Union and Confederate Armies*, 128 vols. (Washington, D.C.: Government Printing Office, 1881–1902), ser. 1, vol. 27, pt. 2:445.

Federal line on Culp's Hill, neither army was able to gain any significant advantage. By 11:00 A.M. the fighting had ceased, and an ominous silence hung over the field. There was nothing to do but wait. As the noon sun beat down on the gentle slopes of Cemetery Ridge, the men of the 20th lounged in the grass, prepared and ate their lunch, and checked their weapons as they awaited the attack they knew must come.

At 1:00 P.M., or shortly thereafter, the anxious anticipation came to an end as the hard cough of a Rebel signal cannon pierced the silence. A few moments later another gun rang out, and then every battery along Lee's front was firing on the center of the Union line. Approximately fifteen minutes after the Rebel batteries opened fire, the Yankee guns began to reply, jarring the ground with every thundering blast. For nearly two hours the cannonade continued. Union troops on Cemetery Ridge hugged the ground and waited for the shelling to end. Fortunately for the Federals, the Rebel guns were once again aimed too high, so that most of the shells passed harmlessly overhead, bursting some distance in rear of the main line. The 20th, however, did suffer a few casualties during the bombardment.

At about 3:00 P.M. the Confederate batteries at last fell silent (the Union guns having ceased their firing some time earlier to reserve ammunition), and the Federals on Cemetery Ridge scurried into line of battle. Every man in Meade's army knew that if the Confederates were going to make any kind of a major assault that day, now was the time to do so. Gazing through the haze of smoke that blanketed the field, the men of the 20th scanned the Rebel position for any sign of movement. Then, from the shaded woods that covered Seminary Ridge, they appeared. Three divisions, totaling some fifteen thousand Confederates, emerged into the bright sunlight, dressed their ranks, and stepped off across the no-man's land that separated the two armies. Abbott and his men stared in awed silence as the gray troops marched steadily forward, in perfect formation, with their bright red battle flags leading the way. And as the faint strains of "Dixie" drifted across the fields from Seminary Ridge, the Rebel advance began to take on more of a parade-like air than that of a desperate assault.

Very soon, however, that appearance vanished as Federal batteries opened up with solid shot and shell, cutting massive holes in the advancing lines. By the time the Rebels began crossing the Emmitsburg Road, the Yankee guns had switched to the more deadly canister, mowing down the Southern infantry with a murderous efficiency. While most of the Union infantry began to open fire at one hundred yards, the 20th, along with the rest of Colonel Hall's brigade, was restrained from firing until the last moment. As Abbott recalled in his official report, "The men were kept lying on their bellies, without firing a shot, until orders came from Colonel Hall, commanding the brigade, the enemy having got within 3 or 4 rods of us, when the regiment rose up and delivered two or three volleys, which broke the rebel regiment opposite us entirely to pieces."[41]

With the attack on their front completely repulsed, and realizing that the Confederates had suffered every bit as heavily as the 20th had in its attack on Marye's Heights the winter before, the Bay Staters began to cheer madly, shouting "Fredericksburg! Fredericksburg!" The celebration had hardly begun, however, when Abbott's attention was directed toward the clump of trees some distance to the right where the Rebels had breached the Union defenses. Immediately and instinctively, Abbott and several other officers of the 20th rushed to the front of the regiment and led it over to the threatened position. The troops stormed into the vortex of some of the most vicious fighting of the war—fighting so desperate that Abbott later remarked: "The rows of dead after the battle I found to be 15 and 20 feet apart, as near hand to hand fighting as I ever care to see."[42]

Although the Battle of Gettysburg ended in a Union victory, it had cost the 20th dearly. Over half the enlisted men had either been killed or wounded; of the thirteen officers who entered the engagement, only three remained unharmed.[43] Once again Henry Abbott had been in the very center of the storm and, once again, he had escaped without injury. As the senior of the three officers who were able to report for duty after the battle, Abbott found himself in command of the regiment—a position he would continue to hold until the day of his death.

Following Gettysburg, the two contending armies once again returned to war-torn Virginia, where they continued to jockey for position. On October 14, 1863, Abbott and the 20th were again subjected to the fury of battle, as General A. P. Hill's Confederate Third Corps ambushed the Federal Second Corps near Bristoe Station. Though taken by surprise, the Union troops quickly formed into line of battle behind the protection of a steep railroad grade, enabling them to deliver a devastating fire into the advancing Rebels while taking relatively few casualties themselves. Hill's attack was thus

[41]Ibid.
[42]H. L. Abbott to his father, July 6, 1863.
[43]Ibid.

easily repulsed, and the Army of Northern Virginia was compelled to retreat to the south side of the Rapidan River, where it went into winter quarters near Orange Court House.

Compared to Gettysburg, the engagement at Bristoe Station was a relatively minor affair, but to Henry Abbott it had some personal significance. For the first time on a field of battle, Abbott was in command of his regiment. Moreover, and underlining the significance of that moment, Abbott was able to lead his troops into battle with the gold maple leaves of a major tacked onto his shoulders, having been mustered in at that rank four days earlier.

On November 26, having spent several weeks patrolling the Rapidan, the 20th was again on the march as Meade crossed the river in search of Lee. However, when the Confederates were found to be securely positioned behind earthen entrenchments along Mine Run Creek, it was quickly realized that an attack could only end in disaster. Rather than wasting thousands of lives in what would certainly have been a hopeless assault, the Federal commander wisely chose to end the campaign and march his army back to its encampments north of the river. So with 1863 rapidly drawing to an end, and with no prospect of another battle until the following spring, the Army of the Potomac went into winter quarters near Brandy Station.

Although Abbott did his best to keep himself and his men occupied by holding daily drills and inspections, his duties as regimental commander had significantly decreased during the winter lull and, as happened with many soldiers during long periods of inaction, he began to grow homesick. Considering that he had not seen his family for the past eight months, Henry's feelings can certainly be understood. He loved his family very much and his separation from them caused him no small amount of pain. When writing home, however, Henry very often attempted to conceal his true feelings with bold statements of bravado. Yet, as the following excerpt from a letter to his mother reveals, those attempts were usually futile: "How I wish I were sitting by you at that coal fire you speak of. You mustn't bring up those pictures of home, because though I am naturally of a warlike & ferocious, & not of a domestic turn, it makes me for a moment forget . . . that I am really just where I ought to be."[44]

Fortune, it seems, often smiles on the downhearted; on December 10, Abbott was granted a fifteen-day leave of absence to visit Boston. However, in what certainly must have been regarded as a blessing in disguise, Abbott was stricken with chronic diarrhea while at home

---

[44]H. L. Abbott to his mother, Sept. 21, 1863.

and was granted a twenty-day extension of his leave, thus allowing him to spend the holidays with his family.[45] And while in Boston, Henry undoubtedly received an endless number of invitations to attend Christmas parties. He went to at least one ball and, in all probability, took a trip up to Lowell to court Mary Ann Welch, whom he was becoming increasingly attracted to.

But by mid-January the celebration was over. With his furlough nearly expired, Henry realized the time had come to say goodbye to his family and friends and return to the army; however, leaving his family for the front was something that Henry clearly did not enjoy. He had seen battle; he had faced the enemy in the streets of Fredericksburg with a coolness that defied all logic; he had seen men die a hundred times and had narrowly escaped death himself on several occasions. Yet the emotional strain of bidding farewell to those he loved was more than Henry could bear; before he left, this noble young soldier "broke down and wept like a child."[46] He would never see his family again.

Shortly after Abbott's return—and much to his great delight—Wendell Holmes rejoined the army, having finally recovered from the wound he had received at Second Fredericksburg. Although Holmes had recently accepted a position on General Horatio Wright's staff in the Sixth Corps and was no longer affiliated with the 20th, he and Abbott continued to spend their off-duty hours together, often engaging in argumentative discussions on a wide variety of topics. In one particularly heated late-night debate, the two men sat in Abbott's hut arguing about the nature of the universe. "The universe is spatially limited," Holmes told Abbott. Abbott insisted it was not, and an intense shouting match ensued. Holmes grabbed a pencil and some paper and said he would prove it through calculus. By this time the other officers in the hut were rolling with laughter and egging the two on as the shouting continued. Soon after, there was a knock at the door. It was a messenger from the colonel of another regiment encamped across the field. "What in God's name were they celebrating at two in the morning?" was the inquiry. "This was a war, not a lecture forum."[47] Obviously such diversions were necessary for these men to maintain some measure of sanity amidst the insanity of war; for as everyone knew, when the dogwood

[45]Service Record of Henry L. Abbott, National Archives.

[46]Bruce, Twentieth Massachusetts, 337.

[47]Catherine Drinker Bowen, Yankee from Olympus: Justice Holmes and His Family (Boston: Little, Brown and Co., 1945), 192–93.

bloomed and the tree buds blossomed, the army would begin another offensive against Lee, and the killing would continue.

As that rainy April came to an end and the muddy Virginia roads began to dry, the Army of the Potomac prepared to embark on what would prove to be the bloodiest campaign of the war—a campaign that would begin in the deep, dank woodland of northern Virginia and culminate in the parlor of a farmhouse at Appomattox Court House. The Battle of the Wilderness—the first battle of the campaign—would signal the beginning of the end for the Army of Northern Virginia, and for the Southern Confederacy as a whole. And it would abruptly end the life of Henry L. Abbott—the "bright, particular star" of the Army of the Potomac.

EDITORIAL NOTES

Few collections of Civil War letters possess the high degree of historical content and literary quality that characterize those of Henry Livermore Abbott. During his three years of active service, Abbott participated in ten major engagements and reported most of what he saw in his letters home. Moreover, as one of the most renowned regimental officers in the army, Abbott frequently visited the headquarters of a number of generals and acquired a clear, overall picture of military operations. This hobnobbing with general officers also provided Abbott with the opportunity to draw some interesting character sketches of several of the army's commanders. All of this, of course, adds materially to the quality of his correspondence.

As a Harvard graduate, and as a young man with certain literary tendencies, Abbott possessed a remarkable ability to express himself in writing. He was keenly observant and bluntly candid in regard to his feelings as well as his opinions. As a result, his wartime letters are superbly written, especially when one considers the circumstances under which he wrote. For instance, the pens that he used were generally of a poor quality, often splotching the paper with ink. When campaigning, paper was scarce, forcing Abbott to write many of his letters on the backs of military order forms. Furthermore, most of his letters were written at the end of a long, hard day of drilling or picket duty, and at least one missive was penned while Abbott was on outpost duty, sitting outside in a drizzling rain. And, of course, the emotional strain that Abbott constantly endured must also be considered as an obstacle to his writing. Hundreds of miles from home, facing the possibility of death on a daily basis, Abbott was acutely aware that every letter he wrote might very well be his last.

Despite their superior quality and overall historical worth, Abbott's letters have largely been ignored by historians. In fact, prior to this book, only three publications have given his correspondence any attention at all, and then only in a limited fashion. Over 90 percent of the letters that comprise the main body of this work have never been published. Mark De Wolfe Howe's *Justice Oliver Wendell Holmes, Vol. 1: The Shaping Years, 1841–1870* (Cambridge, Mass.: The Belknap Press of Harvard University, 1957) contained excerpts from a few of Abbott's letters, as did Thomas E. Rice's article "The Bright and Particular Star," a biographical sketch of Henry Abbott which appeared in the May 1987 issue of *Civil War Times Illustrated.* Finally, in "The Abbotts of Lowell, Massachusetts in the Civil War," an article written for the Lowell Historical Society in 1941, William Greene Roelker included excerpts from the wartime letters of all three Abbott boys. The Civil War letters of Henry, Edward, and Fletcher Abbott are in the manuscripts collection at the Houghton Library, Harvard University.

Despite the interesting nature of these works and the admirable effort put forth by their authors to bring Abbott's letters to light (particularly in the latter two accounts), they have barely skimmed the surface of the collection. *Fallen Leaves* is an attempt to give Henry L. Abbott and his letters the recognition they so clearly deserve.

Because of the quality of Abbott's letters, my duties as editor have been less of a task than I had expected. Yet, because of certain writing peculiarities, slips of the pen, and, to a much lesser extent, errors of spelling and punctuation, it has been necessary for me to implement minor corrections in the letters. It should be stated, however, that while I have sometimes found it necessary to insert or delete a comma, break up long passages into paragraphs, and omit certain repetitive statements, I have in no way changed the substance of anything that Abbott wrote.

The policies I have adopted in editing the letters are as follows:

Following the common usage of his era, Abbott often made two words out of one. For example, he wrote "any thing" for *anything*, "every body" for *everybody*, "any more" for *anymore*, and "in side" for *inside*. I have maintained the original form.

Abbott frequently used the symbols "&" for *and*, and "&c" for *et cetera*. The original form has been maintained.

Throughout most of the letters, Abbott spelled *until* as "untill" and did not correct himself until 1863. The original form has been maintained.

Abbott habitually reversed the "i" and "e" in such words as *believe* and *receive*. Those errors have been corrected.

In many run-on sentences, I have replaced the comma separating the clauses with a semicolon for clarity.

Abbott often inserted commas where they should not be and omitted them where they should be used. I have corrected this only where the original form materially hampers the clarity of the sentence.

Words habitually or intentionally misspelled (except the "ie" words previously mentioned) have been left in their original form. Words misspelled once but spelled correctly at other times (excepting proper nouns) have been corrected.

In those cases where the author has left out a period, question mark, etc., the correct punctuation has been inserted.

Abbreviations have been kept in their original forms.

When possible, all persons mentioned for the first time in the letters have been identified in footnotes, which have also been used to include other explanatory information provided by the editor.

That Abbott ever imagined his letters would one day be published in book form is doubtful. Yet, when reading his correspondence, one might believe that he was writing with posterity in mind. This is well illustrated by Henry's response to his father upon learning that his letter on the Battle of Ball's Bluff had been circulated for friends and neighbors to read:

> Now, papa, you really have a great deal of paternal partiality. I know my letters must be very entertaining & interesting to the family circle, (how I wish I could drop in for one evening only, with the whole crowd there) but when you come to read that miserable old production of mine about the battle to strangers . . . , I must say I think your fatherly fondness is getting ahead of you. . . . Why, if you don't look out, I shall begin pretty soon to try to write well.[1]

During the six years I have spent editing this book, I have quite naturally developed a certain fondness for Henry L. Abbott. In his letters I have found a timeless bond through which I have gained an intimate knowledge of this gallant young man. Through his writing he has poured out to me those hopes and fears that were originally intended only for his family, and, as a result, he has carved a niche in my life. If, in editing his letters, I have helped convey this feeling to the reader, then my task has been completed and the purpose of this book has been fulfilled.

[1]Henry L. Abbott to his father, Nov. 23, 1861.

ONE

MY TASTES
ARE NOT WARLIKE

Fort Independence, Massachusetts, May 1861

Dear Papa,

There are a crowd of fellows from the battalion who are going to have commissions in Gordon's regiment. Henry Russell,[1] one of them, began to drill the same time that I did, & I don't think he drills any better. In fact, though I don't know half so much as an officer ought to, I really believe I know as much as half the officers who get commissions. Consequently I want to know if you will see if there isn't a spare commission I can get in Gordon's regiment. I don't pretend to be on my military, warlike pluck & that kind of thing, but I must say that I hate to have all this military parade wasted.

We are having an extremely pleasant time down here; the grub is getting very good as well as the weather; the work is just hard enough to give you a rousing appetite & if one's family lived in Boston so they could come down on Sunday, it would be as pleasant a way of passing the summer as one could conceive of, if it weren't for one thing, that one seems to be wasting his time down here possibly when he contemplates the prospect of being ordered back to town, without doing any thing whatever. Now Gordon's regiment is officered by gentlemen, a great many of whom I know, & by sober respectable fellows who more do suit a staid graduate like myself than harum scarum young fellows who haven't yet sowed their wild oats. Carrie says that you are going to try & get a commission for Fletcher[2] and if we all three were in the same regiment it would really be bully.

[1]George H. Gordon was then colonel of the 2d Mass. Infantry, in which Henry's brothers, Edward and Fletcher, held commissions as captain and 2d lieutenant, respectively. Henry S. Russell was then 1st lieutenant in the 2d Mass.

[2]Henry's sister Caroline, then twenty-two, was the oldest of the Abbott children. Henry refers to her in his correspondence as both "Carrie" and "Carry." Both spellings have been preserved. Fletcher Morton Abbott, then eighteen, was fourth among the Abbott children. He was commissioned 2d lieutenant in the 2d Mass. on July 8, 1861.

By the way, nothing will be allowed to be sent to the garrison after Tuesday night, so I have written mamma to send me what I asked her to send before, & I wish you would let her put in a bottle of Lacryna Crystina.[3] You have got lots of it now, & it will be [the] last chance to send any thing. Your oranges are delicious. I am extremely obliged to you for them. But they only last a little while & so I shall have to resort to my former remedy.

This letter I suppose isn't very intelligible, but I know you will excuse it when I tell you that I was on guard all night, that the table has got the shakes, that the paper is miserable, that the pencil I don't know what to say of it, except that it induces me to believe that pencils, like language, were given [to] us to conceal as well as to express &c. Under such circumstances I think even your hand writing would get shaken out of its regularity & look as if it had been on a big drunk, as this of mine does.

Your aff. son,
H. L. Abbott

Fort Independence, Massachusetts, May 1861

Dear Papa,

I hope you don't imagine for a minute that I could be so selfish as to begrudge in the slightest the attention & care you have been bestowing on Ned & Fletch who both really need it. In fact, I thought after I wrote that it was very inconsiderate in me to trouble you at a time when you must necessarily be so much occupied by so many different affairs all coming upon you at once. My only [excuse] is that a fellow down here in this crowd gets into a terribly thoughtless way, thoughtless that is, of every thing but dinner & drill. But now that I have once applied to you & you have expressed your willingness to get me a commission & to spare the expense, I can only say that nothing is further from my mind than giving it up, that is of course so long as I have your consent.

You say that I have been with mamma so much more than the others, that she will miss me very much. I shouldn't be telling the truth if I said I were sorry for it, for I shouldn't think very much of any man who would be glad that his parents didn't miss him. That I have mamma's love would be the chief consolation to my distress at parting from her. But I really don't think that she would miss me so much as I should [miss] her. But of course painful as such things are,

[3]A popular wine of that era.

31

they are not consideration enough to keep a man from doing what he has made up his mind to do as his duty.

I'll tell you what I am very much grieved at, that you should have such a very small opinion of me as you intimate in your letter, that I should be contented with playing the soldier down here. I must say that for you every day my respect has been growing, particularly since these troubles began, & I am really hurt that you should think me a mere trifler. I don't pretend to have [the] enthusiasm of Ned & Fletch. Indeed I confess that I know my self to be constitutionally timid. But history shows a great many men who have conquered that kind of thing, & when I look back I don't see any instance where I have displayed a want of physical courage where it was absolutely necessary. My tastes are not warlike like Ned & Fletcher's, but literary & domestic. I can think of nothing more odious than the thought of leaving home & profession for the camp. I don't think I should ever have tried the thing untill there was an actual necessity for every able bodied man, if it hadn't been for Ned & Fletch enlisting. But now that I have once begun, the prospect of backing out without doing any thing is still more odious. . . . I should be ashamed of myself forever if I didn't do something now.

As for Fletcher Webster's regiment,[4] I can't imagine any thing more disagreeable to go in except the not going at all. But still I should accept a commission there with the greatest of pleasure if there is no longer any chance of [getting a commission in] Gordon's regiment, as I suppose there is not. Certainly if every thing were wintergreen & I had never joined any company at all, I wouldn't go in such a regiment as Fletcher Webster's untill the direst necessity called for it. But now I have once plunged in, I rejoice at the chance.

I was going to try to go over to see Ned's company at Roxbury [on] Wednesday, but now mamma & Carry are coming down, I shall put it off till after they have paid the visit. Tell them to come if they can on Friday, for that is to be the great gala day when the ladies of Boston present us a banner. However if they can't come that day make them come some other. No pass is necessary. Only ask for me as a relation. Why can't you come with them? I really think you would enjoy it very much. . . .

Your aff. son,
H. L. Abbott

[4]Fletcher Webster (son of Daniel Webster) was colonel of the 12th Mass. He was killed in action at Second Bull Run, Aug. 30, 1862.

Fort Independence, Massachusetts, May 1861

Dear Papa,

Have you had time to see any thing about that commission, or did you find every thing blocked? Tom Robeson[5] from our mess has got a 2nd lieutenant's commission in Gordon's regiment and [has] gone to town since I wrote. But I suppose that all the other commissions are taken & he got his through strong family influence.

I heard of Ned's company from several fellows who were down today. It was complimented very highly, said to be composed of very large fine looking men, though I heard of some rather singular wars not down in the manual. But generally they all seemed to think that Ned made an extremely fine officer.

I don't know any thing about the expense of a commission but if it is any thing of consequence of course I can't expect you [to] do any thing in the matter after all the cost you have been at so far. This was a matter I didn't think of when I applied & . . . I certainly shouldn't wish to trouble you, because I know you have had your share & more too.

Tell mamma I am expecting a letter from her but don't want to hurry her if she hasn't the time. Please give my love to Carrie & the rest. . . .

Your aff. son,
H. L. Abbott

Lowell, Massachusetts, July 11, 1861[6]

Dear Mamma,

I write to tell you that I have accepted the offer of a commission I have got me. I had made up my mind to get a commission a month ago & was only waiting for a chance. I came to the conclusion that it was the thing I ought to do, that nothing could possibly be so good for me in the way of experience as going in the army. . . .

After I finally made up my mind, there were a good many circumstances [that] made my determination stronger. Every day I had to go through things that you don't know of. There were other reasons

---

[5]Thomas R. Robeson was a 2d lieutenant in the 2d Mass. He served with distinction in that unit and was subsequently promoted 1st lieutenant and captain. He was killed at Gettysburg, July 3, 1863.

[6]Henry, who was in Lowell on recruiting duty, was writing to his parents who were vacationing at Center Harbor, N.H.

besides. I felt that I had never done any thing or amounted to any thing in the whole course of my existence, & that there was no better prospect in view for a long time, if at all. And what is more, that seemed to be the opinion of every body else. I couldn't help concurring with every body else, & so got disgusted with being nothing & doing nothing, & resolved if I couldn't do much, to do what so many other young men were doing. . . .

However, I had determined to wait for Stevenson's regiment,[7] but when Ned's & Fletch's regiment went, it was pretty hard to stand the idea of they being down there fighting while I was at home doing nothing; & as Stevenson's regiment seemed one of those things that were never to be, & as a good chance offered itself, I finished the business, because I knew if I refused & no opportunity came along afterwards, I should probably repent my refusal very much hereafter, without the chance of repairing my error.

To wind up, I really think it is the best . . . I could do, & the governor[8] thinks so too, I know, for he advises every young man who comes to him to take a commission if he can get one. Of course it is every man's duty to develope himself as much as he can if he doesn't do it at other people's expense. . . .

I didn't take [the commission] till I was sure that if I didn't take it, somebody else in the battalion would have it who didn't need it any more than I did. . . . I have kept nobody out who needs it really, that could have possibly got it. And what is of most importance, I didn't take it without coming to the conclusion that I should do so without expense to your feelings, that it would be done without objection on your part, and if there could have possibly been time, I should not have taken it, by any manner of means, without first getting your consent. But I knew that as soon as you saw the motives that influenced me, you wouldn't hesitate a moment about giving your sanction.

I knew this for three reasons. Because you gave your cheerful consent, however hard it was in the first place, to the other boys going as soon as you found it necessary. Because these things are happening so often nowadays that you wouldn't really realize that I am ac-

---

[7]Thomas G. Stevenson, who had served as major of the Fourth Battalion, Massachusetts Volunteer Militia (M.V.M.) at Fort Independence, was commissioned colonel of the 24th Mass. on Aug. 31, 1861. He was later promoted brigadier general and was killed at Spotsylvania Court House on May 10, 1864.

[8]Henry, like many other New England boys, often referred to his father as "the governor."

tually going. It isn't as it was when the [war] first began & taking a
commission was venturing into some unexplored region full of perils
& uncertainties. Now it seems a matter of every day life. It is nothing more serious than going into trade or a profession. The edge is all
taken off. Every body has got so used to it that nobody minds it [at]
all. . . . I shall come home after 2 or 3 years with everything all
right after all, a space not [as] long as I was at Cambridge, where you
were kept in a good deal more worry & trouble than you will be
under the present circumstances. And what is most of all, I know
that you have got so much strength of mind that if you found I had
got a commission to Hades instead of the land of the sunny South, &
was bound to go, you wouldn't, like a great many weak women without character, feel any useless regrets about it, but [would] shut right
down & say that if it had got to be done it must be done & there was
an end of it. Being troubled about it, of course, is useless, as it can't
do any good, & consequently ought to be dropped entirely.

For all these reasons & because I was emphatically, positively
obliged to go by the strongest considerations, I know you will be glad
that I have done what I have done, & so expect to find when I get
up [to Center Harbor, New Hampshire], which will be very speedily
indeed, I hope. In fact, the reason I haven't been up before, was not
only on account of expense to the governor but because I was afraid
I might give up my military ideas, & knew I should repent afterwards
most exceedingly when I found every body else had gone.

My commission is second lieut. in the 20th (Col. Lee's)
regiment,[9] now at Dedham [Massachusetts]. . . . I am going to try &
get up next Saturday or Sunday. Perhaps I may not be able to, so I
wish you would write any way, to make every thing sure. Give my
love to Sallie[10] & the children & remember me to every body. I am
at present recruiting in Lowell, Lawrence, Andover, &c.

Your aff. son,
H. L. Abbott

[9]William Raymond Lee was commissioned colonel of the 20th Mass. on July 1,
1861. Although he had attended the U.S. Military Academy at West Point (where
he knew both Robert E. Lee and Jefferson Davis), he did not graduate; he resigned
two weeks before commencement in order to search for his father who, suffering
from a "brain attack," had disappeared. Nonetheless, Lee chose to stick with the
army for a short time and saw action in the Seminole War in Florida. At the out-
break of the Civil War, he was working as a civil engineer in Virginia.

[10]Sarah Livermore "Sallie" Abbott, the second daughter and seventh oldest of the
Abbott offspring, was then eleven years old.

I just saw Peter Haggerty.[11] I never saw him in such good condition before; you would hardly know him. . . . He says everything is getting on very well indeed.

Boston, Massachusetts, July 27, 1861

Dear Mamma,

I haven't yet got that letter that you promised, though expecting it for a long time. I have just got a letter from Carry which I should say was written before she got my letter. I have just got a letter from Fletch. I should think he was rather homesick. He says he has written 3 letters but got no answers. 1 to Mary Clark. . . . if answers have been sent & not received by him, the letters must be rewritten & sent again. They [the 2d Massachusetts] are doing picket duty & living on pretty tough feed. He has had command of his company for two or three days on account of illness of superior officers. He is evidently deeply in love & does, I dare say, considerable sighing in private, a boyish affair I suppose which won't last long when he gets fairly at work.

We shan't get off till Oct. probably, so the gov. thinks I had better not go up to Center Harbor at all & as expenses are so great I suppose it is better to . . . wait till you get down which, he says, won't be till the middle of August. I hope however for your sake, you will stay till Sept. For I know how disagreeable it is to go off just in the midst of the hot weather.

How is the little devil of a Grafton? I want to see him immensely & also I wish you would ask Arthur[12] why he has discontinued his amusing & instructive letters. Fletcher's letter by the way is really so stunning, so perfectly natural . . . with some comical spelling & illustrations, similes, &c, that I must send it up to you immediately.

I hope you people up there will answer his letter, & I suppose you have, & that it hasn't reached [him]. I should like to come up & see you firstrate but I suppose it is impossible. I expect a letter any way. Remember [me] to Carry, the Clarks, & all acquaintances. . . .

Your aff. son,
H. L. Abbott

By the way, please be careful & not let Fletch know that I have showed his letters or alluded to their contents. . . .

[11]Peter Haggerty was aide-de-camp to Gen. Benjamin Butler.
[12]Grafton St. Loe Abbott, the tenth Abbott child, was then four years old. Arthur St. Loe Abbott, the ninth Abbott sibling, was then seven years old.

Boston, Massachusetts, July 27, 1861

Dear Papa,

I was obliged to come in town this morning after all, as Lieut. Macy[13] is down with severe cholera morbus. I wanted to see you about getting a sword & sash. We are to wear swords hereafter at dress parades. Now Sam[14] has got a sword that Fletch gave him & as he won't need any sword in the autumn when he gets to Boston, why couldn't you ask him to send me his sword & thus save the expense of buying one. I think I can borrow [Lt.] Col. Palfrey's[15] till Wednesday, which would be time enough to send Sam's, if he is willing.

As for the sash, I believe the class[16] give sashes, though I am afraid every body is out of town & I shan't hear any thing about it. However I can wait for that. I made inquiries about buying out an officer, & I don't believe it can be done. Still I will do all I can.

I send enclosed a letter from Fletch. It is meant to be confidential, I suppose. But I don't believe he would object to having you see it, though it was not written evidently to be shown. However, I wouldn't let him know. It is such an admirable specimen of truthfulness . . . that I know you would like to see it as much as any thing you ever read. The slightest [illegible word] are so true to nature & is so opposite to the artificial style of most letters, that I know you will be as much delighted with it as I was. It is a good deal like the letters you read in good novels; very little like most of the . . . letters I have ever read. . . .

Your aff. son,

H. L. Abbott

You said you were going to give me a pistol before I went, you know. . . . if you get one, I think Allen's is better in every way than Colt's except that it won't carry so far which is of no importance, besides being $5 or $6 cheaper. If you get one I wish you would get 2 or 3 hundred cartridges at the same time for so many improvements are constantly being made that it is sometimes impossible to get them a year after buying [the gun].

---

[13]George N. Macy was then 1st lieutenant of Co. I.

[14]Samuel A. Abbott, then fifteen, was the sixth Abbott offspring.

[15]Francis Winthrop Palfrey was commissioned lieutenant colonel of the 20th Mass. on July 1, 1861.

[16]Abbott refers to the Harvard class of 1860.

Camp Massasoit, Massachusetts, [17] *August 7, 1861*

Dear Papa,

I am much obliged to you for [the money for] the sword & sash. I was in hopes to have saved the expense, but shan't be able to wait any longer, so I shall get them today.

I got a letter from mamma yesterday & she wants me to come up to Center Harbor [on] Saturday very much. Now if you do not wish me to go of course you have only to say so, but if you are willing I wish you would send me a note before Friday night so I can obtain leave of absence, which would be very willingly granted on such an occasion, particularly as I haven't shirked any thing yet & mean to stick close after this.

Your aff. son,
H. L. Abbott

Camp Massasoit, Massachusetts, August 8, 1861

Dear Papa,

I have just got the pistol. I am extremely obliged to you for it. I find it carries remarkably well, better I think, as you say, than Allen's. I shall keep the cartridges as you recommend, untill I get South. The case that comes with it is very pretty & what is of more importance very convenient indeed. In fact it is just the thing that is desirable, and just what every man wants. You say nothing about it in your letter, but I suppose it is a present from you & [I] feel very much obliged for this piece of kindness on your part.

I suppose [Shrine?] & Brown have sent in the bill for sword & sash. I might have got each [for] $2 cheaper, but the articles for that price were of a very much inferior quality. . . . There was also a sword suspending strap that I bought at the same place of $.75. I wish you would drive out and see us with Mr. Dean if you have nothing else to do [on] Sunday. I think you will find the men very much improved in appearance by the new uniforms though only a fatigue dress.

Your aff. son,
H. L. Abbott

[17]The nucleus of the 20th moved to Camp Massasoit, near Readville, Mass., on July 10, 1861.

Camp Massasoit, Massachusetts, August 13 or 14, 1861

Dear Papa,

I have got to trouble you again for some money. Our mess is obliged for the present to pay weekly. The last assessment is $3., & as I was obliged to pay 2 or 3 persons' passages home, my last liberal supply from you is exhausted. The next week's assessment will be done very soon and other incidental expenses so that I think I shall be obliged to ask you for $10. This of course I only mean to borrow, for after you have come down so in other expenses of outfit, it would be rather rough to expect you to pay for the rations too. . . .

Did you get my note last week? I hardly expected you out on Sunday, because I supposed you would go to Center Harbor. However, I thought you might possibly be able to come out & we should be very happy to see you at any time. You will find I think great improvement in the drill of the men.

My pistol carries remarkably well. It makes a hole through a shovel as round and smooth as is made by a machine.

The colonel, major[18] & one of our Nantucket privates captured yesterday 1 sergeant & 15 privates who had been lured away [by] the tempting offers of the New York Irish [Brigade], as well as the New York recruiting sergeant who [lured] them off, the latter being safely lodged in jail to be tried by civil process. I don't think the New York fellows will come fooling around Col. Lee's regiment very soon again. We are going to shoot the deserting sergeant if we can.[19] Please come out & see a dress parade whenever you get a chance.

Your aff. son,

H. L. Abbott

Camp Massasoit, Massachusetts, August 26(?), 1861

Dear Papa,

We shan't probably go [to the front] till the last of the week. Still it is just as well to be prepared. I wish you would hurry down mamma & Carry immediately, because you know it may be the last chance. . . . if you would be kind enough . . . have the [errand] boy

---

[18]The major of the 20th was Paul J. Revere (grandson and namesake of the patriot). He received his commission on July 1, 1861.

[19]The "deserting sergeant" was a man named Buguey of Co. C. His fate is unknown.

go & . . . take my 4th Bat[talion] uniform to Snell . . . on Tremont St. . . . tell him to build me a suit of flannel of exactly the model of the regulation suit he built, particularly about the regulation style, of a very fine flannel . . . to be done & sent by an express that will carry it promptly by Friday. [Also get me] 2 pair of army shoes at Rice who has my measure, which has been the same for 2 years, [and get me] an iron bedstead from Clapp, Fulls & Brown [on] State St., corner of Congress. The other things on Fletcher's list you can get according to your discretion, if you will be so kind.

We save the expense of camp chest as there is only one allowed to all the officers. I hope you won't try to get half the things on F[letcher]'s list but only those you think most important; a couple of silk handkerchiefs wouldn't go bad. . . . I am very sorry indeed to give you all this trouble, but I shan't be able to get them in [town] myself. Our company [is on] the right of the line. But you musn't mention it, as it is in strict confidence.

Your aff. son,
H. L. Abbott

My trunk will do. Don't forget 2 hundred cartridges & [percussion] caps. . . . Don't forget a razor & strop. Shan't want the collars.

Camp Massasoit, Massachusetts, Sunday, September 1, 1861

Dear Aunt Elizabeth,[20]

I was very much obliged to you indeed for your slippers. Did you ever get my note thanking you for them before this? They are just the things necessary. Nothing could be more comfortable. Whenever I put them on after a hard day's work, I shall remember your kindness to me.

I was very sorry indeed not to be able to see you, particularly when you were so near. However, I suppose it was impossible and I shall have to take my farewell of you by letter. I have been calculating all along upon coming up to bid good bye to all my Lowell friends before I went, but this hasty departure has dashed every thing. I am going to ask you to do it for me. Tell them all that I hope, notwithstanding, they won't have forgotten me if I come back after a 3 years war to see them again. I trust & know I shall find you well & happy, if you will only take care of yourself & move

---

[20]Elizabeth Livermore was the sister of Henry's mother, and was then fifty-seven years old.

round amongst your friends. . . . Remember me particularly to Dr. & Mrs. Edson, & believe me that I shall always be your

very affectionate nephew,
H. L. Abbott

I had saved up a photograph of myself in military rig for you, but I find it gone now that I was about to send it. I suppose I have lost it. I send you inclosed a song written by a friend of our Nantucket boys for our company to sing.

Washington, D.C., Friday, September 7, 1861

Dear Mamma,

We are here all safe in Washington, after being exceedingly well received in New York & Philadelphia. When we got to Baltimore, our company as a precaution, measure marched with loaded muskets, without there being however the slightest necessity for it, whatever.[21]

Baltimore is as quiet as if . . . all her inhabitants had been turned to stone. With the exception of 2 or 3 boys who gave faint cheers for General Scott,[22] we didn't find, in a march of a mile & a half through the city, that our presence excited any emotion of any kind whatever. It didn't even collect a large crowd.

Baltimore finds Uncle Sam's hand very heavy. Any body with U.S. on his cap can travel any where. No matter where he goes they all toady him as if they belonged to a conquered province. The fact is the police force has completely paralyzed the mobocratic spirit. The police bullyrag the town awfully. Yesterday they arrested a lot of young swells for having the audacity to wear secession cravats. When we were in the station the police whipped off an old broken down vender of pies, because one of his rivals said he was a rank secessionist. They have got them completely under their thumbs, & Baltimore is now as safe a place to travel in as any in the United States.

We got here in Washington at 4 this morning; a place, as you no doubt remember, where when you first arrive, you think you must have got into the wrong cars and suddenly come upon Lawrence,

---

[21]Throughout the war, Baltimore remained a hotbed of Confederate sympathizers. The need for martial law first became apparent on Apr. 19, 1861, when an angry mob attacked the 6th Mass. as it marched through the city while changing trains for Washington, D.C. Although the exact number of casualties is not clear, at least four soldiers and nine civilians were killed in an exchange of gunfire.

[22]Lt. Gen. Winfield Scott was then general in chief of the Union army. He retired on Nov. 1, 1861, at age seventy-five, being superseded by George B. McClellan.

Mass., till you see the capitol, when you reflect that though there are mills in Lawrence as ugly, there ain't any so large. So much for Washington . . . a beastly place under martial law where they arrest officers & men alike in the streets without a pass after 8:30 in the *morning.*

Going into camp this afternoon a mile out of town, when I shall soon write to the governor, the next letter to Carry & the next to Sally. Sam I suppose won't want one, as he couldn't come to bid me good bye when I went off.

We are all rather seedy as the colonel, with his usual shrewdness, has managed to have the cars go 3 miles an hour in the day, so as [to] keep the men in the car overnight; decidedly the most convenient way of disposing of the men, but rather rough on the officers who get very little sleep or to eat.

I was rather blue at first but feel in stunning condition now & expect a letter from you immediately with an account of your going into the new house.[23] Give my love to all the family, my lady friends, Miss Jackson, Miss Sargent, . . . &c.

Your aff. son,
H. L. Abbott

Camp Burnside, Washington, D.C., Wednesday, September 11, 1861

Dear Papa,

I have been waiting to write you till we should get fairly settled in some place or other, but as we seem as much unsettled as the 2nd [Massachusetts], I have made up my mind to do it now. We got [to] Washington Saturday morning you know & reported to General Burnside.[24] In the afternoon we marched 3 miles out of town, or rather in town, to a hill surrounded by forests. The place is called Kalorama, which means beautiful view, I suppose because there is no view at all. Here we encamped—I of course, after having had no sleep for two or three nights & being on my feet all day, was put on guard 2 days after being on guard before, without guard tents or any thing else. However I didn't grumble because we have now got to the enemy's country.

[23]The Abbotts were then moving from their long-time residence at 128 Stackpole St., Lowell, to 6 Arlington St., Boston, just across the street from the Public Gardens.

[24]Ambrose E. Burnside, then a brigadier general, was temporarily commanding Federal troops in the vicinity of Washington.

Second Lt. Henry L. Abbott. This photograph was taken in Matthew Brady's Washington Studio, probably in September 1861. *Courtesy USAMHI.*

The colonel was made provisional brigadier general of the regiments encamped in the neighborhood. Assistant Adjutant General Myers came out to see us & was so much delighted that we were immediately reported for General Lander's brigade[25] & the next day, Monday, we started for new ground 3 miles off, Camp Burnside, where we now are. . . .

Today General Lander came to see us & paid us a good many compliments & ordered us to march tomorrow across the [Potomac] river, where the army is.[26] General Lander is an old army officer which is certainly a comfort. Just now, since I have begun to write, the report has come that the heavy firing we have heard all day is the noise of a battle, 4,000 [men] on each side. The issue unknown. The colonel says from General Lander that we shall have our share tomorrow, & I hope the next letter I write will announce a victory, as I have no doubt it will.

Our present camp is on high ground with a view of Washington. We came to it through what seemed immense forests. At every half mile's interval, crowds of half clad savages who called themselves Pennsylvania & New York troops, came running down. Immensely big fellows, good natured, friendly, & unsophisticated; that is to say, without the slightest notion of military etiquette or discipline. Privates would come up & without so much as saluting, ask us officers questions as if they were actually thirsty to know something of the outer world. When they found we were from Boston, they universally manifested the greatest delight & enthusiasm. They all said, "I know you came from Boston, your clothes are so good & you've got rifles."

You have no idea of the admiration there is for Massachusetts men out in these ragged . . . regiments; it is gratifying to one's pride, you may imagine. There were thousands of men along the route of 3 miles & nearly every regiment was ignorant of the neighborhood of the rest. As we came along, though we came right out from amongst them, they asked where we were from & where bound, with as much ignorance as if we were foreigners suddenly coming in to strange country.

The neighborhood of Washington is a perfect hive of soldiers encamped, some in the woods & some in intervals in the woods, but

[25]Frederick W. Lander's brigade then consisted of the 19th Mass., 20th Mass., Battery B 1st Rhode Island Artillery, and the 1st Mass. Sharpshooters. It would later be joined by the 7th Michigan.

[26]The bulk of the Army of the Potomac was then encamped in the vicinity of Alexandria, Va.

all completely concealed, Lancers, Cavalry, Infantry, all kinds, dirty ragged & ill mannered, but brown, cheerful & goodnatured. You have no idea how singular it seems to march along a common bridle path through woods where all seems as wild & uninhabited as the forests of Maine, & all of a sudden come upon 2 or 3 thousands of men; so it was all the route. We came upon camp after camp in the same way.

In the city you rarely see a soldier except at the railroad station. Every thing goes on the same as usual; you would never suspect from appearances that there was an enemy within a thousand miles. Go 3 or 4 miles out & you find the woods bristling with soldiers & camps, all wearing . . . an air of the most perfect security—in one place the officer of the guard [is] playing cards . . . on his post—& but a short distance off [we hear] the booming of the cannon & the noise of the skirmishes. Then, across the river, is the [main body of the] army encamped together. Altogether it is the strangest mixture of war & peace & 4th of July. The only thing that seems to wake men up is when their regiment is ordered to cross the river to beat the enemy & then you hear the most tremendous cheering. Indeed, when you are so near the foe, every thing seems so awfully tame except advancing to the attack, that the desire to . . . cross the river is universal amongst officers & men alike. I have always wanted to have a speedy engagement in order to try myself . . . [but] not because I like fighting. But now it is a different feeling, the same that every body else has, that the greatest happiness is to be ordered over the river & that we shall be awfully indignant if they get through a battle without us. I suppose the fact is we are all very impatient & think every thing listless & humdrum except fighting, & when we do get fighting I suppose many of us will be equally anxious for the humdrum camp again.

I am writing this letter lying on my stomach with the paper & candle raised on a box & as I am rapidly getting paralyzed in this uncomfortable position I think I will end this long letter. I have made it a long one because I don't believe I shall be able to write another for a very long time. I have already got to write a letter to Carry, besides 4 other female letters & 3 male ones, . . . which will probably take all my spare time for the whole 3 years I am sworn into service for.

Give my love to the children & to mamma & Carry & tell the latter to remember me to Miss Jackson & Lowell. . . . George

Perry,[27] I believe, bestows a small fortune upon the letter carrier whenever he gets one of those square little envelopes, so I would advise Carry not to write too often unless she wishes to have an impoverished husband.

Your aff. son,
H. L. Abbott

[27]1st Lt. George B. Perry, Co. D, was then unofficially engaged to Henry's sister Caroline. The couple would be married on Oct. 5, 1864.

TWO

BALL'S BLUFF:
Now We Shall Have Our Revenge

Camp Benton, Maryland,[1] *September 24, 1861*

Dear Mamma,

I think it peculiar that I haven't got a single letter from home since I started. I have written 3, the first to you the Saturday we reached Washington, the next to the governor the day we got to Camp Burnside, 3 miles from Washington, the next to Carry as soon as we got to our present situation, Poolesville. Carry said in her last that none of you had got a single letter from me. I suppose that is the reason you haven't written, though I think you might have favored me any way.

I fancied at first that my letters might have been stopped in the post office, because they contained descriptions of our whereabouts which I find is contrary to law, but as all the other fellows have done precisely the same thing & as their letters have reached home, I am entirely at a loss to know what in the devil is the cause of the accident. The last letter had money in it for Carry to get some photographs taken with you. . . . If she hasn't got it, I will send some more.

I hope I shall get a letter from you at last & find out how you all are & whether you have got into the new house or not. By the way, while I think of it, will you ask the governor to buy me an eight dollar army trunk? I find mine is too heavy to stand inspection. Also a plain black leather sword belt. The varnished one I bought for $4.50 is entirely used up, besides not being regulation. I will send the money as soon as we are paid off, because I don't want the governor to be at expense for me, now [that] I am fully able to support

---

[1]On Sept. 12 the 20th Mass., along with the rest of Lander's brigade, left Washington for Poolesville, Md., thirty-five miles northwest of the capital. Reaching its destination on Sept. 14, the brigade reported to Brig. Gen. Charles P. Stone and became part of his Corps of Observation. Camp Benton was established the following day about 2 miles from the Potomac.

myself, because I think it would be rather sponging. I will send my [old] trunk back. Send the [new] trunk by Adams' express to Pooles-ville if possible, if not, to Washington, marked Lieut. H. L. Abbott, 20th Reg. Mass. Vol. No comp[any] I on it.

We have been on the banks of [the Potomac] river bivouacking for the last week, & have just got back. The [enemy] pickets are very friendly. They are playing the same thing on us that they did on Ned, hurrying us off at all sorts of hours to all sorts of places. How-ever it is good fun & varies the monotony. Ned & Fletch are within 10 miles, but we officers are not allowed to leave the camp except on duty, because the general says we are on outpost. Rotten rough isn't it? They are both on furlough in Washington now.

Give my love to papa & the rest of the family, & my respects to Miss Jackson & Sargent, if you happen to see [them], & to the charming little Miss Annie Sargent if she has got back. Please ask Mrs. Stackpole why she doesn't write according to agreement.

Your aff. son,
H. L. Abbott

Camp Benton, Maryland, September 25, 1861

Dear Mamma,

I got your 2 letters together & one from Carry & one from papa, last night just after I had written mine complaining of getting none. I was very glad to get them you may be sure. Your description of the house almost makes me homesick, though it is still pleasant to hear all about it. How intensely comfortable it must be. However, we shall enjoy it all the more when we get back after the 3 years war.

I wish whenever you write you would tell me all about home. Though we are having a deuced nice time here, it is certainly most interesting to hear about the pleasures of civilized life. I believe . . . in the long run, [that] I am rather more fond of the latter than the former. Still I like this life better now because it is a change & be-cause I am in so much better condition, [with] so little ailments of any kind. . . .

Just as I was reading your letter last night about 7 o'clock & before I had time to read Carry's, we were summoned by the assembly to fall in & we were dispatched down the river & have just got back this morning. Caspar's[2] company with George [Perry] is still on the banks with one more [company]. All the others but one were sent

[2]Caspar Crowninshield was captain of Co. D.

with ours under Frank Bartlett's[3] command down to the river. Now when you take out 6 or 7 wagoners & a dozen or so on guard, we have only about 30 [men] left in our company, evidently of very little use, & yet they send us on every expedition. It is very plain to the most stupid that we are sent so that Frank, as senior capt., may take command. Very flattering to him, isn't it? A young man of 21 years, taking command of a battalion of 7 companies, all the other captains older than himself & one of them a major under Steizel [?] in the German Wars. If there were a vacancy . . . there isn't the slightest doubt they would make Frank major. The colonel said yesterday to the general, in the hearing of our sergeant . . . that Frank was an officer in whom he could place the most implicit confidence in all situations & under all circumstances, [and] that he knows of nobody whom he could trust so well in the most trying & dangerous posts. Pretty good that, hey?

Last night Frank acted as colonel at dress parade, Macy was adjutant, & I in consequence was in command of the right company. It was [illegible word], I tell you, when parade was dismissed & all we officers marched up to the col. to hear Frank say, "Gentlemen, I don't think of any thing more, I won't detain you any longer." The best of it is, too, we all have to keep on a grave face, salute him in the most reverential way & then retire as if we had just been permitted a conference with the grand noble. After parade was over, they wanted to know, in a chaffing way, if Company I was in command of this regiment. You may believe it is really comfortable to have such a capt. He & Macy deserve to be remembered.

Remember me to all my friends, married & single, particularly the female portion. By the way, one thing that I wrote the letter for & which I nearly left out, was to caution you to take care & lay off after working so hard on the house. If you ain't careful you won't be well enough to enjoy it now that you have got it. . . . Send me *Vanity Fair* every week, will you? The last was delightful. . . .

[No signature]

Camp Benton, Maryland, September 25, 1861

Dear Papa,

I got your note the same time as the other four, & very much delighted I was to get it. Carry says you are coming to Washington in two or three days, & I shall be still more delighted to see you. If you

---

[3]William F. "Frank" Bartlett was captain of Co. I, in which Henry served.

had come a little sooner you might have seen Ned & Fletch in Washington. They have been on furlough for a day or two, but are on duty again, I suppose. . . .

You say Sam thinks my clothes will fit him. I hope he will take them by all means & I trust he will use them tenderly, for I still have a great affection for them as the relics of a bygone civilization. You also say Sam was a better scholar, according to Mr. Chase,[4] than Ned or I. [This] I am glad to hear. . . . I can say so candidly. If I any longer cared to shine as a scholar I have no doubt I should be envious, but I have lost all ambition, for the present, for any thing but the military. I am now completely absorbed in that, & have no interest for any thing else. If you should say that Sam outstripped me in that, which by the way I think he would, if he had studied it as much as I have, for I think his tastes are decidedly military—then I should really burn with envy. But now I can only say I am heartily glad that he is doing so well. If he only goes on in the same way & doesn't get any absurd notions of being a tough nut, he will certainly distinguish himself in college. . . . I trust he will keep his taste for lady's society. That I think the greatest preventive, & the best thing for him. I hope by the time I come back I shall find him a sophomore in college, high in rank & immense of stature.

We are getting on swimmingly here now. The blushing honors are falling very thickly on the youthful capt. who has command of Co. I, & very deservedly too. Nobody I ever came across . . . had a more decided taste for the military.

Very few of the [honors], I notice, do the ignoble second lieuts. get. The col. roughs us poor second lieuts. awfully. For instance he makes a general remark to all the officers assembled about their conduct, & then adds, "of course all you capts. are all right. It is these young lieuts. (pointing to us) that I mean particularly. They are very heedless & need a great deal of looking after" &c. One of his [Lee's] dodges, you see, [is] to hit the capts. over the heads of the second lieuts., & yet, . . . by treating the capts. as if they were above suspicion, make them act accordingly. However, it is rather disagreeable, as the position of a scapegoat . . . [is] to say the least undignified, & the assumption . . . that the little Irish pig Sweeny[5] is better than we are [is] too monstrous, even for such docile & well disciplined brutes as we are.

[4]C. C. Chase was principal of Lowell High School.
[5]Capt. Henry J. Sweeny, Co. G, would resign on Oct. 3, 1861.

50

However, the colonel is a regular old brick & I think we could all bear being snubbed every day for the sake of being commanded by such a bully old fighter as the col. Why he is the greatest possible favorite with the general. Indeed, I should think our regiment commanded the brigade. The general is hobnobbing all the time with our col. They have made Dr. Bryant[6] brigade surgeon. They have made Quartermaster [Charles W.] Fulsom brigade commissary. They have made Adjutant Pearson[7] active asst. adj. general. And I expect to hear shortly that they have invented a new office & made the col. assistant brigadier general. The fact is, whenever the general has a vacancy, he fills it out of our regiment. The field & staff, to use a vulgar but forcible expression, have effectually rung in with him. And as a penalty, they are forced to take all sorts of confidential midnight rides with him, for the general is a man of ceaseless activity & has no idea of doing business in the day that can be . . . done in the night.

He [Lander] is a very large man & rides a tremendous horse, the same one he rode at Phillipa.[8] By the way, they say he is the hero of Phillipa. . . . He doesn't confine his efforts, however, to the field & staff. It seems to be his particular delight to send us off to bivouac on the river when it is actually so cold that the men walk about half the night to keep themselves from freezing. However, we all like these midnight excursions . . . because it varies the monotony. You will judge what kind of a man he is in short when I tell you that he has a most violent prejudice against allowing any body in his command to sleep quietly during the time allotted by the Almighty for sleep.

Tell Carry that the part of the river where George [Perry] is, isn't so cold, for it is completely sheltered by trees, so that [he] is very comfortable. . . .

The men of our company are getting on stunningly. They are really the best set of [men] that could be . . . desired. I have actually got very much attached to them. In fact I don't rough them half so hard as I did when I first went to camp. It is really hard for me to

[6]Henry Bryant, the regimental surgeon, was promoted to brigade surgeon Sept. 19, 1861. The assistant surgeon, Dr. Nathan Hayward, then became regimental surgeon.
[7]1st Lt. Charles L. Peirson.
[8]"Philippa" is actually Philippi, W.Va., where forces under George B. McClellan—on whose staff Lander was then serving—drove off a Confederate force under Col. G. A. Porterfield on June 3, 1861. This action led to the Federal victory at Rich Mountain on July 11, 1861.

Field and staff of the 20th Mass. Vol. Infantry, 1861. Standing, *left to right:* Surgeon Henry Bryant, Lt. Col. F. W. Palfrey, Qtr. Mast. Charles W. Folsom. Seated, *left to right:* Maj. Paul Revere, Adjt. Charles Peirson, Col. William R. Lee, and Asst. Surg. Nathan Hayward. *Courtesy USAMHI.*

punish them. Why it is a fact that I very often find myself rebuking them on drills in a pleasant, goodnatured way, instead of the proper short, sharp, curt military style. One can't help it; they are such a fine set of fellows.

I suppose you think I am giving you rather more than you bargained for, writing such long letters, but now that I have written . . . about the general & colonel & camp, you may congratulate yourself that my letters will be much shorter. Give my love to mamma & the rest.

Your aff. son,
H. L. Abbott

Please send all the *Vanity Fairs.* . . . Send newspapers three instead of one a week. No matter if it is old.

Brig. Gen. Frederick W. Lander. *Courtesy USAMHI.*

Camp Benton, Maryland, September 26, 1861

Dear Aunt Lizzie,

I don't very often get a chance to write, but tonight [I] have a firstrate one, as I am on guard, that is officer of the guard of the regiment. I have to sit up all night & as [I] only have to patrol about the camp occasionally, I have lots of spare time. This is the first time I have been on guard since we left Washington, as they have reserved our company to go off on exploring expeditions. Perfectly safe they are, as the pickets are very friendly & don't fire on each other.

These expeditions are getting [to] be very stupid, as there is considerable marching to be done, frequently on an empty stomach. For instance, you are sitting quietly in your tent, enjoying a comfortable smoke & thinking it is about time to turn in, when an order comes that you must be ready to start with your company in 15 minutes on a march 7 or 8 miles up the river. Rough but healthy. We are all in bangup condition. I never was so well in my life. Those slippers of yours are extremely comfortable. They are just the thing.

We are within ten miles of Ned & Fletch. I saw them both for a long time on the march past the camp. But now we are not permitted to leave camp even to see them. Severe, isn't it, particularly as there doesn't seem to be any reason to apprehend an attack for some time. Either side which attacks is sure of getting a most tremendous flogging. So there is no prospect of a mill at present. The Rebels will probably have to begin it & get a deuced good beating. I hope so & then we may possibly winter further south—dine in the halls of Richmond perhaps, though not at all probable. There is every prospect of remaining here all winter. By the way, the very spot we are encamped on used to be a rebel encampment & Gen. [Joseph E.] Johnston's headquarters at Leesburgh [Virginia] are only 5 miles distant in a straight line, about 7 by the road.

How are you getting on? Have you any more neuralgia? I hope you will be able to keep your house warm & comfortable this winter. And about your house rent, has Mr. Gordon lowered it any? I should think he would as I suppose all rents must have fallen tremendously of late. How is Lowell now? Do you have as many invitations out as usual to dine? And by the way, speaking of dining, I am at this present time awful hungry & wish most heartily I had some of your cake. It makes my mouth water to speak of it. Well, good bye, tell me all the news when you write.

Your aff. nephew,
H. L. Abbott

Carry's engagement I heartily rejoice at. George is a deuced good fellow & you will like him very much.

Camp Benton, Maryland, October 1861

Dear Mamma,

Your letter as usual was stunning. I only wish you would write me oftener but I suppose you have no time. I got a letter from Aunt Elizabeth together with yours. She writes a very nice letter, indeed a firstrate one. She speaks of Ned opening a recruiting office in Lowell. How is Ned getting on with his recruits? I should imagine it rather a tough job to scare up recruits in Lowell, particularly when so many other Lowell companies are going from the place.

I am very much obliged to you for sending the trunk; I suppose the pipe is in it, though I have got neither as yet.

You speak of Miss Jackson & Maryanne Welch calling. I should like to see them immensely. Please give my love to them. It was very kind of Miss Jackson to send her love. You see I have now no hesitation in sending mine. I got a letter from Maryanne Welch day before yesterday. You may imagine how delighted I was to get it. A letter from any body at home while out here is hailed with rapture, even though you didn't think much of the person before you came; but when you get one from a friend you value so highly, as I do Maryanne, it is really [a] supreme pleasure.

I remember that night I wrote, there was a good deal of tom fooling signalling done & we were ordered to pack our trunks & be ready to start at 3 in the morning. We packed our trunks & slept with one eye open according to command, which means with your boots on. Of course we didn't go. We never do. If the general happens to have a toothache or eats too much supper & is restless, he calls up the brigade to make an advance or a retreat. . . . I suppose there is a sort of dreary satisfaction in the thought that when you are uncomfortable yourself, you can, at a moment's warning, make 3,000 human souls uncomfortable also. At least I don't see any other way to account for these [numerous] marches against invisible foes &c.

Just think if Gen. Scott chose to play it on in the same way; whenever he felt a pain in his little toe he might make a twinge radiate through a circle [of] 200,000 [men]. But then he is a much greater man than Lander. However, I make no doubt Gen. Lander will achieve greatness very soon, if he goes on in the same brilliant way as heretofore. However, there is some danger. He forgets the fable of the [word obscured by inkblot] who played off dying [inkblot].

I thought when I began I had nothing to say but I find I have managed to scribble a sheet. By the way, about the governor's nomination.[9] Is he going to take it? You musn't blame me for these blots, but the celebrated English pen which the governor gave me. It is certainly a very fine pen, with the exception of that little peculiarity of blotting.

Your aff. son,
H. L. Abbott

Be sure & give my love to all the children & tell Sally to write, as well as to the rest of the family & all my friends.

Edwards Ferry, Maryland, October 16, 1861

Dear Papa,

We (that is, George's co. & ours) are down here about ½ mile from Edwards Ferry, detailed to support Rickets' battery. Indeed there are no companies left in camp now. They are all scattered along the river, in one place & another. We shall probably stay here a week.

We are having a stunning time. The weather is beautiful in the day time; in the night rather cold which makes it so much better because it allows us the luxury of a regular old fashioned fire.

The men made for us a California lodge, of this nature: At the back of the tent is an open fireplace dug into the ground, from which the smoke is conducted out by a stone passage under ground, terminating in a large conical chimney made of stone & mud, about a dozen feet behind the tent. We have roaring fires by this means in our tents, without being troubled at all by smoke, in the morning & night.

We have an hour's drill . . . in the morning & then a bath in the [Chesapeake & Ohio] canal, dinner, one hour's drill in the afternoon, supper & then the company goes down to the ferry or spends the night in a barn, for the purpose, I suppose, of supporting the ferry. I spend most of the day in chopping down big trees (we are encamped in a wood) & the consequence is that my hands are covered with blisters, which together with this horrid pen must be my excuse for what I am rarely guilty of, wretched writing.

I suppose in a few days I am to be a first [lieutenant]. When Sweeney's resignation happened I declined promotion, because it

[9]Henry's father was nominated unanimously for attorney general of Massachusetts in Sept. 1861, but he declined.

would have taken me out of the company, so Billy Milton[10] went ahead of me. But now Col. Palfrey thinks I can fix it so as to take a first [lieutenancy] & yet be obliged to leave my company only for a short time, which is certainly very pleasant news for me. . . .

I shall have to trouble you for $50. The government at Washington has concluded to turn an honest penny in the following manner: First lieuts. are to receive money from the time the company numbered 42, up to the first of Sept. Capts. & 2nd lieuts. from the time the company numbered 101. By this admirable dodge no company officers in our regiment will receive any pay except the first lieuts. We poor devils who have been 3 weeks without a cent in our pockets, anxiously waiting [for] pay day, are to receive absolutely nothing. My company numbers 60 & will probably never be full during the war. Consequently, as far as I can see, I shall be dependent on you during the whole war for any support. I don't suppose any body went into the war for the sake of the money, but it is a little rough to be shut down on in this way when you have been waiting so long without a cent in your pocket.

I have been delaying sending home for money because I expected it every day, but can't do so any longer. I must have some to pay for [my] servant[11] & subsistence. I wouldn't send it by express for my trunk has never got as far as Washington even.

Ned, I suppose, is having a gay time. I see by the newspapers his regt. is just paid off. How is his recruiting getting on? Give my love to mamma & tell her I haven't had a letter for some time, also to the rest, [and] the little ones.

Your aff. son,
H. L. Abbott

Edwards Ferry, Maryland, October 19, 1861

Dear Mamma,

I got you & the governor's letters just now, after I had sent one to the governor. I have just got time to write [a] few words in answer before the mail goes.

The trunk has never yet reached Washington. Now if it was sent long enough ago to get here, remembering that freight trains are

[10]2d Lt. William F. Milton, Co. G, was promoted 1st lieutenant of Co. C on Oct. 12, 1861.

[11]Abbott, like many well-to-do officers, had a servant to perform menial chores while in camp.

slower than passenger, then I would humbly suggest that somebody should go & have a row with the expressman & see if something wouldn't turn up.

The buffalo [robe] was something that I have been thinking of for a long time & have only waited to be paid off to get one. I am extremely obliged to the governor for anticipating. It seems he sent everything before a fellow thought of it himself. I only hope it will get here. I believe you have to allow 2 weeks for passage to Washington.

I am very much flattered by people telling me that my writing is very much like the governor's, though I flatter myself that it is considerably plainer. I am very sorry to hear that you are troubled with styes. What awful bores they must be. Why don't you try the efficacious remedy of salt & water that will almost always cure the worst, you know.

I expect to find Sally a graceful & slender young lady with the most finished manner & address by the time I come back, & tell her the most effectual way of becoming so will be to renew the long & interesting correspondence we kept up when she was at New Hampshire. Did Arthur get any answer to his letter? Tell him to write again, as also Frank,[12] who has never yet written at all. I send inclosed a note I got from Jimmy Nesmith. It is so funny a specimen that I thought it might amuse them. Be particular & give my love to Grafton & Holker,[13] & tell Grafton to be sure & not forget me, as I am growing a fierce & hairy moustache, one of those wild untrimmed ones, & Grafton shall have the pleasure of pulling it when I get back. . . .

Your aff. son,
H. L. Abbott

Camp Benton, Maryland, October 21 or 22, 1861

Read the second sentence to yourself.

Dear Papa,
We miraculously escaped without a wound. All the officers of our co. that is. *Half the men* [of the regiment] *killed & wounded.*

[12]Franklin Pierce Abbott, the eighth Abbott child, was then nine years old.
[13]Holker Welch Abbott, the eleventh and youngest of the Abbott children, was then three years old.

Abbott's first letter on the Battle of Ball's Bluff, hastily penned just hours after the fighting ended. *Courtesy Houghton Library, Harvard University.*

Now read to yourself. George Perry is *unwounded* but a *prisoner* with the col., major & adjutant & Dr. Revere.[14] We have [heard] from the rebels that they are *well treated.* There are a hundred of the regt. [which] came out [safely]. 2 or 3 capts. killed, & half the officers wounded.

Your aff. son,
H. L. Abbott

[14]Edward H. Revere, brother of Paul J. Revere, was then assistant surgeon of the regiment. He was killed during the battle of Antietam on Sept. 17, 1862, while performing surgery on the battlefield.

Camp Benton, Maryland, October 22, 1861

Dear Papa,

I suppose you have by this [time] got my telegraphic dispatch & know that we are all safe. I will give you a brief description of the affair, only brief because I am rather played out by 2 days hard work.

It seems that on Sunday the quartermaster of the 15th Mass. [had] got across [the river] & discovered that there were no pickets on the other side; accordingly to them was given the honor of crossing to attack a rebel camp about 2 miles off from the shore. One company of a hundred men from the 20th was ordered to follow the 15th & take possession of the opposite height as a reserve. Co. I & 57 of Caspar's men with Caspar [Crowninshield] & George [Perry] were the reserve.

Sunday night the passage was made by the 15th. We followed, getting over about 5 o'clock [A.M.] & taking the heights. Now look at the absurdity of the thing. To cross the river we had two row boats that together carried over 30 men at a time. We landed on the hill [which was] almost perpendicular & thickly wooded. When we get on the top, we are drawn up on the only open space there is, about wide enough for a front of two regiments, & about a short rifle shot in length, surrounded on every side by large, unexplored woods. It was in fact one of the most complete slaughter pens ever devised. Here we were kept, while the 15th marched off to surprise the rebel camp.

In the meantime we sent off scouts which resulted in our first sergeant, [William R.] Riddle, being shot in the arm. The 15th, of course, lose their way, are attacked & send word they are surrounded & we must cover their retreat. It was rather an uncomfortable thing. A hundred men in an unknown country, surrounded by the hidden enemy & cut off virtually, by the badness of transport, from reinforcement. The col. told us there was no doubt it was all up with us.

The 15th, however, held their ground nobly till now, when they fell back on us & shortly after we were reinforced by the rest of our regiment . . . (making only 300) & by Baker's brigade[15] & a couple of howitzers, who came in by boatloads of 30. After a while, however, they got a boat which carried 60, so that the reinforcements came in faster.

---

[15]Col. Edward Baker (U.S. senator from Oregon and personal friend of President Lincoln) commanded one of the three brigades in Stone's Corps of Observation. His outfit, termed the California Brigade, consisted of the 1st, 2d, 3d, and 4th California regiments. Although Stone was in overall command of the troops at Ball's Bluff, Baker was directly in charge of the troops on the battlefield.

First Lt. George B. Perry, who was engaged to Abbott's sister Caroline. *Courtesy USAMHI.*

Now to begin with the order of battle. I have no right to criticize it. . . . It will be enough to describe it. The uncovered space I have spoken of was the battle ground. Part of Baker's brigade was drawn up on the right flank, on the edge of the wood, with the 15th. The rest was drawn across the opening, back towards the river, 30 feet from the top of the bank. 15 feet behind them the 318 men of our regiment were drawn up in a second, parallel line, under command of Gen. Baker. The two howitzers [were] in front. . . . The rebels had 2 inf[antry] & one cavalry regt.; how full is not known.

. . . 2 of the regts. on our side were left in open view, when they might just as well have been in the woods, while the rebels were conveniently posted in the woods, just at good rifle shot, from which they didn't venture out till the conclusion of the fight.

In the first half hour, the gunners & horses of the howitzers were all killed; the line in front of our regiment was broken & fled so that we were the only force in the open field & from 2 [P.M.] till 6, we kept that field under a heavy fire of rifles & musketry. It seemed as if every square inch of air within six feet of the ground was traversed by bullets as they whistled by us. Tremblet's[16] company got the worst of it. The col. tried to save ours as a reserve. But we foolishly hung all our company's great coats on the trees just behind us. Their red lining was so conspicuous as to draw the enemy's fire at a great rate. Though we were lying down, our men were shot on every side of us. And yet Capt. Bartlett, though standing up nearly all the time, wasn't so much as scratched.

The fight was made up of charges. You would see our capts. rush out in front & cry forward & their companies would follow them at full speed under a tremendous fire till they were obliged to fall back. And this was repeated over & over during the 4 hours fight.

Our company made the last charge. The general [Baker] was killed, shot by 5 balls; nobody knew who was the senior in command & Col. Lee ordered a retreat. But we were determined to have one more shot. So Frank [Bartlett] ordered a charge & we rushed along, followed by all our men without an exception, & by Lieut. Hallowell[17] with about 20 men, making about 60 in all. So we charged across the field about half way, when we saw the enemy in full sight. They had just come out of the wood & had halted at our

[16]Capt. Henry M. Tremlett, Co. A.
[17]1st Lt. Norwood P. Hallowell, Co. H.

advance. There they were in their dirty gray clothes, their banner waving, cavalry on the flank. For a moment there was a pause. And then, simultaneously, we fired & there came a murderous discharge from the full rebel force. Of course we retreated, but not a man went faster than a walk.

When we got back to the wood, we found the whole regiment cut to pieces & broken up, all the other forces gone & Col. Lee sitting under a tree, swearing he wouldn't go another step, but had rather be taken prisoner. However, we got him to go & we all started down the bank, every body knowing, however, that there was no chance of an escape. The col. ordered a surrender & had a white flag raised but the rebels fired on us & we were obliged to retreat to the river's edge, the rebels pouring down a murderous fire.

When we got down [the bluff] we had lost the col., but heard that the adjutant [Charles L. Peirson] & major [Paul J. Revere] had got him into a boat & carried him across. After that, of course, we had only to look to our own safety. We rallied our men & then proposed to swim across [if] they could all do it. We found there were four that couldn't swim, so we were obliged to stay with them, and we sent the rest over. It was hard work to make them leave us, but we insisted upon it, & most of them reached the opposite shore in safety, notwithstanding a heavy fire opened on the swimmers immediately.

With the rest of our men & with Capt. Tremblet & his men, we marched along the shore, picking up about 50 men of Baker's [brigade], meaning to surrender ourselves, if we could only get a chance. After we got a mile & a half we found an old nigger who got us a boat & in this we sent across by fives the 70 men with us & then went over ourselves. And so we escaped.

The col., major & adjutant are prisoners, it seems. . . . Capt. Dreher is nearly dead, shot through the head.[18] Capt. [John C.] Putnam's arm is amputated close to the shoulder. Capt. [Alois] Babo is killed. Capt. Schmidt [George A. Schmitt] has 3 bullets in the legs. Capt. Crowninshield a slight flesh wound. Lieut. Putnam will probably die, shot through the stomach.[19] Lieut. Holmes[20] shot through

[18]Ferdinand Dreher, Co. C, recovered.
[19]2d Lt. William L. Putnam, Co. E, died on Oct. 22.
[20]This was the first of three wounds Holmes would receive during the war. He was then 1st lieutenant of Co. A.

Col. Edward Baker, a personal friend of Abraham Lincoln, was in direct command of Union forces at Ball's Bluff, where he was killed. *Courtesy USAMHI.*

Two casualties of Ball's Bluff. Capt. Alois Babo (seated at right) was shot while attempting to swim back across the Potomac. Lt. Reinhold Wesselhoeft (standing at left) valiantly attempted to rescue his wounded friend, but both men drowned in the process. *Courtesy USAMHI.*

the breast, will recover, as will Lieut. [James J.] Lowell, shot in the thigh. Lieut. Wessleheft is dead.[21]

We are now in camp trying to rally enough men to form a company, so as to join it to the two companies that were not engaged & make a battalion of 3 under the command of Col. Palfrey, who was not in the fight, but has since crossed the river with the two unengaged companies.

Gen. Lander has just got back from Washington & is in a horrible rage, swearing that the thing is nothing less than murder. Gen. Banks'[22] column crosses here tomorrow & there will probably be a retreat of the rebels. The little midnight adventure of ours has started the whole thing; now we shall have our revenge.

The good of the action is this. It shows the pluck of our men. They followed their commanders admirably, except in the last charge that we made. Cas[par Crowninshield] wanted to go with us but his men, who had been pretty well cut up, refused to follow. He swore & raved awfully, but it was no go.

The men of our company couldn't possibly have behaved better. They never fired once without an order. They never advanced without an order, as all the rest did. They never retreated without an order, as some of the others did. In short, they never once lost their presence of mind, & behaved as well as if on the parade ground.

Give my love to mamma & the rest.

Your aff. son,
H. L. Abbott

Camp Benton, Maryland, October 24, 1861

Dear Mamma,

I have written several letters already to notify the family of my whereabouts & George's, because I knew you would be so anxious. I

[21]2d Lt. Reinhold Wesselhoeft, Co. C, and Capt. Alois Babo, who had recently replaced Sweeny as commander of Co. G, had both attempted to swim across the river without removing any part of their uniform or equipment. While the pair was midstream, a volley was fired at them from some Rebels atop the bluff. Babo was shot and Wesselhoeft valiantly tried to save him, but both drowned. Wesselhoeft's body was not recovered until thirteen days later when it finally washed ashore, along with other Federal dead, some twenty miles downstream.
[22]Maj. Gen. Nathaniel P. Banks was then commanding the Dept. of the Shenandoah. The 2d Mass., to which Henry's brothers belonged, was a part of Banks's command.

hate to lose the chance of sending this one, which is going by a special messenger, & may inform you where the others fail. The telegraph of course has, before this, assured [you] of my safety. George is equally safe as far as wounds go, but is undoubtedly a prisoner with the col., major, adjutant & Dr. [Edward] Revere. He will be well treated & released on paroll not to engage again in the war, which will bring him home much quicker than any thing else, I have no doubt. Nobody regards his case as a very hard [one], being situated as he is. It is the col. we grieve for. I could cry now as I think of it.

I was in the house at 2 o'clock the night before [the battle], waiting as a messenger with him [Col. Lee] & Col. [Charles] Devens of the 15th. Col. Devens seemed like a man who had made up his mind that he was going on a forlorn hope. But [Lee] was in the merriest of moods. He joked & quoted Shakespeare & appeared transported at the idea of at last getting into action.

At the same time, he didn't omit the mention of a single circum-[stance] that would help to make us safe. I never heard of [a] more clearsighted, cooler or more satisfactory statement of a plan than was his. He discussed every possible emergency & suggested the action appropriate for it. Nothing escaped him. You can't imagine any thing clearer. He enumerated every case that could possibly turn up, a thousand things which had escaped Col. Devens, & for each he had the appropriate course of action. He wound up every thing by the assertion that it must be distinctly understood beforehand that in case of defeat, no retreat was possible. We must either conquer or die. I remember he urged this upon Col. Devens a good deal oftener than was apparently agreeable to the latter. This was about the expedition to conquer the camp by surprise in the morning, without reference to any thing in the afternoon, because no battle such as that of the afternoon was contemplated. And it was because he was in such high spirits that I am so sorry for him.

The reverse was terrible. It was an awful blow. He exposed himself in every way during the action but wasn't hit. And after our defeat was certain . . . he sat down under a tree & refused to leave the field. It was with difficulty [that] we got him to go down. All we want now is another fight to avenge his capture. I don't think it too strong an expression to say that we are burning for a chance.

I saw Fletcher yesterday. He was in good spirits. Ned has not reached the camp. The 2nd was ordered down here to cross at Edwards Ferry when there were already about 6,000 men thrown across by canal boats. Just as they [the 2d Massachusetts] reached the ferry, however, they were sent back again to Conrad's Ferry, about six miles above us, where they are now. The whole force on the Virginia side was then immediately brought back by General McClellan's orders, who, by the way, slept in our camp last night.[23]

Now look at the difference between him [McClellan] & [Charles P.] Stone. Gen. Stone orders this advance, without any boats or any thing else for the passage . . . [while] on the other hand, McClellan comes & gets them back in the following way which, by preventing confusion & panic, alone saved our army from the total rout always consequent upon raw troops retreating before the foe, especially across a river.[24]

He had one hundred men . . . just the number the canal boat would hold, waked up at a time, with orders to march as if for picket duty or something of that kind, keeping the men actually going in perfect ignorance of where they were going till they positively reached the water's edge.

The movement was begun by the men nearest the river & carried [out] in regular order up to the advanced guard, so that no regiment was passed by any other regt. & no regt. knew that any other had crossed till itself was fairly on this side. You see they didn't give any body any chance of getting panic stricken. It undoubtedly preserved our forces from annihilation.

[Lt. Charles Lindsay] Tilden's co., one of the 3 not in the fight [of the 21st], was in the advance & he was one of the last to cross. Lindsay was under fire with his company while over there & stood it with remarkable coolness.

Now all I have to do is to tell you about the dead & wounded, which [is] so awful melancholy because we got licked in that infernal slaughter pen instead of whipping the scoundrels. Of the 315 men we took in . . . nearly one half escaped to this side. We brought out one half [of] our company, but amongst the killed were 3 of the noblest fellows that ever were born, men that we loved. However, we are cheerful as we ought to be, of course, that it was no worse.

[No signature]

[23]McClellan assumed command of the Army of the Potomac on July 25, 1861. He would replace Scott as general in chief on Nov. 1 of that year.

[24]Here Abbott refers to the withdrawal of the left wing of Stone's forces which had crossed the Potomac at Edward's Ferry, a short distance downstream from Ball's Bluff. Palfrey, commanding that portion of the 20th not engaged in the battle, was sent to reinforce these troops early on Oct. 22; however, all forces were withdrawn that evening.

Camp Benton, Maryland, October 26, 1861

Dear Papa,

I have sent a draft to Mrs. Norman, my servant's sister. If you will be kind enough to honor it I will send you the sum as soon as we are paid, which I believe is going to be immediately.

I suppose by this [time] you have got my other letters & know all about us. George is the only line officer who is taken prisoner, but we have the satisfaction of knowing that he acted gallantly during the action & is now with the col.

Your aff. son,
H. L. Abbott

I saw Ned today. [He] just got here, all right.

THREE

AN ADMIRABLE
LOT OF FELLOWS

Camp Benton, Maryland, November 4, 1861

Dear Mamma,

Your letter breathes a very natural indignation against the officer who is responsible for the blunder of the 21st. I am afraid however that the public will have to rest in ignorance. . . . It is evidently considered that it would be injurious to the service to have a public examination into the conduct of an officer who, though he may have made one stupendous mistake through carelessness & neglect, and apparently laziness, has enough other good qualities to make his dismissal a loss to the service.

I have fully made up my mind who the man [to blame] is, upon I think very good grounds. A certain person's own defense, I should say, shows very clearly that that person, to put the most favorable construction upon it, shifted upon another person the responsibility of deciding whether or not an advance should be made.[1] Now I don't accuse that person of being conscious that he was ignorant how to proceed, for his subsequent conduct upon an important occasion involving the fate of 6 or 7 thousand men proved him to have great generalship. But I do accuse him of great & inexcusable laziness & negligence, when, being within ten miles of the scene of action, instead of coming to see about the thing himself, he orders his subor-

---

[1] Abbott undoubtedly blamed Stone, as many did, for placing the burden of the battle on Baker when Stone himself should have been at the scene of action. Due to the severe casualties inflicted on his troops at Ball's Bluff, the death of Lincoln's friend Baker, and other political reasons, Stone was imprisoned without charges on Feb. 9, 1862, following a one-sided investigation by the newly formed Joint Congressional Committee on the Conduct of the War. Though Stone was guilty of mismanaging the battle, he hardly deserved to be imprisoned. (If that were the case, half of the Union generals would have wound up in jail at some time or another during the Civil War.) Stone was freed on Aug. 16, 1862, and later served as chief of staff to General Banks during the Red River campaign.

dinates to decide the matter for him. I have not the slightest doubt from the indisputable generalship of the person I refer to, that had he seen to the thing himself, instead of leaving it to inferiors, we should have been saved from destruction. I don't think he will be careless again. And I do think he has great abilities. Therefore I conclude that the service would suffer in losing him.

How are your eyes now? You wrote in your last that they were better but not yet well. It must have been a very bad case to trouble you so long. . . .

I got my trunk day before yesterday. It seems the mistake was in trying to send it to Poolesville instead of simply sending it to Washington. It went as far as Georgetown, where it was brought to a halt & nobody knew where it was till one of our teamsters happened to see it there & brought it in.

The buffalo robe I can't praise too much. The shoes were, what I considered to now impossible, better than the previous ones; the pipe was there too. But the trunk is what I admire most. Though much more expensive than the one I asked for, there is no other fault to find with it. It is the lightest I ever saw & yet [as] strong, apparently, as the heaviest. I think the governor is unmatched in his taste for trunks & sheer bother.

Ned gave me a stunning belt, too, when he came on, so that I am royally equipped, & as the gloom of the battle is passing away, feel very cheerful again. How does Carry feel? Tell her to write. By the way, you don't know how the regiment misses the little col. Though the drill &c is improving because it is now in the hands of Frank Bartlett, who is doing wonders, instead of Col. Palfrey, yet we feel sadly the difference between Col. Lee & Col. Palfrey.[2] Don't forget my love to my female friends.

H. L. A.

Camp Benton, Maryland, November 7, 1861

Dear Papa,

I have just got your letter. I suppose it must have been on its way for a long time. Probably as long as some of my letters are in getting to you. For instance, immediately after the battle I sent home letters by all the means I could get, calculating upon about half getting there. The telegraphic dispatch you say, too, never reached you.

[2]During Colonel Lee's captivity, Palfrey served as acting colonel and Bartlett as acting lieutenant colonel. Macy assumed command of Co. I.

Brig. Gen. Charles P. Stone was in overall command of Union troops at the Battle of Ball's Bluff. *Courtesy National Archives.*

Frank's [Bartlett's] letters never reached home either. And for the very fact that he sent a so much more elaborate one is the reason I took so little pains with the letter which you say was circulated extensively. I never dreamed of its going out of the family circle, when so many other better ones I supposed would reach home at the same time. I am very glad you didn't print it, not only from "innate modesty" but because I did in it [a] gross injustice to the California regt. Whether they did well or not I won't say, because I shouldn't be speaking from personal observation. The mistake I made was to call the men who were placed in front of us & who ran away, California, they being in reality Tammany,[3] though at the time I wrote we all . . . supposed them to be California [men] & only discovered our mistake afterwards by finding out the dress of the two regts. If you get my next letter you will find that I corrected the mistake as soon as possible, though, of course, the remedy isn't much better than retracting in the presence of one man an insult offered before a thousand. Still it is all I can do.

The letter [about the battle] is full, too, of other inaccuracies, being written before consultation with others, as I hate, you know, letter writing, particularly when elaborate. Others, evidently, who were on the left of the line, know more about the special detail, though the field was so small I could easily tell the general outline.

All these stories you see in the newspapers about the ferocious red-whiskered rebel who shot Gen. Baker & all such poppy cock, of course, you don't believe. When Gen. Baker was shot his blood bespattered Caspar Crowninshield. So you see we have good authority for all our accounts, & I advise you to believe nothing at variance . . . with them.

Above all, be sure to disbelieve all ridiculous yarns about a certain California capt., formerly of Boston, then of New York, whose previous occupation was so loathsome that his name would pollute a gentleman's page. . . . Discredit every thing told of that fellow, except the fact that he was carried off the field to a place of safety about 15 minutes after the battle began, showing a slight scratch on his arm, but not showing his sword, which he left on the battle field. Pah! I have wasted too many words for such a creature.

You know I told you that I didn't believe I was physically brave. In fact, I was pretty sure I should be frightened on the field of battle, though I hoped my feelings of duty, pride & honor would keep me up. The fact is, however, that on the battle field I was very much

[3]The 42d New York was also known as the Tammany regiment.

surprised to find that I wasn't frightened at all. Indeed, it would be hard to be frightened when men whom you are accustomed to think more ignoble than yourself are cool all round you. To tell the truth, I am rather sorry I wasn't considerably frightened, because if I had been I might have had a chance to see whether I could command any amount of will, moral courage, &c. Besides, in my efforts not to be subdued by my fear, I might have rushed into the other extreme & have done something gallant & glorious, whereas the fact is I wasn't excited enough to be able to do any thing better than my men who were with me.

All the stuff you see in the newspapers about "young Abbott, son of Judge Abbott," is all blow & poppy cock. I no more deserve to share Frank's praise with him than any of his privates do. The fact is, I am completely disgusted with these newspaper notices. There are plenty of other officers in the regt., Hallowell for instance, who deserve more praise than I do, though they haven't had the distinguished honor of being posted by the newspapers. Frank, however, you may be sure deserves all he gets. In a word, you had better disbelieve all the stories & all the puffs in the papers, except those which have the sanction of this regt., & then you will be safe.

I suppose this letter to most persons would be horribly stupid, because it is so egotistical, but I know that you will like to hear how I felt because your last letter was such a kind one. And speaking of letters, I think that one of Ned's is wonderful. The idea of such a stately, reserved old boy as Ned breaking down so. I am glad you showed me the letter. It only confirmed me in my opinion that this is the kind of man who feels the most. Indeed, I think the only reason of our disagreeing at times was his protecting way, which I rather resented, though I had . . . the lurking belief that it rose from affection, as now I am sure of it. I trust to God I shall never be on the same battle field with either him or Fletch. It would, I think, be horribly distressing. My next battle field I shall wear a present of his, a beautiful sword-belt, the best I ever saw.

All your things came safe, each perfect in its kind, the trunk particularly. I wish you could have gone to congress. I think you are needed really. There can be no doubt. . . . How are mamma's eyes?

Your aff. son,
H. L. Abbott

I forgot to say that Frank's official account in the newspaper is the only trustworthy one, except that printing has turned the plan of the battle upside down. George [Perry] is reported by southern papers, a prisoner, unwounded.

Camp Benton, Maryland, November 12, 1861

Dear Papa,

I send you enclosed a receipt for $260. If you will be kind enough to present it at the major's office, you will get the money. My pay was $298. Next time I shall send a larger proportion out of the pay.

Now I want you to deduct from this the following sums & invest the balance; put it in the bank or what you choose. Of course, when I am earning such a magnificent salary myself, it would be shameful for me to be an expense to you, so I want you to take out the following:
$50.
Trunk
Shoes
Robe

Then, as this is the first good sized sum of money which I ever earned, to share my elation . . . I want you to give Sam a present from [me] of $10. Sally $5. & each of the little devils a quarter apiece. I want you to give it in their own hands personally. Sam, of course, is old enough to manage $10. properly, and as Sally,—girls of her age generally, I confess, I don't think ought to have $5. in their pockets as a general rule, but Sally is so wise & discreet a little maiden, that I have no more doubt of her ability to handle $5. than I have of my own to handle $300. You needn't be afraid I am going to tip them regularly at every payment. I only do it now because this is the opening of my earnings, just as a man would do if he came into a fortune. So please be sure & put it into their own hands & don't put it into a five cents savings bank, will you?

I shan't probably want any more clothing from Boston. My best dress suit is magnificent cloth, not shabby in the slightest degree, & as I only wear it at parade, there isn't any prospect of its wearing out. For the rest, I get my clothes [from] the quartermaster, which answers regulations exactly, except that it is a little coarser.

By the way, Macy sends now to Nantucket about a thousand dollars for his Nantucket boys. Good boys, aren't they? Indeed, it would be impossible to get a better set. We never hear an oath or a growl . . . of any kind in the whole company. I think they behave even better since the battle. . . .

I saw Ned here Sunday. I have got permission to go & see him next Sunday, though he said that they are expecting to go to Charlestown [Virginia], the capture of which is beginning to be rumored. Shouldn't it be glorious if both our regts. could go together through the gates of Charlestown?

Poor Sergeant Riddle has just had his arm taken off. . . . We are going to give him a commission, though he isn't to be told of it yet, so you musn't say any thing of it, for fear it might get back to him.[4] Mrs. Bartlett wrote him a letter a while ago.[5] He was very much delighted to get it. As he is a very nice respectable fellow, I think mamma might take advantage of his being in my company to consider him an acquaintance & write a letter to him. At any rate, I should be very much obliged to her if she would, when she has a spare moment. He was the first man shot in our regt., about 8 o'clock in the morning when out scouting, in the right arm. The elbow was all knocked to pieces & finally, after 3 weeks suffering, the arm is cut off, just above the elbow, & he is now, I think, much better. Another of our men will have his right arm cut off in a day or two. They all bear their wounds with remarkable fortitude. The Englishmen & Irish of the regt. suffer less than the Yankees, though I think the latter bear it as well.

I have got lots to say about the house & Boston & particularly the girls, but I haven't time. Only be sure to tell Carry to remember me to Miss Jackson & [Miss] Sargent & to the Welches.

Your aff. son,
H. L. Abbott

Camp Benton, Maryland, November 17, 1861

Dear Mamma,

I was very glad to hear from you again; indeed, I think I could hear from you very much oftener, without getting tired of it. But I am very sorry to hear that you still suffer from your eyes so much. It must be exceedingly disagreeable & interfere with all you have to do. . . . Still, I think you might stop the thing by going to somebody who thoroughly understands it, a regular oculist, for instance.

And speaking of that, who is your regular doctor, now you have got to Boston? You see there are lots of things I am ignorant of by being away from home, especially since such a great change in domestic affairs has been made by the moving. I want to know too, what kind of servants you have got. Whether you are bored with them still. As you say, I need one of our old conversations to get me fully up on existing arrangements. Still, I have pretty conclusively made up my mind not to come home till the war is over, even if I

---

[4]William R. Riddle was commissioned 2d lieutenant on Nov. 25.
[5]Mother of W. F. "Frank" Bartlett.

get a furlough, unless I am wounded, & perhaps not then. Because, you see, not to speak of natural anxiety to be at the seat of operations & to accompany everything right straight through, just imagine how much gladder we all shall be to see each other, if separated for a period of 3 years or so, than if the edge of the meeting is taken off by previous visits home. Why you won't know me with my mustache & imperial, though I shall know you and the governor & Carry, but shall hardly be able to recognize Sam & the rest. Quite dramatic, you see. Quite too much so, at any rate, to be defeated by any little furloughs. This is the way I console myself at the prospect of 3 years absence, or rather the way in which I shall console myself, when I need that sort of thing; for now, I can assure [you], I have no desire to leave.

We are all . . . interested in the advance that is going to be made. I hope & trust . . . that we shall have a chance at them as well as the lucky fellows who have got Beufort.[6] Just think what a glorious revenge, if we could only give the rebels a second edition of Beufort. . . . However, I have no doubt whatever that we shall have our chance some time or other. . . . I suppose I have blown about enough now, & I will turn to other topics.

In the first place, I am going over to see Ned & Fletch tomorrow. I have got a promise from the col., so I consider the thing safe. It will be the first visit to the Second [Massachusetts] since I have been out here, though they have been within 12 miles of us all the time. Rough, isn't it?

In the second place, I want to thank you for your kindness in making the stockings. Very gladly they will be received by the men, you may be assured. Please be sure & thank Hattie Gordon for the pair she knit. Tell her I shall bag that pair for my private property, if you will put a mark on them, so that I can tell them. Thank papa very kindly for the mittens; nothing could be better. I am very much obliged to Carry for working so hard to make stockings for my men; she is certainly very patriotic and warm hearted. The best way of thanking her is to tell [her] that a letter has been received making us sure that [the] colonel, George, & the rest are exceedingly comfortable. I am sure they deserve it, for no men could have behaved better on the field. Now that they are beginning to exchange prisoners, we are all in hopes that we shall soon get our stunning little col. back again. If I should see him again I should be as glad as at a victory.

[6]Beaufort, S.C., fell to Union forces on Nov. 9.

By the way, when you send those stockings & mittens, can't you put in the bundle my thick undershirts? I was a fool not to carry them. Or better still, some thick woolen shirts like those I carried with me, only thicker, & made for wearing collars, a luxury which I now habitually indulge in. If you could also put in a cheap prayer book, which, though I am . . . a dutyful son of the church, I am ashamed to say I do not possess. I won't deceive you into thinking that I mean to read it as often as I ought, by any means. I ask [this] for me because, in case one should be seriously wounded, it would be needed. As a matter of precaution, too, I am going to make my will this morning, though I suppose it is rather crowding things. Still, it has always been my plan to be guided by the dictates of prudence, you know.

Give my love to the governor & Carry & Sam & Sally & the little dev[il]s. How I should like to give them a hug again, & also to all female friends; don't forget the latter [and] be sure & ask Mary-anne Welch why she has given up writing to me. What have I done to be forsaken so ignominiously, ask her?

Your aff. son,
H. L. Abbott

Oh, tell papa not to forget in the list the $50. paid to my servant.

Camp Benton, Maryland, November 23, 1861

Dear Papa,

I do believe you are the best governor going. Ever since I graduated from college I have been thinking so more & more. When I remember how often I have been a self opinionated, self conceited donkey to you, I wonder how you still can be so good to me as you are. I feel very deeply the kindness of your last letter, you may be sure, or else I shouldn't let myself out in this demonstrative kind of way; for I inherit your supreme contempt for fellows who are always doing it. But I think it makes one feel better once in a while.

Now, papa, you really have a great deal of paternal partiality. I know my letters must be very entertaining & interesting to the family circle, (how I wish I could drop in for one evening only, with the whole crowd there) but when you come to read that miserable old production of mine about the battle to strangers, & such distinguished ones as Judge Bigelow . . . , I must say I think your fatherly fondness is getting ahead of you. No joking, it was really a very slovenly production; however much you might like it, uninterested parties like the judge, I am afraid, would be bored very considerably by it, & you know the idea of being even the innocent cause of bother to the bigwig before whom I am going to stand up some day, gives me a great deal of trepidation. Why, if you don't look out, I shall begin pretty soon to try to write well.

I think Ned takes after you in writing letters, for he certainly has the knack of doing it most excellently. I read considerable portions of your letters to Frank [Bartlett]. He says he likes to hear your letters very much, because you always write so easy, as if you were talking.

How much it is like Fletch to want to buy a horse with his sole remaining $50, for Grafton. It is just like him; he is altogether too generous. He & Ned have been obliged to spend a good deal more than I have, because they have led so much more interest[ing] a life. And then, you see, they have been spending their own money, while I was living on what you sent me. There is no particular praise due me for the way I have saved my money. It is only because I have happened to hit upon a method by which it is easier not to spend than to spend. . . . As soon as the wounded get well & Thanksgiving is fairly past, I shall even have a redundancy in my purse, for there is nothing here to spend it on.

By the way, speaking of Thanksgiving, I want to give you a description of the day, though it must be strictly private, for I shall censure most severely the conduct of a noble superior, merely by relating it.

In our regt. we gave the men a . . . dinner of roast turkey & plum pudding, & then most of the company officers gave their men something to drink. We gave our 35 men 5 bottles of whiskey, & I am happy that there wasn't the slightest trouble resulted therefrom. But in the 19th [Massachusetts] there was considerable more fun. They had a great dinner, to which I was invited . . . , but didn't go. In the evening they had a ball to which came a large number of very vulgar & respectable tradesmen's wives of Baltimore. Col. Hinks[7] & his noble crowd of officers slung them round with considerable force, as is, I presume, the fashion they parade at home. About 8 o'clock, Col. Hinks came into the drinking tent (I forgot to say that the dancing hall was a tolerably spacious apartment, with a wooden floor under foot, & tent flies overhead, with two drinking

[7]Edward W. Hinks was colonel of the 19th Mass.

tents connected.) Well, in the drinking tent he [Hinks] joined Billy Milton & myself. In a moment, we were joined by Brig. Gen. Gorman, also.[8]

The contrast between the col. & [Gorman] was startling. The former is a stout, thickset, very vulgar looking fellow, showing, however, in his face, considerable resolution, energy & pluck; vulgar, resolute & *drunk* completes him. Gen. Gorman, on the other hand, appeared to be a very mild, courteous, old fashioned rustic gentleman, conspicuous, as far as I could see, for a sharp nose, a small mustache, a big collar, a big belly, & a buff sash, besides being sober.

The noble col. drank whiskey several times. The gen. & myself, being altogether milder individuals, drank champagne. The Col. toasted the 20th, which he was kind enough to say he had rather command than any other [regiment] in the vol[unteer]s. The general deigned to tell Billy & me how different would have been the result at B[all's] B[luff] if he had been there. The col. said his reputation had been assailed . . . & it made him a demon, but still he had rather lead the glorious 20th into action &c &c. The gen. said the col. took things too hard. And so it went on till Billy & I, who were delighted at first at the novelty of ringing in with a col. & a brig[adier], got played out & left. The col. was soon put to bed. I have described the scene so that you may have an idea how disgusting it was to see a Mass. col. drunk, & before several privates, too. There was also a drunken Mass. major & a drunken New York col. making fools of themselves there. It was sickening, I assure [you]. But don't breathe a word of it, for heaven's sake. All I am afraid of is that [General] Stone will get hold of it, & so get ahead of Hinks in their controversy, in which, at present, Hinks has most decidedly got him. Stone is an old woman, though a gentlemanly one. Hinks is low, of course, but is at any rate a man. . . .

Your aff. son,
H. L. Abbott

Camp Benton, Maryland, November 30, 1861

Dear Mamma,

I have just got your last letter. You tell me that you had rather a solemn Thanksgiving without any celebration. The day of rejoicing & no rejoicing therein must really be somber. I am sorry that you

[8]Brig. Gen. Willis A. Gorman commanded one of the three divisions in Stone's Corps of Observation.

had so serious a time of it though. I can assure you I feel very much the kindness of you all in remembering us & praying on account of our absence. . . .

I hope now you won't let Christmas be spoilt by any thought of our absence. For I dare say, we shall be enjoying ourselves. Thanksgiving, certainly, I had a very nice time indeed. Certainly the idea of being scattered so on that day as we are, & away from the family isn't cheerful in the extreme; but still, take it all in all, we had a very pleasant time. A nice dinner & a swig of rum.

All my men behaved excellently too. They are certainly an admirable lot of fellows, that is, what is left of them. One of them died this afternoon of wounds [received] at Ball's Bluff. The doctor says he was the most uncomplaining of all in the hospital. In fact, for the last day or two he hadn't been able to complain. I have [seen others] that die in the same way. For [several] hours before they [die] they lay with their eyes half closed, the skin as tight over their face as a drum head, with the hiccoughs in their throats, actually catching for breath, just barely able to gasp, "water." They seem to be neither dead nor alive, neither fully conscious, nor yet entirely unconscious, oppressed with terrible suffering which they have [not] the strength to complain, however much they suffer, just like a man buried alive or partially suffocated. Almost the last thing Barber[9] said was to ask to have his wife's letter read to him. He was just barely able to gasp it out. It had been read to him several times before. It was written under the impression that he was doing bully, & asked when he was coming home &c. His death was particularly melancholy because he was a very valuable fellow in the company.

We have just got a list of the rebel prisoners, 108 in number. The number of killed, wounded & missing was in our regt. 183, so that we have about 80 killed & wounded of the 300. I hope we shall have our turn soon. Don't you?

I shall be extremely obliged for the shirts. These thin ones are getting to be rather cool. I supposed your eyes had got all well by this time. You must have had a severe attack to have it last so long. I consider it a perfectly good reason for not writing often, though I will do you the justice to say that you write as often as I do.

Poor old George, I suppose, is rather low [in] spirits. However, he will soon get exchanged I have no doubt. Whether they would hang the prisoners in any contingency, I hardly can make up my

---

[9]Pvt. Alexander M. Barber died on Nov. 21.

Headquarters of the 20th Mass. at Camp Benton, near Poolesville, Md. Capt. W. F. Bartlett stands in front of the door. *Courtesy USAMHI.*

mind. I am certain we shall never hang the privateers.[10] Annoying & aggravating as their plundering is, I don't see . . . why we should have ever contemplated hanging them any more than any other rebels taken prisoner. The only reason they are pirates is because they are rebels, & rebels are always treated as prisoners of war untill the war is over. Then when we are successful, we can single out our proper objects for hanging. Certainly it won't be the poor private sailors & soldiers, who have acted, however wrongly, in obedience to

[10]At this time the U.S. government was considering whether or not to hang a group of Confederate privateers recently captured by the navy. The Lincoln administration had determined that these men were not regular sailors, but were, in fact, pirates and not entitled to be treated as regular prisoners of war. When the Confederates got wind of this decision, they responded by stating that they would hang an equal number of Union prisoners—to be chosen by lot—if the Federal government carried out its dastardly policy. Lots were drawn, and Colonel Lee, Major Paul Revere, and assistant surgeon Edward Revere were among those prisoners placed in a condemned cell to await execution. In the end, however, the U.S. reconsidered its policy and decided to treat captured privateers as regular prisoners of war. The Confederates, therefore, cancelled plans to execute the Union prisoners and returned them to regular confinement.

their superiors & in accordance with their notions of right. So long as we allow to Jeff Davis the de facto sovereignty by treating his soldiers whom we capture as prisoners of war instead of prosecuting them before civil courts & hanging them, so long we must recognize the de facto power of issuing letters of marque & sending out privateers.

By law, the armed traitors we take on land are just as much subject to hanging as the pirates we take on the ocean. The reasons we don't hang the former are entirely political. We are afraid of retaliation & of instituting a cruel & bloodthirsty system of warfare. . . . Trying the privateers in the first place was a blunder & I think the government will acknowledge it by desisting in their proceedings. It is certainly disagreeable to have people say that you are bully ragged, but if I were Old Abe, it would be still more disagreeable to think that I had stretched 3 or 4 necks on a matter of pride. Some people say we shall have the best of it yet, because we have got Mason & Slidell;[11] that is, we can hang the most & get the better of it in the end. The idea of the good natured Old Abe pursuing such a fiendish policy as that is laughable, don't you think so?

Give my love to all my friends & to the little devils & the governor & tell the [governor] how much obliged I am for the gloves. . . . I told the men they were a present from him & they swell round in them very proud indeed. . . .

Your aff. son,
H. L. Abbott

Camp Benton, Maryland, December 13, 1861

Dear Mamma,

I got your parcel safe, for which I am very much obliged. The novel I have never read before, but I presume from the fact that you send it that it must be a very good one.

Miss Lee, you say, asserts that I am coming home on a furlough. I don't know where she could have got the impression. I have no idea what ever of coming home untill the war is over & I confess I haven't even felt much inclination to since I have been out here, except that the other day I did have a little touch of homesickness, arriving from peculiar circumstances which made it perfectly excusable.

[11]On Nov. 8, U.S. sailors commanded by Capt. Charles Wilkes boarded the British ship *Trent* and captured Confederate emissaries James M. Mason of Virginia and John Slidell of Louisiana. They were released on Dec. 26 following strong protest by Great Britain.

I was commandant of the Grand Guard & went into a poor white man's house on my rounds. The whole building was just about the shape & size of our old kitchen building in Lowell. There was only one room below, which was kitchen, "sitting room," &c, & one chamber above. In this place lived a man, his wife & 7 or 8 children. Think of it. They were all pretty children, or seemed so at any rate, perhaps because it [has been] so long since I have seen any children. So I relaxed for a moment my usual stern & ferocious military aspect & began talking with them. All of a sudden there peeped down from the chamber above a face so exactly like Grafton's that I actually made about for it & came very near invading the sanctity of the bed chamber by pursuing the little devil in his retreat. He had the same blue eyes & pug nose & long yellow curls & saucy little mouth &, in fact, the resemblance seemed so complete that if I hadn't been with another officer, I believe I should have stayed round till I won the little one's confidence. As it was, I promptly resumed my habitual military aspect & by way of making up for any want of gravity before, I came very near bagging the little one's father on a suspicion of selling rum to the soldiers. However, I went round to the same place once afterwards on duty, & on closer view found that the resemblance was by no means as close as I had fancied.

Indeed, it would be strange if a man of [that] social condition could have a child that looked like Grafton. Still, the incident made me think a little of the pleasures of seeing you all again, old & young, particularly from the association; however, those little round arms of Grafton's would fasten round my neck. The feeling didn't last long though. I think I am beginning to get entirely over that feeling of homesickness which used to afflict me so much, whether for better or worse I don't know.

It is my firm belief that we shall be in Virginia before a fortnight has passed. I am very seriously afraid, however, in fact I am . . . certain, that we, that is Gen. *Stone's* division, won't be allowed to cross till the country has been occupied by Gen. [George A.] McCall's division, which I think is already within 7 or 8 miles of Edwards Ferry. . . . You can comprehend how much we want to revisit the battle field of B[all's] B[luff] & see the spires of Leesburg, to us a miniature Richmond.

Gen. Stone has had a balloon . . . here for the last two or three days. Of course it hasn't gone up yet. In Boston it only takes up an hour or two. But here, you know, military promptitude & decision, I suppose, stand in the way. The gen. remembers that before, on an unimportant occasion, he forgot to look before he leapt, but evidently he is determined that now the great balloon shan't go up without due care & circumspection.

Think what it is to be a great man! The other day the gen. had a drill of infantry, cavalry & artillery. 3 regts. of inf[antry] of which the 20th was one, (I was absent on guard) a squadron of cavalry, & 2 batteries of artillery. It is described as being magnificent & giving one an excellent idea of battle; also, I have no doubt, it was another evidence to the gen's. admirers of his transcendent abilities, for he showed clearly how easily he could demolish the foe, if they would only allow themselves to be placed by him. How nice it is to be a great man.

I could get only one chance to see the 2nd while they were in this neighborhood. Fletch came over the Sunday before they went to Frederick [Maryland]. I have just heard that all Banks' division have crossed [the Potomac] somewhere below McCall. If that is the case, they have got ahead of us. I hope we shall soon be up with them.

Do you know that I have never yet got one of the stockings sent by Carry? How were they directed? I have been putting off . . . writing to her to wait for the stockings, but they [were] not forthcoming. Do you know also that every one of you owes me a letter, the governor & all? Please give my love to all the family & to my friends & tell Aunt Elizabeth that I find my slippers a great comfort. I wear them constantly.

Your aff. son,
H. L. Abbott

Tell Sam I am very much obliged for his photograph. I think it a very good one. . . . Frank & Macy would hardly believe that he was a younger brother of mine of fourteen.

Camp Benton, Maryland, December 16, 1861

Dear Papa,

I am happy. I am first lieutenant, detailed as acting captain of Co. I.[12] I have now entire command of my boys. And I really believe that they are as glad as I am, for tonight, after dress parade, there was the uncommon sound of loud cheering; & old [Leander F.] Alley, my first sergeant, who is a regular old salt & used to be first mate [on] a whaler, & is usually a gruff old fellow who isn't given to flattery, told me there wasn't a boy in the company who wasn't glad of it;

[12]Abbott was promoted 1st lieutenant on Nov. 25, with commission to date from Nov. 8, 1861.

rather unmilitary, I suppose, but still allowable because Alley is a man who never takes any freedom or presumes, or any thing of that kind.

It is very much owing to him . . . that the company is kept in such good order, being an old whaler & used to [enforcing] obedience. Indeed, I believe he keeps in his tent a long flat stick, known as "Alley's Spanker," & when the boys don't behave they catch it. Why, we haven't had one from the company in the guard house since we left [Camp] Massasoit, & I think any body will allow that I am very strict with them.

Such things as this, for instance. Col. Lee always wanted to be very liberal in religious matters. So he assembled the regt. & instructed them that prayers would be read every Sunday, but that nobody should be forced to go. . . . Well, that worked very well for some time, till finally the audiences became very slim & dwindled down to about sixty. Still, my company all turned out because they knew their officers wanted them to. Finally there were 3 one Sunday who didn't fall in. Of course, one couldn't do any thing directly, after Col. Lee's order, so I made the 3 do all the water carrying during the services & for an hour or two afterwards. And since then nobody in my company has availed himself of the col's. permission to stay away from religious services. . . .

About other things I am very strict with them & yet they are such a good set of boys that I never have a word of complaint from them of any kind, not even looks; for you know the best disciplined men can, if they choose, without saying any thing, . . . express a great deal in their looks. In fact, I am perfectly well satisfied, & that must be my excuse for pouring out such a lot of egotistical stuff. Besides, I know that it will be interesting to you to hear it, even if it would sound egotistical to a stranger.

We have just had a fresh batch of 17 for our company. They seem to be a good set of men & make our company, about half of whom are on extra duty, up to 75. Isn't that pretty gay?

Speaking of recruits reminds me to ask you have you had Capt. Tremblet [Tremlett] to dinner yet? There are rumors of his not coming back. I hope they are not true, for I think him one of the pluckiest, most resolute, most determined fellows I ever met. If you see him I think you will agree with me that he is one of those men who impress you with the idea of force.

Have you seen Capt. Putnam yet? The heroism with which he has borne the loss of his arm equals any thing connected with the whole affair of B[all's] B[luff]. But really, after reading the lives of Havelock,

Capt. Henry M. Tremlett. *Courtesy USAMHI.*

Hodgeson,[13] &c, I am convinced that B[all's] B[luff] was no fighting at all. We only thought so because we were green at it. Why here in the lives of the Indian heroes, a young fellow comes out to India & in his first letter home records 3 terrific battles he has already [been] engaged in,—and not such fighting as we have [had] in this country so far, at long distances, but real fighting, where a fellow has a chance to get excited & gets two or three sabre cuts, a regular hand to hand conflict, & then marches 3 days on a road which runs through forests & marshes where a battery plays on him from every turn in the road & a volley of musketry comes from every clump of trees; one continual fight from the time you set out till you get to your journey's end. It seems as if all the fighting we have done since the war began, if all put together, couldn't compare with . . . the least of these battles. Have you ever thought so?

Macy goes as capt. to Co. B, a German co. I have no doubt he will make a good capt. My young second [lieutenant], Arthur Curtis, I think, as well as I can judge from such short notice, is going to make an excellent officer; just the fellow I should desire.

[Lt. Herbert C.] Mason has just told me that you wanted to know whether I should like to have a Christmas dinner sent on. I think I have no right to give you people at home the trouble, for I suppose we officers shall have a festive dinner ourselves. Still I am very much obliged to you indeed. Tell mamma I shall answer her last letter immediately & shall also write to Carry.

Your aff. son,
H. L. Abbott

Camp Benton, Maryland, December 20, 1861

Dear Papa,

Your letter interests me so much that I must reply at once. . . . About Caspar [Crowninshield], I assure [you] I am horribly indignant that an officer should go away & slander the regt. he belongs to by saying that one of the officers didn't behave well.[14] The most he ever said here was under the inspiration of whiskey (I don't mean that he was tight at all, but when not after a drink, he was very close & prudent)—that a certain officer in the regt., whom you don't know &

[13]Sir Henry Havelock (for whom the headgear was named), 1795–1857, commanded British troops in India. Maj. Gen. John S. Hodgson, 1805–70, commanded troops in H. M. Bengal Army.
[14]Crowninshield transferred to the 1st Mass. Cavalry on Nov. 25.

I don't care for, behaved very shabbily. That was all. He never said any thing of the kind openly even of one, much less did he put it in the plural number. And now to go home & cast a stigma upon the whole regt.,—for when he doesn't particularize, the suspicion attaches to all—is base & dishonorable. As for the boat exploit, I am sure, if I recollect aright, none of us attached any great importance to that till the newspapers chalked it up, & then Tremblet's friends & those who are jealous of Bartlett, seem to be trying to transfer the laurels from B[artlett]'s brows to T[remlett]'s. I suppose, seeing that I was with the expedition & Crowninshield wasn't, I am as good authority as he,—and I assert that in my opinion Bartlett was indisputably the originator & commander of the whole. Crowninshield never expressed his opinion in camp, publicly at any rate, but I can easily see why he expresses it in Boston. Prudence, of which he has great stock, dictated a proper reserve at camp, which is broken, though, by his jealousy at finding himself only second fiddle to Bartlett at Boston. . . .

Now about Caspar's being the last to leave the field & there being no firing from the tops of the banks into the river. The first statement I deny; the second I agree with. About the first, the facts are these. When our company made the last advance, while we were still advancing, I looked behind to the left & saw Caspar vainly endeavoring, by words & actions, to rally his broken & dispirited handful of men to make another charge. They wouldn't go on, & he of course wasn't fool enough to rush without them. After the charge . . . made by us, when we came back, there wasn't a single officer of the 20th on the open field.

In the edge of the woods were the col., major & adjutant. We stopped & assisted the adjutant & major in inducing the col. to leave. Caspar was not only not on the field behind us, but he was not in the group at the edge of the wood. Where he was, I don't know. But this I do know, that here at camp he never claimed to be the last man on the field. . . . However, he does report that considerably after the battle he crept up the bank & getting behind the tree, surveyed the field on which he says there wasn't a rebel to be seen. Perhaps that is what he refers to, though it isn't my idea of being last on the field . . . though I think it shows greater daring. This assertion . . . I have always believed hitherto, because I have always considered him a man of honor & a gentleman.

But about the rebels firing down the banks into the river, I agree with Caspar entirely. I don't believe any thing of the kind. I don't remember whether I asserted in my accounts of the battle that the

Capt. Caspar Crowninshield. *Courtesy USAMHI.*

rebels did so; I dare say I did, for such was my opinion during the time in question, as well as of all the rest present, & for [a] considerable time after the battle. . . . But upon hearing Caspar's account of going up & seeing the field empty, which, by the way, I have only heard very lately, & upon considering other . . . convincing proofs . . . I am satisfied the shots which fell in the river came from the rebels while still occupying their old position of the battle. Still, you couldn't tell that at the time.

Indeed, I have no doubt that if Col. Baker had been possessed of a spark of military genius, the field would have been ours; if, leaving Baker as he was, the guns had been properly handled, or if . . . the other regiments on the field had fought as well as ours, that is, untill one third of their number were dead or wounded, on the field mind you, not after the battle was all over by being made prisoners, as was the case with [the] 15th, Cal[ifornia] & Tam[many regiments], . . . we should have won the day.

I think statistics show that our men fought well. As for the rest of the whole, now that I have got agoing, I may as well relieve myself by saying that it was a most miserable blunder from beginning to end, both on Gen. Stone's part (who is very incapable I think, & is entirely destitute of moral courage I know) & on Baker's part.

I think the 20th behaved well, but from what I myself saw on the field & from the list not of *prisoners*, but of *killed & wounded*, I should say that the other regts. didn't behave well, owing I suspect, on the part of the 15th, to their col., who though not a coward, hasn't the grit he ought to have. As for Gen. Stone, I won't run him down openly, because those bloodhounds of abolitionists are at him,[15] but I say to you privately that I believe him to be a nincompoop & so regarded by McClellan; the consequence of which is, I am very much afraid, we shan't have a chance, as long as we are in his [Stone's] division, to revenge B[all's] B[luff].

Caspar's not coming to see either you or the Perrys I think a more open manifestation of his selfishness . . . than I supposed him capable of. But in regard to his being dull, I think you are entirely mistaken. . . . I consider Caspar one of the ablest young men of my acquaintance. He certainly possesses a very clear insight into human nature. In several cases, when I have differed with him at first,

[15]The committee investigating Stone's actions at Ball's Bluff was composed largely of radical Republicans and chaired by staunch abolitionist Sen. Ben Wade of Ohio. Since Stone had, in the fall of 1861, returned a fugitive slave to his master in Maryland, he was put in disfavor with the committee from the beginning, although his action obeyed current U.S. law.

events have afterwards proved him right. He has also strong common sense, very good taste, considerable humor, & whenever he has a mind to throw off the heavy German air of stupidity, he can be one of the pleasantest men I ever met. . . .

On the other hand he is perfectly selfish & indifferent to everybody else, though ordinarily too shrewd & wellbred to show it. This power of concealing his feelings, joined to his deuced pleasant address, is what has made him so popular. He never alludes to himself, which misleads most persons into supposing him free from vanity. I first suspected this at the fort, from seeing how jealous he was of Col. Stevenson, one of his rivals before the war, [who] shot ahead of him so.

Now it is simply because his vanity (his leading passion) has been wounded that he has left the regt. His jealousy of Bartlett overcame him. He saw Bartlett reorganize the regt. after the battle & make it better than it was before. I say Bartlett because Frank entirely governs Palfrey, who is very superficial [and] ready to lean on any strong man. He [Crowninshield] saw Bartlett do all this & properly get the praise of it, while he did nothing & got praise accordingly, for Bartlett is as much superior to Crowninshield in military matters, as Crowninshield is [to Bartlett] in social matters. And that is the reason Caspar left. His pride won't let him be second fiddle & his energy isn't enough to make him first, & consequently, with all the ability he possesses, he will never be successful. . . .

Now pray do excuse this very long letter, for I have been waiting to have a conversation with you on private affairs of this nature for a long time. . . . I hope you will have a pleasant Christmas. You don't know how much I should like to be with the whole family on such a day, that is, if I could without leaving camp. Please be sure & burn this letter just as soon as you have read it. Give my love to mamma & the rest.

Your aff. son,
H. L. Abbott

Camp Benton, Maryland, December 21, 1861

Dear Aunt Lizzy,

I believe that you still owe me a letter, but to show that I am not proud . . . I am writing again. I hear that you have been staying at Uncle Welch's. How is the old gentleman? When you write tell me all about your present condition. How your house & every thing is getting on. I should think, except for the loneliness, it might be very comfortable there now; that is, if you have been enjoying the same kind of weather that we have, for here it has been uncomfortably warm, though the cold weather is just setting in. . . .

There is no news stirring here in particular. I suppose you know all Banks' division has left these parts for Frederick [Maryland]. Consequently there is only a small picket force of 4 or 5 thousand men about here now, just about enough to do picket duty on the 16 miles of river left to their charge. All this shows conclusively, I am afraid, that McClellan doesn't contemplate any business for this division, & that we shall have to rot in inglorious peace & quiet. Hard luck for us, but I suppose we have had our turn & have got to give somebody else a chance now. I suppose you like such news very well however, for I don't think you are very glad to have me in a fight.

How is everything in Lowell getting on? You be sure & give my love to all my friends whenever you see them, won't you? I should like immensely to visit the city once more. I should hardly be known I fear, for I am very effectually disguised by a mustache & imperial. I believe you don't like whiskers, so I shall cut them before I . . . see you. Don't you think that a great sacrifice?

The abolitionists are making a great row in Congress, but they will get floored as they deserve, with that miserable old humbug Charley Sumner[16] at their head. I haven't seen any men or officers in this part of the loyal army who are willing to fight for abolitionists, though I hope we are too good soldiers to disobey if such are the orders. . . .

Your aff. nephew,
H. L. Abbott

Camp Benton, Maryland, December 31, 1861

Dear Papa,

I am writing to you in order to get you to interest yourself about Capt. Bartlett particularly & Col. Palfrey in a minor degree. I think from all the indications I have had that you enjoy considerable influence, or at any rate did enjoy considerable influence with

[16]Sen. Charles Sumner of Massachusetts was the undisputed leader of the Republican abolitionists. On May 19, 1856, in his "Crime against Kansas" speech, Sumner venomously denounced Sen. Andrew Butler of South Carolina, a proponent of slavery. Three days later, Butler's colleague Cong. Preston Brooks retaliated by repeatedly beating Sumner over the head with the butt of his cane as the senator helplessly sat at his desk on the Senate floor. It took Sumner over four years to recover from his injuries.

Gov. Andrew.[17] And I know, papa, that you give me credit for sufficient insight into character to be able to form some judgement where
I have had such excellent opportunities as lately for forming a judgement, so I am going to tell you my opinion in hopes it will have
some weight with you. Of course entirely unsolicited by the parties interested.

It is simply this. It would be a most outrageous shame to think for
a moment of following any other than the regular course of prefer-
ment, making, namely, Palfrey colonel & Bartlett lt. col. Palfrey, I
candidly confess, isn't a man of uncommon abilities, but decidedly
better than the average of cols., for he is a gentleman, well educated, able to make the most of fair abilities, & what is of most
importance, has the most intense regard for appearance, undisturbed
in any strong passions which would make him forget to do what
would look to be right, so that if he were all alone, the chances are
he would be much oftener right than wrong. His desire to appear just
& equitable in the eyes of men & officers in most cases makes him
so, as he is possessed of sufficient discernment to discover in most
cases what is just and equitable.

And now comes the necessary infusion of vigor that is needed, in
Frank Bartlett, a person of more natural military aptitude & genius
than anybody I have ever met. I think this quality is universally allowed him by friends & enemies of whom he has a good many since
his reputation has grown so wonderfully. Not only military aptitude,
but the power of governing men with vigor & firmness, so that they
not only look up to him in every moment of doubt but also love him.

Company I is proud of the last. The men are under the most admirable control, not merely in the camp, but on the field of battle,
where, when the [rest of the] force was in a busy flurry, firing in all
directions, they didn't fire a shot till word of command from him.
Ask anybody here about the improvement of the regt. since Bartlett
has managed the drill. . . . Since Palfrey & Bartlett have had charge
of the regt. you see a complete change all through. Instead of
blacked boots & washed hair being confined to one company, you see
all companies alike in that respect. Instead of the majority of the
men being merely a pack of Broad St. & Northstreet roughs who are
just working along as little as possible for their pay, kept under by
discipline & ridiculing all appeals to the better feelings, you see them
actually vying with each other who shall be the best soldier, most

[17]Gov. John Andrew of Massachusetts

Col. Francis W. Palfrey, 20th Regt. Mass. Vol. Infantry. *Courtesy USAMHI.*

tidy in his equipments & most active in his duty. And all this done with very little punishment. . . .

Palfrey gets along with the men amazingly well & they are really fond of him. When some really hardened cases come up, then Frank comes in, & they are treated with a strong & energetic hand that quells them effectually. Palfrey has good sense enough to see that such cases demand prompt treatment, such as tying a man up by his thumbs & keeping him in a cell on bread & water with the mercury below freezing. He sees that it is necessary & allows Bartlett to do just as he chooses, as in fact he usually does. Palf's desire of popularity never allows him to interfere with Frank carrying out the proper discipline.

In a word, I don't see how the regt. could be possibly more cheerfully obedient than it is now & when I remember what a crowd of roughs most of the men were who came into camp, I am really [illegible word] struck how they could be brought into their present state. It is really impossible that the government of the regt. could be changed for the better, & justice surely requires that they be continued permanently in the places where they are now acting, Palfrey as col. & Frank Bartlett as lt. col.

I know, papa, you will interest yourself in the case, & I hope successfully.

Your aff. son,
H. L. Abbott

FOUR

A LETTER IS A GODSEND

Camp Benton, Maryland, January 11, 1862

Dear Papa,

I write to ask you to send on by bearer Corp. [John W.] Summerhayes my rubber boots. It is impossible to get them here. Mamma
will tell you how deuced muddy it was when she was here, from the
melting of the snow.[1] The next day it got so bad that you couldn't
step out side the tent without going over your shoes in mud. As I was
on guard & couldn't remove my equipments for 24 hours, I was in a
box & made up my mind immediately to send for rubber boots. As
the corp. has to start immediately, I can only say good bye.

Your aff. son,
H. L. Abbott

Very much obliged for your phot[ograph] & the paper.

Camp Benton, Maryland, January 17, 1862

Dear Papa,

I have only time to say a few words. I have sent on by [Capt.]
Charley Whittier, who is, by the way, about the best line officer in
the regt.—$100. My savings this month hasn't been so large as the
time before, not because I haven't tried as hard & economized it as
much, but because the expenses have been so much heavier. The
wounded men had to have many things, & then Christmas &
Thanksgiving both coming in the same period took the cost of two
dinners for the men.

Considering everything, therefore, though I felt rather cut up at
first, I think I have economized tolerably well. My full pay was $225 &

---

[1]Abbott's mother had been visiting Frederick, Md., during the first week of January. Henry, along with his brothers, had obtained a short leave of absence in order
to visit her.

Josiah Gardner Abbott. *Courtesy Library of Congress.*

I sent home $100. Had it not been for the extra expenses, I should have sent home $175, or rather had $175 left after all expenses & sent home $150. Please give Sam $5, Sally $1, and each of the young ones .25. I should like to come home immensely, but it is absolutely impossible.

By the way, I have never got an answer to the letter I sent you about Frank Bartlett & Col. Palfrey. The col. says too [that] he has written you but never got an answer. I hope mamma has got home safe with Fletch. . . .

Your aff. son,
H. L. Abbott

Camp Benton, Maryland, February 5, 1862

Dear Mamma,

You needn't apologize for your letter. It was the best that could be written, just what I want to hear about precisely. It is the next thing to going home. I wish, whenever you write, you would write just the same kind of letters.

Fletcher, I suppose, must have had an immensely good time. I can easily imagine how he enjoyed himself [while on leave]. Did he go to see Miss Mudge, or has he forgotten that little incident? Sally, with her French, &c, will be a regular young lady by the time [I] get back. By the way, what did she do with the money I sent her this last time? I hope she will enjoy it. When I read that little anecdote about Frank, I can see the whole scene just as plainly as if I were there. Is Frank as warlike as when the war first began? Grafton and Arthur you tell me about, but Holker, the fatty, you say nothing of. However, I suppose he isn't much more than a second edition of what Sam was at his age. Tell Frank and Arthur they must write me. It is a long time since they have done so.

I suppose Carry can't see the justice of letting Charley Peirson back before they do George.[2] Well he will come soon, I fancy. Charley Peirson we expect soon at the regiment. The others I don't know about. We should all like to see the old col. above all things. I suppose the plucky little fellow must be pretty used up by prison hardships by this time.

Aunt Elizabeth owes me a letter; tell her the next time you see her. By the way, do you know who sent me a Christian Society almanac?

[2]Peirson, the first captured member of the regiment to leave Richmond, was exchanged on Jan. 27.

I have just come off the hardest week's duty I ever had in my life. With 97 men & 2 lieutenants under me, I had to guard eight miles of the Potomac on the tow-path between the canal & the river. I had to make personally the entire rounds of the whole, making six-teen miles every night, starting at 12 o'clock, through the most hor-rible mud that the mind of man can conceive of. During the course of the week I was tipped over in a crazy boat by a stupid fellow & had to swim for it. I almost ruined my sword & belt by tumbling down in the ruts during my midnight rounds. I got my feet so sore that the last night of all, I couldn't stand on them & had to come when relieved in a wagon—& to crown all, one night, at half past eleven. . . . dark as pitch & blowing great guns, I was burnt out, losing my blouse, all my shirts & drawers, stockings, . . . both pair of army shoes, brush comb & lots of little things, & a borrowed pair of rubber boots, saving my bag at the expense of singed hair & a very slight burn on the neck. Luckily I have got 2 pair of shoes left & have got all the other things from right here in the regiment.

Billy Perkins I have seen nothing of.[3] I suppose he thought the going from here to Washington too bad. Several persons have given it up for the same reason. The mud makes Poolesville almost inaccessible.

Your aff. son,

H. L. Abbott

When the boots or the book comes, please send 2 boxes Roussell's shaving cream.

Camp Benton, Maryland, February 5, 1862

Dear Papa,

I didn't for a moment ascribe your not answering my letter to ne-glect; I knew you must have too much business on hand. And now I hear from mamma that you have had one of your old nervous head-aches, from working too hard I suppose. What you need is a visit to the Army of the Potomac. Say, I hope you will, as soon as you can make time, by any means. It would be the best thing for you, you know. . . .

I am horribly afraid we shan't see any more service & that the fighting will all be done in the rear of the Southern Potomac army. I don't mean, of course, that I love fighting for itself, but I do ear-nestly long to be in a grand battle. If a fellow should go through this

[3]William F. Perkins, a newly commissioned 2d lieutenant, joined the regiment on Feb. 11.

war & never be in any thing but that murderous little skirmish where we got licked, it would be outrageous. I think we should have a good right to complain. But such seems to be the prospect now. A little while ago I thought from what Col. Palfrey gleaned at headquarters that there was a strong prospect of an advance, but I am afraid it is hopeless.

I suppose you know that military dandy, Stone, isn't to be confirmed, not because he is inefficient, but because he has offended the abolitionists. They talk of Fremont & Steyel & Gen. Burns, an old army officer, for his place.[4] The latter I hope. I don't want any abolitionists or foreigners. They may do very well to lead on the mythical hordes of the West in mythical battles, but they ain't the kind of men we need here.

I am equally rejoiced with you at the battles in Kentucky[5] & the ejection of Cameron.[6] If they would only put it through by an advance. But I suppose the roads are too poor here. We cannonade each other down on the river here nearly every day now. But fighting at long distances, Gen. Stone's favorite style, is rather weak & of course, when the river is between, will never lead to any thing. What do you think of the Burnside expedition?[7] Do you think it will do any thing?

I am very much obliged to you for looking after me in the way of clothes. But I don't think I need any thing now, except the rubber boots, & those boots I need shockingly. There is an express now between here and Washington, but it costs all most as much as the boots are worth. Only send them by the first person coming & that will be enough.

Your aff. son,

H. L. Abbott

---

[4]Maj. Gen. John C. Frémont (the "Pathfinder") was then in command of the Mountain Department. Brig. Gen. Julius Stahel was in command of a brigade in Frémont's department. Brig. Gen. William W. Burns was then in command of the Third Brigade (Baker's old brigade) in Stone's division.

[5]On Jan. 19, Federal forces under Brig. Gen. George H. Thomas defeated Confederate troops under Brig. Gen. George B. Crittenden at Mill Springs, Ky.

[6]Secretary of War Simon Cameron resigned his post on Jan. 11 rather than face formal charges of corruption. Cameron was then appointed minister to Russia, and Edwin M. Stanton accepted the position of secretary of war.

[7]Brig. Gen. Ambrose E. Burnside was then leading an expedition against Roanoke Island, N.C. See James I. Robertson, Jr., ed., "The Roanoke Island Expedition: Observations of a Massachusetts Soldier," Civil War History 12 (Dec. 1966):321–46.

Camp Benton, Maryland, February 13, 1862

My Dear Mamma,

If you only knew how glad I am to get your conversational letters, you would write oftener. I don't know what you mean by saying that you haven't heard from me lately. I was under the impression that I had written twice to your once. I got tonight, at the same time, two of your letters, one dated Jan. 9, the other Feb. 10. A mistake on your part or the mail's?

Isn't this glorious news, the Roanoke victory and the capture of a second fort with 5,000 men? Could any thing be better? The 24th [Massachusetts] have had a chance to get ahead of us.[8] Lewis, too, has seen fire. I wish we could [get] particulars as to whether the 24th suffered [losses] or not. The governor has always been right in his political prophecies and I begin to think he was in saying that the war would be ended in spring. I have all along wondered how he could believe such a thing possible. But I see now very plainly that it is possible. The men are all wild with enthusiasm. We took them out on the parade [ground] & read the telegram and cheered them & they did it well. If we could only have a fight now! I can fully comprehend how Ned feels at not getting a lick at them. Both the 20th & 24th have had a turn, and it [the 2d Massachusetts] only awaits for a fight. . . . But I don't believe Banks' division will ever fight, nor ours either as long as we have such an infernal old pompous asinine idiot as Gorman to command.[9] May the Lord deliver us from destruction if we go into battle under such an old fool as Gorman, for in man there can be no help, except from the fact that as soon as the battle commences, the hero of Bull's Run & *Edwards Ferry* will ride rapidly to the rear in order to secure a commanding eminence to view the battle from. See paragraph 780 *Revised Army Regulations* which recommends for the position of a commanding general a lofty eminence in the *rear*, well out of cannon ball range.[10] You can see how incapable a poltroon the general is, to surprise me out of my usual rule not to write home letters censuring my superior officers.

You are wrong, mamma, about Gen. Stone. You know my opinion about his incapability, but to doubt his loyalty is simply ridiculous. I

[8]The 24th Mass. was a part of the Roanoke expedition.

[9]Gorman had assumed command of Stone's division upon the latter's incarceration.

[10]The editor could not find this reference anywhere in the *Revised Regulations for the Army of the United States, 1861* (Philadelphia, 1861), although it may have appeared in an earlier edition.

wouldn't send a private to the guard house on such absurd charges as have been trumped up to enable Charles Sumner to have a gentleman dragged away in the night from a dying wife & shut up in a prison. Every decent man here feels shocked beyond expression.

I don't think you are foolish at all in what you say about the enemy crossing [the river] & capturing us. I think it perfectly possible, if they chose to do so, of which there isn't much chance at present. For, though the regiments of this division are amongst the finest in the service, I candidly believe, they are few in number (not more than 5,000 effective & a few useless batteries that can't come within two miles of the line of any thing they aim at) while there is no help within a day or more's march. However, thanks to these glorious victories, we can sleep as securely as at home. I wish we couldn't. I can't say enough about these victories. If we could only follow them up.

You must be in a great state of excitement in Boston. Victory, but probably bought at the expense of some men Boston mothers will be sorry to lose. I hope and trust Lewis isn't among the number. Sad for Mrs. Stackpole if he is. And if he isn't, glorious. Write as soon as you can and tell me what they think in Boston.

This mud and drill and inaction here is horrible while other people are fighting their great battles. We want something more than that little skirmish over on the bluff. Wish with me that we shall have it now.

Tell papa how very much obliged I am for his care in ordering army shoes. It is very kind of him indeed. There is nothing else at all that I want. I am amply supplied with underclothes. I shall be very much obliged for the book and soap. It was blouse I said that was burnt, not trunk. However, I have another. I send enclosed a picture of 3 roughs of the bloody 20th, taken to patronize a Dutch corporal. I shall send pretty soon a picture of all [Company] I's bloods, where you will notice that they all have cut their whiskers down to a mustache and chin beard. I recommended it to them last night, and today there wasn't a single different cut of beard in the whole company. Even old Alley, for years the first mate on a Nantucket whaler, a regular old American sailor who despises every thing like poppery, sacrificed his great yellow whiskers. I want to go into battle with the boys. I know they won't go back on me, as long as I don't go back on them.

Your aff. son,
H. L. Abbott

"3 roughs of the bloody 20th." *Left to right:* 1st Lt. George N. Macy, Capt. W. F. "Frank" Bartlett, 2d Lt. Henry L. Abbott, near Poolesville, Md., February 1862. *Courtesy USAMHI.*

Camp Foster,[11] Maryland, February 28, 1862

Dear Papa,

I am very sorry to trouble you, but necessity compels me to ask you to send me, with the utmost possible speed, 2 straps for blankets to be carried on the back, the one to replace my own which I lost at Ball's Bluff, the other to replace [Arthur] Curtis', which I borrowed & which was burnt on picket. It is impossible to get the article here in Poolesville, though there is a large army store here. I have to my experience the futility of sending to Washington, so I see no other way than to trouble you. You had better send them by way of Washington.

The 15th [Massachusetts], when they got to Adamstown [Maryland], plundered the express house it is reported, & I am afraid my boots and book [were] amongst the rest. I think the straps will get here before we move, if sent quickly. If we should go without being

[11]The 20th left Camp Benton on Feb. 26 and reestablished camp later that same day at Camp Foster, closer to Poolesville, Md.

permitted to carry trunks or any thing else, the straps would be absolutely essential.

Banks' division it seems, has crossed [the Potomac] without finding any thing to fight. I don't believe there will be any thing of that kind untill Manassas is reached. We felt pretty blue at first at being left behind, but are promised a share as soon as the fighting begins.

Ned & Fletch must have had a pretty tough time of it, if they marched as our division, without tents. It has been bitterly cold for the last 3 days, particularly here in our new camp at Poolesville, as the place is bleak and the wind tore our tents pretty well up.

Your aff. son,
H. L. Abbott

Camp Foster, Maryland, February 28, 1862

Dear Papa,

The boots & book have both got here safely. As I just sent a letter an hour ago saying that they had not got here, I felt bound to correct the statement. Stunning boots they are too. I had no idea of getting new ones. I merely wished to have my old ones sent. But I ought to have known you well enough to know you would send new ones.

Your aff. son,
H. L. Abbott

Camp Lee (formerly Camp Foster), Maryland, Saturday, March 8, 1862

Dear Papa,

I beg your pardon for not acknowledging before the receipt of the army shoes. They were received 3 or 4 days ago. I meant to have answered immediately, but the fact is that I have been so very busy lately that I forgot it from day to day. Today I got the coat straps. Stunning things they are too. Both they and the army shoes show that they came from the same donor. You always send the most magnificent of the kind, you know. . . .

The straps came just in time tonight. Tomorrow we set out for Leesburg, which I am deeply grieved to say is in the hands of Col. Geary . . . who advanced down & took it, the enemy fleeing at his approach.[12] It is the grossest outrage & insult to us that a parcel of

[12]John W. Geary, commanding the 28th Pennsylvania in Banks's division, was captured in the movement on Leesburg, which fell to Union forces on Mar. 8. Geary would later be released and would eventually be promoted to major general.

pickets should be allowed to come down & take the place, we who have been beaten off once from the place & been lying watching it for six long & dreary months in a muddy Maryland cornfield. There can be no cause for it except that the feelings & rights of a brigade in an army of half a million are too small to be respected.

We have, without bragging, an excellent division & an excellent general[13] who . . . has been telegraphing for the last week to be allowed to go over & occupy Leesburg. And now to have our just revenge snatched out of our hands is mortifying in the extreme. I feel almost as if somebody had slapped my face. However, I suppose I have said enough of our personal grievances when so much is at stake.

I should like to hear immensely how Ned & Fletch & the men of the 2nd are getting on. The troops who evacuated Leesburg & all the troops, we hear, that the rebels are getting, are concentrating on Winchester [Virginia]. Northwest of Leesburg, you know. So we shall perhaps have a big fight there in which we join with the 2nd. I think not, however. I don't believe any thing of consequence will be done till we get to the plain of Manassas. There I know we shall be in at the death. There Charley Peirson says he saw works of immense strength & large numbers [of Confederates]. There we shall have slaughter such as we read of in European battles.

Have you had any letters from the 2nd? Have you got my last, acknowledging the receipt of the rubber boots?

Your aff. son,

H. L. Abbott

I have just got by tonight's mails a letter from Carry dated December 6 or 7, in which I learn for the first time the no. of our house. . . . Please give my love to the little col. & tell him how much we all want him & the major back here, to make us advance.[14]

Cantonment Bolivar, West Virginia, March 17, 1862

Dear Papa,

On Monday we evacuated Camp Lee, Poolesville, marched to the Monocacy [River], took the canal boat, came to Harpers Ferry [West

---

[13]On Feb. 22, John Sedgwick assumed command of Stone's division (now the Second Division, Second Corps). Also Napoleon T. Dana was now in command of Lander's old brigade, the Third Brigade of Sedgwick's division, to which the 20th Mass. belonged.

[14]Colonel Lee, Major Revere, asst. surgeon Revere, and George Perry reached Boston on Feb. 28, but they were still on parole, not yet having been formally exchanged.

Virginia], marched to Perrysville, within 8 miles of Winchester, bivouacking on the spot where campfires of the 2nd were still warm
from the night before. The next morning [we] retraced our steps &
are at present . . . occupying deserted houses in Bolivar, a suburb of
Harpers Ferry, under marching orders bound for the Lord knows
where. Rough wasn't it, to get so near the 2nd & not see them
after all.

We are cut off from our trunks & so are obliged to carry knapsacks
like the men. I don't find it very hard, however, & I don't believe I
shall give out on any march the brigade can make.

Captain [Allen W.] Beckwith, who has always been a disgrace to
our regiment on account of his stupidity, ignorance & vulgarity, &
Lieut. [John W.] Le Barnes, ditto for like reasons, with the addition
of being a long haired abolitionist & spy of Gov. Andrew's, have
both sent in their resignations for fear of being kicked out,—the
former got drunk at Harpers Ferry & jumped his horse out of a two
story window; the latter refused to obey orders with regard to keeping
fugitive slaves within the lines. This removal leaves only *one* of the
regular old 20th officers as the regiment was originally organized, viz.
Capt. Shephard [Allen Shepard], & he, though the poorest officer
on the field, with exception of the two above mentioned, is a thoroughly well meaning, hard working man & a good fellow.

What comes now is strictly private, except to mamma. I have
been offered the vacancy caused by Beckwith's resignation, Co. G,
but have refused in favor of Charley Whittier, who is really about the
smartest officer on the field. I have the most intense desire to be a
captain, I confess. I would give almost any thing for the position, &
what is more, I am not afraid of being able to fill it amongst our
volunteers. It is a pretty hard thing to throw away a chance of rising
in any thing you take hold of, particularly when you see so many
inferiors above you. But to tell the truth, I can't make up my mind
to leave my own company. I have got really attached to the fellows. I
have worked over them since I joined the service & now that I have
had exclusive control of them for 3 months, I can't bear to see any
body else in my place.

If Frank Bartlett had been promoted I should have been captain of
Co. I, the great object of my present ambition. But now I have got
to settle down as soon as Frank comes back to the company, which
will be when the col. & major get here, to be nothing more than a
first lieutenant, in the company which I have drilled & disciplined in
the smallest particulars. A pretty hard pill to swallow, but better
than leaving them.

Now [that] I have had a chance to unburden myself I shall feel better. Write me whether you hear any thing from Ned & Fletch.

Your aff. son,
H. L. Abbott

Fort Monroe, Virginia,[15] *March 31, 1862*

My Dear Papa,

We have got down at last to Fort Monroe, through Washington. We are lying off the fort tonight, & tomorrow shall disembark, I suppose. Where we shall go, I have no idea. Something to do, I hope.

Have you heard lately from Ned or Fletch? They were not in the battle, it seems.[16] Rather hard luck, isn't it, after all their marching & hard service? . . . Tell Aunt Lizzy & Carry that I shall answer just as soon as I can. Here on board, every thing is so horribly crowded & confused, & there is such a mass of topics, that I can't possibly do so yet. . . . The same reasons, with the meanness of the paper, must be my excuse for the shortness of this letter. . . .

Your aff. son,
H. L. A.

Near Yorktown, Virginia, April 9, 1862

Dear Mamma,

Your letter, short as it was, was inexpressibly cheering. We had just got back to our bivouacking station after a hard day's work at reconnoitering—marching & countermarching all day with a bloodless skirmish, the mud up to our knees, the rain coming down all day, back in the dark to a camp without tents of any kind or any shelter, & worst of all without wood. So we were obliged to go over & collect a little wood, & sit up all night round a small fire in a big circle, the rain drenching us all the time. But I can honestly say that your letter & the kind remembrance of the pipe, together with Sally's stunning sugar plums, were a thousand times more refreshing than a bottle of brandy would have been.

[15]On Mar. 24, the regiment broke camp at Bolivar, Va., and marched to Sandy Hook, Md., where it then took a train to Washington, D.C. At Washington, the 20th boarded the transport *Catskill*, sailing from the capital on Mar. 28 and arriving off Fortress Monroe, Va., on Mar. 31. That night the regiment disembarked and went into camp one mile from Hampton, Va.

[16]The 2d Mass. was not engaged in the Battle of Kernstown, Va., fought Mar. 23.

Today, the third day, it is still raining with no prospect of leaving off. And yet, though the men are sleeping & living in mud puddles, I haven't heard a word of complaint. Every officer remarks the same thing. I think this cheerful endurance is perfectly wonderful. All the rest of the army except our brigade have shelter tents, but through a mistake in our brigade neither officers or men, with the exception of the field & staff (in whose tent I am writing this) have been supplied since the march began. Coupling this with the fact that the rations are necessarily short on the march—since rice, beans &c, which constitute a large part of the ration can not be cooked on the march—all together I truly think the men bear it heroically.

We have got here an army of from 80,000 to 100,000 men. I suppose we are only awaiting dry roads so that the artillery can pass to attack Yorktown. There is a man or two shot every day on picket, as there was on our reconnaissance, but other wise you wouldn't imagine we were in the presence of the foe.

There are 4,000 regulars here, but I don't see that they are much better than our regiment—scrubby looking men, though there is no denying that they march at a good slashing pace. Gen. McClellan, whose headquarts. are only a half mile off, rode through all the troops on our first day's march. He was cheered most lustily by all the regiments. Soldiers don't share the hatred which politicians feel towards him.[17] I liked his looks very much what I saw of him. His cap was off all the time as he rode through miles of troops & he looked most smilingly gratified, as he might at the expression of such warm devotion.

Poor Putnam & Riddle, after sticking it out a great deal longer than they ought, have at last been forced by the doctor to go back on thirty days leave to the fort. Gen. Sedgwick says they should resign as it is impossible, as it is ridiculous, for [them] to think of standing such campaigning as we are now having. Dreher still holds out, though he is only for duty when there is prospect of a scrimmage. Several other officers are on the sick list, & so we are rather reduced in that line.

I wish to God Col. Lee were back or Frank Bartlett had command. Don't say that I said so. Billy Milton is a[ssistant] a[djutant] gen. for the general.[18] Pearson is his commissary, & he wanted Charley Whittier as aide, only we couldn't spare him. Tell me about

[17]McClellan was relieved as general in chief on Mar. 11 but retained command of the Army of the Potomac.

[18]Milton and Peirson were serving on General Sedgwick's staff.

Ned & Fletch as soon as you hear, & for heaven's sake write, & tell all the rest of the family to write often. A letter is a godsend. Give my love to papa, Carry, George & the rest. I shall answer Frank's most excellent letter as soon as I can. . . .

Your aff. son,
H. L. A.

Picket before Yorktown, Virginia, April 20, 1862

My Dear Mamma,

In the first place, I am glad you took the precaution to send me a sheet of paper, for it is inconvenient to carry it in my knapsack. Pencil, of course, you will excuse, as I am writing while on picket.

Speaking of picket, the orders now are to practice that barbarous & unchristian warfare, picket shooting. The result is that a man or two is picked off every day, without getting any thing to compensate for the loss of life, slight as it is. On the post where I am, however, I have taken the precaution to put out my extreme pickets without caps on their pieces & [with] orders not to fire, merely to fall back on me. The result is that I am having a very comfortable time of it, while there is a popping of guns going on all round. These men, you see, have [general] orders to fire when they see any body, so they pop away all day, & as soon as it grows dark they mistake every stump for a man, & begin a general engagement, all on their own side, while the enemy, who never dreamed of making an attack, are quietly enjoying our folly, ensconced behind their walls. The last time our regiment was on picket there was a continual alarm on this post, day & night, because they were so anxious to shoot a few poor devils on the other side. Last night is the first night since we have been here that we haven't been routed out of our blankets, once or twice, because our pickets insisted on firing at their own shadows.

This whole country seems to be densely wooded, the houses about 3 miles apart. The peninsula is about 10 miles wide . . . and the rebels' works extend clear across. These works are, I think, considered tolerably elaborate for temporary field works, though of course nothing like the field fortifications before Sebastopol that the allies were so long in taking.[19] These works, at least those which we are engaged at, are placed right in the midst of these immense forests,

---

[19]Referring to the siege of Sebastopol during the Crimean War (1853–56).

with a clearing of a few hundred feet in front. The consequence is that our whole forces are enabled to encamp in these woods within a mile of the works, some regiments within a quarter of a mile, ours about ¾ mile. Each regiment goes on picket for 24 hours every third day, which merely consists of holding the outer edge of the wood in front of the enemy's works. The cover is so good that there is no need of any body being hit unless they choose, or unless the enemy make a sortie, which they haven't done yet & which I don't fancy they will do.

Porter is on the right, we are the center, & Keyes the left.[20] The men have at last got shelter tents, little tents with front & rear open wide enough to lie down in & tall enough to sit up in, officers the same, made for shelter against the sun, not the rain, but very much better than bivouacking as heretofore. So all is comfortable, except being turned up in the middle of the night to stand till you are drenched (it has been raining the last day or two) only to find it a false alarm. We are so near the enemy, however, that the utmost precaution is necessary & any thing is better than to be surprised so shamefully as Grant's army.[21]

Now I have said every thing. If George is still feeble I should advise him in the strongest manner to get a sick leave & not come here, for the going with wet feet, & sleeping in the mud, though good for a well man, might make him go home again, as it did Riddle & Putnam.

It seems from your letter that the governor hasn't got my letter from Bolivar, nor Fort Monroe, and that you haven't got mine from Yorktown. Be sure & write often & tell all the rest to write. You have never been in a situation to appreciate the comfort that a fellow out here gets in a letter from home. It is incalculable & I have fewer than any other man in the regiment. I am glad to hear Ned is all right. Where is Fletch & the rest of the regiment?

Your aff. son,

H. L. A.

[20]Brig. Gen. Fitz-John Porter commanded the Fifth Corps while Brig. Gen. Erasmus Keyes commanded the Fourth Corps in the Army of the Potomac.

[21]During the Battle of Shiloh (Pittsburg Landing), Tenn., Apr. 6–7, 1862, Grant's forces were attacked while preparing breakfast, though they eventually won the battle. Over thirteen thousand of Grant's troops became casualties of that engagement (the heaviest losses then sustained by any Federal army), resulting in severe criticism of Grant by the press and in Congress.

Camp before Yorktown, Virginia, April 26, 1862

My Dear Mamma,

You don't know how awfully we are cut up about Frank Bartlett's loss.[22] Poor fellow, to be cut off for good from a military career when he had so much talent for it. It is aggravating to him to think his future career is ended, but think of us too. There is no use trying to disguise it any longer. Officers & men have said it out here for a long time, & we may as well tell you in Boston what indeed I think Frank Palfrey would willingly acknowledge, & that is simply that Frank Bartlett was the commander of our regiment. He was the one officers & men all looked to for preservation whenever we should get into battle. I don't believe this regiment can disgrace itself by cowardice, but I am very much afraid that we shall make some terrible bull in our next battle. Well, if every thing doesn't go right, lay it all to our loss of Frank.

He behaved with so much pluck. He was a few rods off from me, behind a tree which gave, through an accidental opening in the trees, a tolerably good view of the fort. Frank and I had a shot fired at us the day before, behind the same tree, but it is so common an incident on picket to have shots come near you without hitting, that it was almost impossible to exercise due caution. He was kneeling, looking through his glass, when the ball (an Enfield rifle) struck his knee, passed along, shattering the bone to pieces & stopped just on the surface of the calf. When I came up to him, they had just ripped up his trousers, & Frank sat up & took the ball out of the wound & then picked 2 or 3 pieces of bone out. When he saw the bone, he said his leg was a goner. The ball, as he picked it out, was so covered with bone & flesh that I thought it a huge gobbet of flesh. They found, after they cut his leg off, that the bone was all knocked to pieces, & that amputation, & that promptly, was all that saved his life.

It was a pretty mournful sight for me to see him lying there with only one leg, both as the dearest fellow in the regiment, & as the man that the regiment had got to depend on in battle. But his family ought to feel glad he has escaped so easily, for his conspicuous figure & position as leader of the regiment would have ensured his being knocked over in a general engagement.

Tell papa he owes me a letter, so does Carry & George & Sally. Give my love to the young ones.

Your aff. son,
H. L. Abbott

[22]Bartlett was wounded on Apr. 23.

West Point, Virginia,[23] *May 8, 1862*

My Dear Papa,

I was glad to get your letter at last. I had begun to think that you had cut correspondence entirely.

You have seen now the enemy have evacuated Yorktown. The morning they left was the last of my 24 hours of picket. Shots were fired at us about day break. A few hours later we heard, just opposite from the place we had been religiously guarding all night, . . . shouts & cheers at a tremendous rate. We thought it deuced strange that the enemy should be cheering, for their custom is to yell. But as soon as we heard the tiger,[24] we knew our forces were inside. And then you may believe we were mad to be [illegible word] out of the opportunity of going into the fort.[25] There we were left, for two or three hours, without orders & without any positive information whether the enemy or our forces held the fort, untill we were ordered to march back to the camp.

Immediately we were under marching orders, the next day we marched, so that I had no chance of going inside the fort. I had the compensation, however, of knowing that though the 19th [Massachusetts], from their position on the right of the line, were the first to enter the work, our [regimental] flag was the first that was planted on the parapet. We halted at Yorktown over night, & there I had a fair chance of seeing the [earth]works. The town itself is a scrubby little hole. I never expected, of course, that the works would be any thing like the field fortifications before Sebastopol, but I did think they might have been more elaborate.

The rain, in many places, had washed the dirt so that the parapet was all run over the berm, a very serious defect. The positions of the heavy guns commanding the [York] river seemed to be miserable. Of course, all that I know on the subject I know from the books, & those works, instead of being in advance of the books written 20 years ago, didn't come up to what those books prescribe as the requisites for the most ordinary field fortifications, . . . excluding those designed for musketry alone. There is no doubt that works 8 or 9 feet high & 20 feet at the base would be, if decently defended, impregnable

[23]After the fall of Yorktown, the 20th sailed by steamer up the York River to West Point Landing on the Pamunkey River.

[24]Referring to the battle cry of the Boston Tiger Fire Zouaves, Co. K, 19th Mass.

[25]Although the majority of the regiment took part in the attack on Yorktown and was the first Federal unit to plant its colors on the Rebel ramparts, a portion of the 20th, under Abbott, was doing picket duty.

Capt. William F. "Frank" Bartlett. He would be wounded three times during the war, most seriously before Yorktown during the Peninsular campaign, where a Rebel bullet would cause him to lose a leg. *Courtesy USAMHI.*

to infantry attacks by volunteer troops, but our heavy guns would have knocked them all to pie in no time. None of the niceties which the books lay down as necessary for the preservation of earth works, & which McClellan's Report[26] says were executed with the greatest finish at Sebastopol, were observed here. The books say that a ditch must be at least 20 feet wide to be effective. At no place that I saw was it wider than 10 feet. There were lots of things of the same kind showing great haste.

From Yorktown we came up the York River. Wednesday [we] were drawn up all the morning in line, every body expecting an attack. Nothing, however, but skirmishing.[27] Tonight (Thursday) McClellan, whom we believe in as our Napoleon, is only 5 miles off. The whole regiment has had a bath in the river. We have all got over the complaints of the season, are in bully condition, & expect soon to lick the enemy, who have fallen back on the [Pamunkey].

A week ago I was paid 2 months' out of 4 months' pay. After expenses I had $50 left which I shall have to keep. As soon as I get my last 2 months' pay I shall be able to send it all home. Considering how expensive this marching business is, I don't think I have done badly. Most of the fellows have spent all 4 months' pay.

Give my love to mamma & Carry & George & Sam & Sally & the little devils. I hope I shall get home & hug them pretty soon. 2 or 3 months, at least.

Your aff. son,
H. L. Abbott

West Point, Virginia, May 8, 1862

My Dear Arthur,

Didn't you jump up and clap your hands when you heard that Col. Lee had got back?[28] He said you told him to kiss me for you, but he wouldn't do it because I hadn't shaved for two or three days & he was afraid of getting scratched. He needn't have been afraid of getting scratched, however, for when I leave off shaving 3 days, I get a beard as long as your curls used to be. Keep on writing, Arthur, &

[26]In 1855 McClellan, then a captain, was sent to Europe to observe British and French operations in the Crimea. He later issued a report to the U.S. government on the siege operations around Sebastopol.

[27]Referring to the action at Eltham Landing on May 7.

[28]Lee and the two Reveres returned to the regiment on May 2, just in time to enter Yorktown.

Maj. Gen. George B. McClellan. *Courtesy National Archives.*

tell me all the news, because the rebels have gone & run away & we have got to follow them.

Your aff. brother,
Henry

Col. Lee sends you his love, also to papa & mamma.

West Point, Virginia, May 8, 1862

My Dear Grafton,

You dear little debil, you can write letters can you? How I should like to get home & give you a hug & have your little hands round my neck. Don't you forget me, now, Grafton, & when I get back you shall be the only person who will dare to pluck me by the beard. Now you must be good all the time & remember, when you get mad & begin to cry, it makes the rebel bullets come a good deal nearer to me. I shall see you in 2 or 3 months.

Goodbye,
Henry

Give my love to little fat Holker & tell him to be good.

Camp on the Pamunkey River, Virginia,[29] *May 18, 1862*

My Dear Aunt [Elizabeth],

I haven't got any letter from you since the one I wrote, & then you owed me one. I suppose they have miscarried. . . .

We are getting on very well here. I am in excellent condition. This kind of life, which kills men of delicate health, agrees with me most wonderfully. We expect a grand wind up on the [Chickahominy River], & hope to be in at the death.

The battle of Williamsburg was undoubtedly the severest ever fought on this continent.[30] Our loss in killed & wounded is pretty well known to be as much as 3,000, which, considering the much smaller numbers engaged than in the Western battles, knocks the latter into pie, & compares favorably with the butcher's bill of most European battles, on a small scale.

I expect to get back by November, if the enemy stay & get themselves squelched on the Chickahominy. But if they manage to escape

---

[29]Since landing at West Point, the 20th had been continually marching up the Peninsula and reached the vicinity of White House Landing on the Pamunkey by May 18.

[30]This action was fought on May 5, while the 20th was still at Yorktown.

into the cotton states, we must make up our minds to another spring campaign. It is all very well to talk about starving them out. But they can certainly keep up their army to a comparable size till autumn, when they can get fresh levies enough to wait out the winter season. You musn't believe all the yarns you hear about the Southern Potomac army[31] being demoralized. No demoralized army could retreat in such excellent order as they have. The only place which showed signs of confusion was where they got licked at Williamsburg, & then not so bad as we at Bull's Run. . . . Indeed, I wouldn't have it so. It would be no honor to whip an army so completely panic-stricken as the papers represent the rebel army, & it is robbing us of our just honor to represent it so. I believe, myself, if we do fight, we shall have a most desperate struggle. At Williamsburg they drove us till McClellan came up, though, to be sure, they had superior forces, but even superior forces couldn't have fought if panic-stricken. Besides, they have a most excellent general, one of the best of our old army. . . .

Keep your courage up & never say die, & be ready for me to pay you a visit in Lowell next winter.

Your aff. nephew,
H. L. Abbott

Camp on the Pamunkey River, Virginia, May 18, 1862

My Dear Mamma,

You don't seem to have got the letter I wrote you from West Point. The day after the so called battle I wrote 6 letters, one to you, one to Aunt Sarah,[32] one to Frank, & one to Arthur, & the others I forget to whom. I wish you would tell me in your next letter whether you got them or not, for it is devlish provoking to write letters & not have them received. . . .

Poor George I was deuced glad to see.[33] He isn't looking as well as when he went over to Ball's Bluff. However, I think he will pick up. This is a healthy life. I have never been in such stunning condition since I went to college.

I think my original supposition was right. I don't believe we shall get home till November, at any rate. Military movements are very

[31]This, of course, was the name of the Confederate army under Gen. Joseph E. Johnston, the army which McClellan was then pursuing. It would soon be renamed the Army of Northern Virginia.

[32]Sarah Livermore was Henry's mother's sister.

[33]Perry, having been released from Libby Prison on Feb. 20, had just rejoined the regiment.

slow where there is such an enormous army. If the enemy don't make any show on the Chickahominy & retreat into the cotton states, it will take another spring campaign. . . . What do you think of it?

Your picture of home is really delightful. It almost makes one homesick, though I am not yet by any means sick of campaigning. The weather is oppressively warm, & alternately muddy, almost worse than Maryland mud, if such a thing can be.

Col. Lee is enormously popular with the regiment. He certainly has a charm of conciliating every body about him. All old cliques surrender to him unconditionally. Besides, it is so good to see the head officer work just as hard as his subordinates, always up before any body, & 3 o'clock in the morning is no joke for a man who, though not very old, has suffered so many hardships.[34] Some days, too, he has been in his saddle all day long, so stiff at night that he can hardly get off. He sends much love to all, particularly to Arthur. The major, too, is very welcome indeed. He is a thorough gentleman.

Give my love to all & tell Arthur, Frank, Holker & Grafton that I have written to them.

Your aff. son,
H. L. Abbott

I got a letter from Ned the other day.

Camp on the Pamunkey River, Virginia, May 19, 1862

My Dear Papa,

I just got your letter today. I certainly think there never was any body who itched for military glory so much as you. But it seems to me that the fact of your having 3 sons in the war is the very reason you shouldn't be . . . asking every thing in one venture. As for patriotism, I am sure I don't know of any man who has done more for the war than you have. You have sent 3 sons. You have spent a great deal of money. But what is of the most importance, you have given your whole influence to the prosecution of it. I should say, as every one else would, that you ought to rest satisfied with what you have done, instead of disquieting yourself by thinking you haven't done enough. You don't know how much I am touched by your anxiety for us. I really think it makes you too nervous on our account. There isn't much danger of any thing happening to any of us & we shall come back all right & immensely benefited by the experience we have had.

---

[34]Lee, age fifty-five, was the second oldest officer in the Army of the Potomac, the oldest being Brig. Gen. Edwin V. Sumner, then sixty-five years old.

And it is from the very fact that the first part of your letter was so kind that it makes it so much harder for me to have to differ with you on what you mention in the last part of it. There is now only one vacancy in the regiment, & that has been long promised to Wilkins,[35] one of my most intimate friends, both by Col. Palfrey & Col. Lee. There is no probability of another vacancy untill we have another battle, for officers are not allowed to resign in the face of the enemy. But even if there is, I hope you won't recommend Charley Francis. . . . I devoted a long time with myself before I came to the conclusion to beg of you not to get his appointment in case of a vacancy. After all your kindness . . . I would do almost any thing rather than differ with you on such a point. I hope when you know my reasons you won't be offended.

Charley Francis I think to be, I am sorry to say, a silly young fellow. He was the butt of his class in college. And I don't think it was merely the greenness, that wears off. . . .

Now we are awfully hard up for good officers. I wouldn't have this go any further for the world. But the fact is that all the officers who have lately come back, from the col. down, are most stunningly & amazingly deficient in military knowledge. There isn't one who knows so much as any sergeant in the regiment. They confess it, some of them, themselves. Moreover, 3 of our best officers are absent on staff appointments, which altogether leaves a small minority of officers who know their duty. . . . The consequence is that not only do we absolutely need . . . new appointments of officers of first rate ability, besides military knowledge—for out here there is no chance of learning any thing—but also there is a tremendous feeling among all officers . . . of indignation, as well as of fear that the regiment is going to the devil by the appointment of officers without consulting their [the regiment's] wishes. They all feel that inasmuch as the officers appointed have got to be their associates, they ought to have some voice in the matter.

I can't imagine a more uncomfortable position for Francis than to be out here in this regiment, whereas in a good many others they might think he was a big gun & he could enjoy himself to his heart's content. Besides, though the sergeants haven't any right in the matter & haven't the presumption to claim any, unless the civilian appointed was one nobody could object to, I should hate, as a great many other officers would, to see them stepped over. I have got a stunning first sergeant, a man who has been first mate of a whaler,

[35]Henry E. Wilkins would be commissioned 1st lieutenant on Jan. 6, 1863.

has made a great deal of money, is thoroughly up in all military knowledge, has always done his duty most faithfully & efficiently, & is a devlish smart fellow & I should hate to see a mere boy, without a great deal of sense (I am sorry to say so) & no military knowledge, put over his head. . . .

Write & tell me what you think as quick as you can.

Your aff. son,
H. L. Abbott

FIVE

WITH TERRIBLE FORCE

Camp on the Chickahominy River, Virginia,[1] *May 26, 1862*

My Dear Mamma,

. . . We have been moving through a most beautiful country. Before Yorktown it was hideous. When we got to West Point we were immediately struck with the change, & the further we moved the more beautiful it grows. Our last camping ground was certainly the most beautiful place for a country house I ever saw in my life. We were encamped on [an] oval hill, just about large enough for a division of 1,000 camped in close column, bare of trees, except here and there a squad with the fruit trees which shaded the house belonging to some rebel doctor.

The plain all around the hill [was] an open field for a quarter of a mile or so, then these dense forests with every variety of green. The cresting of the hill [was] marked so plainly from the plain below that some how or other it seemed just like being on an island. Just in rear of the house, the most superb view. The hill straight down 100 feet, & below the plains thousands of glittering stacks of arms & little dots of tents, these tremendous forests looking more like the ocean than any thing else. . . . in short, you can imagine how stunning it must have been to tempt me to describe it.

We, that is the 20th Mass. & the 106th Pennsylvania under command of Col. Lee, yesterday scoured the country along the Chickahominy for 15 miles—an absurd & nonsensical idea of that old fool Sumner.[2] The country had been all secured by other troops, and here we were making fools of ourselves, up to our knees in mud, tearing our faces with brambles, every now & then heroically rushing on to the charge, only to find that we had come upon our own men. It was all very natural, however. Here we were led up to the

[1]The regiment left its camp near the Pamunkey River on May 21.
[2]Edwin V. Sumner commanded the Second Corps.

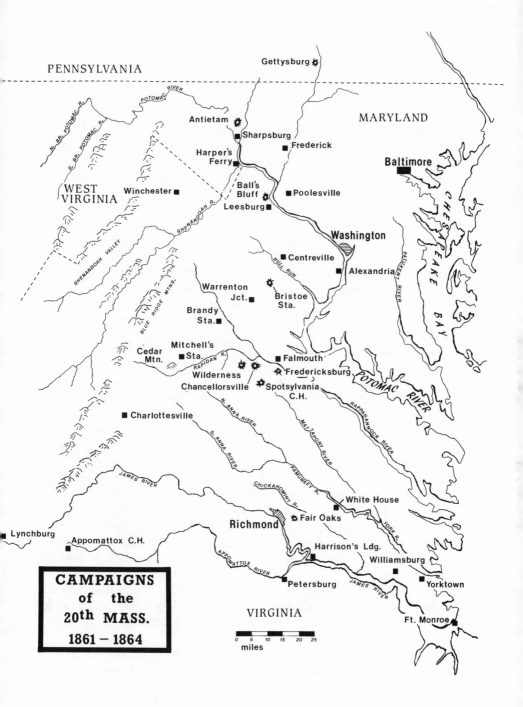

PENNSYLVANIA

Gettysburg ✷

MARYLAND

POTOMAC RIVER

N. BR. POTOMAC R.
S. BR. POTOMAC R.

Antietam ✷
Sharpsburg ■
● Frederick

Baltimore ■

Harper's Ferry

WEST VIRGINIA

Winchester ■

Ball's Bluff ✷
Leesburg ■
■ Poolesville

SHENANDOAH R.

SHENANDOAH VALLEY

Washington

● Centreville
■ Alexandria

BULL RUN

CHESAPEAKE BAY

PATUXENT RIVER

BLUE RIDGE MTNS.

Warrenton Jct. ■
✷ Bristoe Sta.

Brandy Sta. ■

Cedar Mtn. ■
Mitchell's Sta. ■
RAPIDAN R.
Wilderness ✷✷
Chancellorsville ✷
■ Falmouth
✷ Fredericksburg
✷ Spotsylvania C.H.

POTOMAC RIVER

Charlottesville ■

N. ANNA RIVER

S. ANNA RIVER

RAPPAHANNOCK RIVER

MATTAPONY RIVER

JAMES RIVER

PAMUNKEY R.

CHICKAHOMINY R.

■ White House

Lynchburg ■

Appomattox C.H. ■

Richmond
✷ Fair Oaks

Harrison's Ldg. ●

YORK R.

Williamsburg ■

APPOMATTOX RIVER

■ Petersburg
JAMES RIVER

Yorktown ■

CAMPAIGNS of the 20th MASS. 1861 – 1864

VIRGINIA

0 5 10 15 20 25
miles

Ft. Monroe ■

123

burnt railroad bridge, our knapsacks left behind, Gen. Sumner going there in person, & ordered to sweep, by a line of skirmishers, what appeared to be an immense forest, Co. I and one of the Pensyl. [companies] being the skirmishers while the regiment marched up the road on the flank of the wood, our pieces loaded & primed, which latter is never done except when [a] fight is expected. Well into it we went as heroically as possible, scrambling through mud & briers, snakes, turtles, high brush & low brush, & after 3 hours hard work, emerged torn & muddy to find our own baggage trains quietly moving along in front of us. This was repeated over & over till by night, we marched back to where our division had moved, to find that the great Sumner had forgotten his promise to have our knapsacks brought, & we had . . . to sleep all night without blankets, tents or any thing else, under a dew that is almost a rain that wets your jacket through in an hour. The old jackass had read in a newspaper, I suppose, about Banks having left this part of Virginia infested with guerillas, & so he thought he would do a big thing & sweep them out of this part of the country, at any rate.

It seems, as I thought, from the official accounts of killed and wounded, that the Williamsburgh [battle] was one of the hardest that has ever occurred on the continent. I see from the accounts of killed & wounded of the different regiments that very few regiments suffered . . . more than the 20th at B[all's] B[luff]. Our loss then was 80 killed & wounded out of 300.[3] The greatest loss of any one regiment at Williamsburgh was less than 200 & this was a full regiment, that is less than one out of five, ours being nearly one out of 3, which fact makes me think that our little affair at B[all's] B[luff], though one of the first of the [Army of the] Potomac, was a tolerably sharp action.

I believe we are considered to have been in the battle of West Point[4] as much as a great many regiments ever are, being in reserve in the third line, on the extreme left, supporting a section of Porter's battery, which Col. Lee says was a very honorable position, though all the time we thought it was only skirmishing going on in front, waiting I think very calmly for the battle to begin, untill the battle was all over. The only missiles that came near us were a [few] shells, while we were eating dinner.

I think it is awful hard for Ned and Fletch to be up with Banks there, when they are so anxious for a fight, which reminds me that a

---

[3]Actual losses for the 20th Mass. at Ball's Bluff were 87 killed and wounded and 111 captured out of approximately 300 engaged, for a total loss of 66 percent.

[4]More commonly known as Eltham Landing, Va., fought May 7.

rumor has just come, announcing the annihilation of Banks' army & retreat beyond the Potomac.[5] However, it doesn't disturb my appetite, as I have still later heard that Banks is in Richmond, our left is destroyed, McClellan assassinated, McDowell[6] victorious, [and] other reports equally trustworthy.

I have just got your letter saying that you very rarely hear from me. This is horribly provoking. I answer every one of your letters just as soon as I get it, & I know that they never get home. It certainly is the most provoking thing in the world for one who writes with so little ease as I do, to have my letters miscarry. I wish, in order to make sure, you would acknowledge the receipt of each letter you get.

How does the governor get on with his horseback riding? I have just written him. Boston must be delightful just now. I must confess the idea of getting home & seeing you all soon forces itself upon me much oftener than I ever used to allow it, though my common sense tells me that 9 months is the shortest time I can expect it.

Your aff. son,
H. L. Abbott

Camp near Chickahominy, Virginia,[7] *May 31, 1862*

My Dear Mamma,

You remember in my last letter that I spoke jestingly of a rumor about Banks being driven into Maryland. That very afternoon we heard from [a] trustworthy source that the news was true & that Gordon's brigade was in the engagement. But that didn't alarm me at all, because I had always thought Gordon was assigned to the command of another brigade & that the 2nd were still in Abercrombie's,[8] & were undoubtedly by this time safe with

---

[5]Banks's command was defeated at the Battle of Winchester, Va., on May 25 by Confederate forces under Maj. Gen. Thomas J. "Stonewall" Jackson. Banks then retreated to the north side of the Potomac.

[6]Maj. Gen. Irvin McDowell had commanded the Federal forces at the First Battle of Bull Run, which ended in disaster for the Union troops. At the time of this letter, he was commanding Union troops which were moving to intercept Stonewall Jackson in the Shenandoah Valley.

[7]This letter was written moments before the regiment was sent to take part in the Battle of Fair Oaks.

[8]Brig. Gen. John J. Abercrombie was in command of the Second Brigade, First Division, Fourth Army Corps of the Army of the Potomac. The 2d Mass. was still in Gordon's brigade.

McDowell at Fredericksburgh. This morning, the 31st, the papers for the first time mention the 2nd as engaged, Carry's note to George arriving at the same time, by which we find that Mudge & Crowninshield were slightly wounded & Dwight[9] taken prisoner & that the 2nd behaved with the most admirable courage, maintaining their position untill taken by an enfilading fire of artillery, though deserted by the cowardly 27th Indiana. Of course the 2nd behaved with more pluck than any other regiment on the field. I always knew they would. And from all the accounts . . . we can get of the whole thing, I am sorry to say that it strikes me most painfully that the 2nd was the only regiment that didn't cut sticks & run in a most abject panic. Thank God they stood to it for the honor of Boston Massachusetts and the army. It won't be long, I know, before they have the chance to whip the rebels who have insulted them, to their hearts' content.

Carry's letter says that Sam has gone to Washington in the Guards.[10] I suppose it was almost impossible to prevent him [from] doing something of the kind & that is as safe as any thing.

I have just heard the most disturbing news that Major Dwight instead of being taken prisoner is killed. It seemed to come from very good authority. But I have made up my mind not to believe it, untill it is confirmed beyond the shadow of a doubt.[11] You must remember that we don't get Boston papers here. Send any having an account, also Ned & Fletch's account.

Your aff. son,
H. L. Abbott

Camp at Fair Oaks, Virginia, June 6, 1862

My Dear Papa,

This, the 7th day from the battle,[12] is the first time I have had a chance to write you. We have just got our knapsacks & before they came paper was unprocurable for love or money.

[9]Capt. Charles R. Mudge and 2d Lt. Francis W. Crowninshield (brother of the 20th's Caspar Crowninshield) belonged to the 2d Mass. Maj. Wilder Dwight, also of the 2d Mass., would be commissioned lieutenant colonel of that regiment on June 13, 1862, but would die on Sept. 19, 1862, from wounds received at the Battle of Antietam.

[10]Samuel Abbott had enlisted for thirty days' service in the M.V.M. He would not see any active service during the war.

[11]Dwight, of course, was not killed.

[12]Referring to the Battle of Fair Oaks, fought May 31–June 1, 1862.

Saturday, the first day we received news that the 2nd was in the Winchester fight, we started for the scene of action here. My letter [of May 31] was written during the battle of musketry, just before we started, for we had been so often alarmed before that we had no anticipation of really fighting. The fight began in the morning by Casey's division being drawn in & cut to pieces.[13] When we started, the fight had ceased entirely, & it was only about a half hour before our regiment marched to the scene of action that the second battle began. We double-quicked up through swamps & forded a brook up to our middles, arrived on the battle field when shells & bullets were making a devil of a racket, formed into line on the left of Gorman's brigade, the front line, after being first run into by [several] horses, one of which jammed Riddle's amputated arm, compelling him to go back to the hospital the morning after the battle. The 19th [Massachusetts] & Tammany [regiments] in our brigade were left behind. The 7th Mich. were on our left. We were formed on the crest of a slight slope, running down to a thick woods, extending ¾ of our front, the remaining fourth being an open plain, followed by another wood, resting on the [Richmond & York River] railroad.

The firing was tremendous from the rebels, but just where we were, rather too high, whether because our regiment fired so accurately as to prevent the rebels before us from taking their usual low aim, or because the enemy, in trying to fire up hill, actually fired too high, I know not. However that is, we lost only about 30 men out of 400 & no officers, while the regiments immediately on our right & left lost 80 or 90 apiece. I had only 4 men hit, one of whom was shot dead. Our whole line, as well as I could see it, not only our regiment, but the scrubby New Yorkers [the 34th New York] on our right, stood up straight in their places, firing low & the most tremendous volleys, no man dodging or kneeling. Our men showed wonderful discipline, firing & ceasing to fire just as they were ordered. . . . The col., lt. col. & all the officers showed great presence of mind & gallantry.

In about an hour we let up on the firing along the line, the smoke partially cleared, & we saw the rebels charging from the woods to take Rickets' battery,[14] which, by the way, did admirably. Instantly there went up a tremendous shout along the line & the biggest volley of the battle sent the rebels yelping into the woods. Then our whole

[13]Maj. Gen. Silas Casey commanded the Second Division, Fourth Army Corps.
[14]This was Battery I, 1st U.S. Artillery (formerly commanded by James B. Ricketts), then under command of Lt. Edmund Kirby.

line charged, the first half the distance in quick time, without cheering, except from old Sumner, who cheered us as we passed, the second half the way taking the double-quick with the loudest cheers we could get up, through the most impenetrable &—excuse the word, it must come—damnable bog I ever went through, clear up to our knees in solid mud. Lots of the men left their shoes. In fact it was a good chance to get stuck, if a man chose to; only one of my men tried it, but a slight prick of the bayonet from a file closer extricated him speedily. So difficult was the place that I don't believe less than one half of the regiment would have given out, going at the rate we were, if on drill. But, kept up by the excitement, not a single man, unwounded, fell out.

Over the fence we went, when the little col. bolted ahead, & I was afraid he would come to grief, but, thank God, he didn't. It was now dark & we had to halt in the wood. Very soon [we] filed off to [the] left, into the adjoining field before mentioned, whither the rebels had run, [and we] drew up here in an oblique line, facing towards [the] next woods, where the rebels tried to make a stand, firing at us. A few volleys cleared them out. Here we found lots of them dead, one in the act of aiming, behind a stump, shot dead through the neck in the act.

It was now dark. We lay on our arms, on marshy ground, without blankets, officers being obliged to sit up, every body wet through as to his feet and trousers, & we had brought our blankets, but gave them all up to the wounded prisoners, of whom our regiment took a large number. . . . My company took 10 unwounded, & 11 wounded rebels prisoner in the woods. Among the former, 5 of the celebrated Hampton Legion of South Carolina, & one Tennessee, two North Carolinans, a Georgia & a Louisiana Tiger.

Among the wounded, Brig. Gen. Pettigrew of S.C.[15] & Lt. Col. Bull of the 35th Georgians. Pettigrew had given up all his side arms to some of his people before they ran away, in anticipation of being taken prisoner, & had only his watch, which of course I returned to him. Pettigrew will get well. Bull had his side arms, of which I allowed Corp. Summerhayes, his captor, to keep his pistol, an ordinary affair, while I kept his sword, an ordinary U.S. infantry sword, which I intended to send as a present to you, but the col., knowing

[15]J. Johnston Pettigrew, who commanded a brigade in G. W. Smith's division, was actually from North Carolina. Although captured at Fair Oaks, he would later be exchanged, only to be mortally wounded at the Battle of Falling Waters, July 14, 1863.

his family's address, wants me to send it to them, & as the poor
fellow is dead, of course I can't hesitate to do any thing which would
comfort his family. His scabbard, however, I found very convenient,
as mine got broken in the battle and I threw it away. I am going to
send you, instead, a short rifle which I took from a H[ampton's]
Legion fellow, who were all around with them & the sword bayonet.
The rest of the rifles we of course turned over to the col., as in duty
bound, except one revolving Colt's rifle, 5 barrels, worth $60 or $70
apiece . . . which one of my men took from a dying officer, & which
I let him keep as a reward of valor.

The prisoners when we took them were terribly frightened, expecting no quarter. It took a great deal of work to reassure them; we
gave them water & food, as well as all our blankets to the wounded.
All the men, without exception, vied in doing kindnesses to them,
though they were horrible looking devils, lank, long haired, clad in
a nasty brick colored stuff that a beggar in the North would be
ashamed to wear. . . . But it was only to show that we were "generous as well as brave," hey? They all told the same tale, forced into it,
fighting for the rich man, when they didn't own no niggers themselves. Only one was sulky. He had just had his eye cleaned out by a
ball. When I told him to move up to a stump, where the others
were, he answered, "How in hell do you suppose I can see the stump
with only one eye?"

The next morning the rebels began the attack on our immediate
left, from the railroad, our new line being at right angles to that of
the previous day. Here Richardson's division,[16] not in the fight before, licked the rebels awfully, fighting 2 or 3 hours, while there were
no rebels in front of us, so that we had to stand & face the woods
all this time, separated only by two or three rods from the fighting,
all this time without firing a shot. I had much rather fight all day,
any time.

Since then we have had rather a roughing of it, today being [the]
first day of dry clothes, having been on picket ever since the battle,
sharpshooting with the rebels. Now we have again bridged the Chickahominy, got some food & luggage, picked up rebel blankets, and are
anxiously & longingly awaiting the final grand struggle which Mac
[McClellan] tells us is to wind up the whole thing. The night after
the victory, we could, I believe, have easily walked over [all] the
soldiers in the world, so elated were we.

[16]Maj. Gen. Israel B. Richardson commanded the First Division, Second Army
Corps.

Please send Ned's account of the battle [of Winchester]. We hear rumors that Banks is taking his revenge. Thank God for that. Tell us all you know about Major Dwight. I felt horribly about the anxiety I know you and mamma must have felt, but this is the first chance I have had of writing, though Palf[rey] managed to send a telegram, which you must have got Tuesday. Love to all, kiss the little ones for me.

Your aff. son,
H. L. Abbott

George was used up & obliged to go to the hospital some time before the battle.

Camp at Fair Oaks, Virginia, June 13, 1862

My Dear Carry,

You have neglected me shamefully, while so many letters have poured in for George, who isn't here, that, upon my soul, I shall soon have to make a bon fire of them.

What a silly girl you are to worry so for George's safety &c. . . . Try to imitate the *manly* good sense of your mother and myself, who so far from getting up imaginary evils, always disbelieve all bad news untill it is conclusively proved, & then try to find some bright side, instead of looking at the black side till one is so blind that every thing else looks black as well. You remind me of an officer out here who is always afraid of "being attacked on our left" or having our "right turned" or "our center broken" or fancying that every bullet whistling past him from some murderously inclined picket is the token of a general engagement, or some thing else awful & impossible. . . .

Remember that George has got a sick leave & will come home as soon as Richmond is taken, leave off half your letters to him & send them instead to me, thereby engaging me to send you those lighter, airy, charming . . . full and frequent letters for which I am so famous, in lieu of George's sentimental lover's nonsense, and you will be all right in no time.

Your aff. brother,
H. L. Abbott

Excuse the horrible envelope. It is all I can get.

Camp at Fair Oaks, Virginia, June 13, 1862

My Dear Mamma,

I have just got your letter of the ninth. It is very singular the governor hasn't got my letter describing the battle. You have no idea what a glorious feeling a victory brings. We were almost drunk with joy & so hoarse from cheering that we could hardly speak. I have often wondered how this enthusiasm they talk about was got, for I couldn't feel it at B[all's] B[luff], though it was a pretty hot firing; neither did I have [it] at this battle, till the charge, & then it came with a rush. Why, we all felt horribly disappointed at the darkness coming on just as we had got our stomachs up for a long fight, & we felt as if we could have walked over the best troops in the world with considerable pleasure, though I dare say, plenty of grape shot might have diminished our ardor.

But what a glorious thing the 2nd have done. I consider them unquestionably the first regiment in the service, regular & volunteer. Their hardships have been immense.[17] Their cheeky little major, they say, was as cool as a cucumber; I have no doubt of it. He has just the temperament for standing fire. A great many men, you know, are brave under fire without being cool. He is both. Ned of course belongs to the bravest of the brave. Every body always knew what he would be. Fletcher's exploit must have been extremely dangerous. To have those confounded little stinging, whistling bullets in front is bad enough, but to be attacked in front and rear would deprive a good many brave men of their entire self possession, particularly such young ones as Fletch.

I am sorry to hear Carry isn't better. She is very foolish to bother herself so much about George. He got a sick leave a day before the battle. He has been for duty once since he came out here, except when there was a prospect of battle. We had been deceived so many times, that when we started for this last battle, he expected to see us back the same night. We had been fooled so often that nobody thought we were going to fight. Luckily for George it was so, for I varily believe that had he been there, the exposure would have killed him.

I am sorry poor little Arthur has got the whooping cough so badly. However, I suppose you console yourself with the thought that they can't do it again. All well regulated families [have] measles & whoop when they are young. A gentleman is always safe in saying that he was christened, had the measles & the whooping cough when he was young. Give my love to all.

Your aff. son,
H. L. Abbott

[17]The 2d Mass. acted as rear guard during Banks's retreat across the Potomac following the Battle of Winchester.

Fair Oaks, Virginia, June 24, 1862

Dear Mamma,

I was wondering why I didn't get any answers to my letters, either from you or the governor or Carry, till I got your letter. I see now the day time has been fully occupied & the night time your eyes wouldn't allow you to [write]. Aren't your eyes any better? It is an awful deprivation to suffer so long with them.

Your dinner party was stunning. How much I long to be at home. The dinner you promise me is inviting as any thing I can dream of, except the greater pleasure of a private family uniting when we first get home. Fourth of July will not see us at home, I hope [we will then be] in Richmond. If the blasted rebels only stay & get licked, I think there is some possibility of our eating the family dinner with you at Christmas.

Life here now is stupid, horribly so. For my part, I liked much better our ten days of picket just after the battle, when we were really suffering hardships & had something to do, at the same time gaining experience in warfare. Here we lie all day on our backs—shelter tents won't admit of a seat—with a scorching heat that actually bakes one up into flakes—too furnace-like even to admit of sleep, and all we have to do is to turn out two or three times, day & night, whenever there is any firing, & get up at 3 o'clock to stand under arms an hour & a half—an awful life of inglorious ease & inaction. It fretted me at first tremendously, but if you will believe it, so strong is my power of adapting myself to circumstances that I have actually got to like this life tolerably well, & have passed the last two days pleasantly enough, lying on my back & reading books lent out to Ropes,[18] drinking very good brandy, sugar & water . . . to keep off the lassitude incidental to this infernal scaly climate, & fancying myself an English officer in the burning sands of India, my costume being shirt & drawers simply, all sorts of preventatives against the sun over my head, & brandy & water by my side. . . . So you see we are having a bully time after all, though if we could only march 10 or twelve times, or lick the rebels, or something, it would be still better.

I send home my pay (there are still 2 months due me) $150. I wish you would give Sally for me $5, on condition that she writes me a letter; Frank & Arthur & Holker & Grafton $2, to be divided

---

[18]2d Lt. Henry Ropes, Co. K, was one of Abbott's dearest friends and brother of the noted military historian John C. Ropes.

on same conditions, & Sam $10, as a compensation for his whooping cough, which, by the way, I hope they have all weathered by this time.

How is Carry? Is George home yet? Poor fellow. Rather a hard going of it to be down ill without having been in battle. Never let him come back again. It is madness to think of it, untill he has had at least a year to recruit,[19] by which time the campaign will be over.

Your aff. son,
H. L. Abbott[20]

Harrison's Landing, Virginia, Sunday morning, August 10, 1862

Dear Papa,

I wish to heaven you could see how comfortable I am here, that your mind would be at ease with regard to me, & I wish the down-hearted, dispirited, cowardly North could be placed here bodily & see the army. It would be impossible for them to resist the contagion. They couldn't help being cheerful & happy.

I can't describe to you the change between the people at home, all down in the mouth, . . . & the army down here, who are just as confident as at the beginning of the war. If you at home could only come here and see us, you would readily believe that nothing but overwhelming odds could beat us. Even I, who was at first entirely prostrated by the horrible heat & the swarms of flies (moskitoes there are now) which cover every thing human & beastly, animate & inanimate, even I have become like the rest & can cheerfully breathe the dust, which covers the ground every wheres, inches deep, eat my breakfast of flies & any thing else, while in revenge the flies are eating me, & pleasantly smoke my pipe while the perspiration is melting off me, the normal condition of the body out here.

---

[19]Too ill for active duty, Perry was given the lighter responsibilities of recruiting in Boston. He would be discharged for disability on Sept. 30, 1862.

[20]June 25, 1862, the day after this letter was written, marked the beginning of the Seven Days' campaign. Following relatively minor engagements at King's School House, June 25, and Mechanicsville, June 26, the right wing of McClellan's army, isolated on the north bank of the Chickahominy, was defeated at the Battle of Gaines' Mill, June 27. That loss compelled McClellan to withdraw his army from the immediate vicinity of Richmond to Harrison's Landing on the James River. During the retreat a number of rear-guard actions were fought. At the Battle of Glendale on June 30, Abbott was severely wounded in the right arm. On July 2, he went home to recuperate but rejoined the army on Aug. 9.

This is the army that most of you at home look on as doomed.
You think there that the Southern army is playing with us as a cat
plays with a mouse, & that we only continue to exist through their
gracious pleasure. Don't believe it. Look at our regular camp discipline, our policing, our dress parades, our good clothes, our shining
arms, our two hours drill, our comfortable feeds (potatoes, vegetables, & in our regiment, very good soft bread) but most of all, at the
perfect absence of all downheartedness or gloominess amongst the
men. The great head of our army inspired his generals, they theirs,
untill it radiates through the colonels & company officers to the
men.

The rebels, with their vile butternut clothes, illmade & illfitting,
their wretched food, & personal filthyness, can't be in as good spirits
as we are. We are the men, you know, who have been killed off by
work in the trenches & such bosh. If the people could only know
how the army despises the liars who have stuffed them with those
ridiculous tales & how thoroughly they believe in McClellan—even
those who didn't before, having come to that opinion since they saw
his management in the Seven Days fight—they would sink a good
many of rottens . . .

Harrison's Landing, Virginia, August 10, 1862

My Dear Mamma,

(Continued from letter to the gov.)

. . . and think that possibly there might be still something left between them & destruction.

Our regiment has got up to 350 & will soon have 400. I think the
whole army is considerably increased, though I don't know certainly.
We have, however, only 11 company officers & 1 field officer for
duty. The major is sick a bed, & Cabot, Tremlet, Whittier, Messer[21]
& Perkins lie in the hospital, as yellow as oranges, giving themselves
up however, very cheerfully it seems to me, to be the prey of flies,
heat & dust. The small number of officers in the regiment has made
the work too hard for them.

Macy & Ropes are as cheerful as ever & say the fates are against
them. They can never get sick or wounded, so as to see their friends
once more. Neither of them have been home since they first came
out you know. Col. Palfrey is also well & happy.

[21]Capt. Charles F. Cabot, Co. F, who would be killed at Fredericksburg, Dec. 11,
1862, and 2d Lt. Nathaniel T. Messer, Co. D, were among the injured officers.

The excursion to Malvern Hill they tell me was an awful hard thing, forced marches & so on.[22] We came quietly back again when the rebels appeared in force. Gen. Sedgwick said we bore off the palm on inspection the other day & looked like veteran regulars.

Before this reaches you (this is strictly private . . . unless the event shall already have happened when the letter reaches you) we shall probably be at Fort Monroe, on our way to join [Gen. John] Pope's army, where I shall have a chance to see Ned & Fletch.[23]

I saw Gen. Dana at Philadelphia.[24] We had to stay over night there on account of only one boat leaving Baltimore, which we were too late for. He is terribly done up, sick a bed & weak as a child. Indeed, from the freedom with which [he] spoke of my superior officers, & from the incredibly extravagant way in which he praised the 19th [Massachusetts] & Col. Hinks (Hinks & he are rivals & he has to do the magnanimous) I should decidedly think he was a little out of his head. From what they say in the division here I should imagine, between you & me, that Dana, though a magnificent officer for organizing & disciplining a regiment, isn't what he might be on the field of battle. Brave enough of course, but in other respects perhaps not equal to what you would expect from him. . . .

Harrison's Landing, Virginia, August 10, 1862

My Dear Carry,
(Continued from letter to mamma)
Sally's letter reached here after I left, as did also a letter from the governor & Aunt Sarah & Billy Perkins. Give the envelope to papa, to show him how the husband of his friend, the one-eyed beauty Mrs. Goodwin, writes. I haven't another Yankee in my company who could write such a miserable scrawl if he tried, though Goodwin is really a very good looking fellow.[25]

I tell you, Carry, I felt horribly blue after leaving the family . . . particularly without giving the young ones a farewell kiss. Tell them all to write, Sally also. Has Sam got to go? Tell him to make all the

---

[22]On Aug. 4, McClellan sent the army on a reconnaissance to Malvern Hill. It returned to its camp at Harrison's Landing on Aug. 7.

[23]Although Henry did not yet know it, his brother Ned had been killed at the Battle of Cedar Mountain on Aug. 9.

[24]This occurred on Abbott's return trip to the army. Dana, his brigade commander, had apparently been away on sick leave.

[25]Pvt. Charles F. Goodwin, Co. I.

cowards enlist. War isn't nearly as bad as it is painted. I was a coward before I went & now I ain't.

How is your back? You must look out for that & mind my advice. What has George done about his leave?

I left Wilkins & Curtis at Baltimore to get some recruits for a day & came on the boat with some of the most intense snobs & scrubs that the mind of man can imagine, from Pennsylvania of course. They remind [me] of their exact opposite, Ogden Codman. I wish he were well enough to be out here. . . .

The col., Grosvenor, of the [7th] Mich., is kicked out for running away at the last battles, the major [of the 7th] ditto. . . . [26]

How do you like my style of letters by chapters? A very happy idea I think. . . .

Your aff. brother,
H. L. Abbott

I forgot to say my arm is doing remarkably well.

Newport News, Virginia,[27] August 24(?), 1862

Dear Papa,

Untill I got the newspapers & mamma's letter day before yesterday, I thought Ned only wounded. I got your letter yesterday. Today we finished our march & I can answer. It came upon me with terrible force. I could hardly believe it. I thought Ned would surely come through all right. I wish to God I could have seen him on the battle field. Tell me all about it as soon as you can learn. I know how awful the blow is to you, for he was the best son you had & was so sure to have been a great man. It is very hard to think that we will never see him again. If I could only have seen his body. Every time my company is drawn up it reminds me of Ned, for I have been thinking lately of getting it into fine shape to show to Ned when we got up there. Do let me know all you find out about it.

Your aff. son,
H. L. Abbott

[26]Col. Ira R. Grosvenor resigned his commission on July 8, 1862. He later became lieutenant governor of Michigan.

[27]The regiment, along with the rest of the Army of the Potomac, left its camp at Harrison's Landing on Aug. 16 and began the march across the peninsula reaching Newport News, Va., on Aug. 22. Abbott's statement that "today we finished our march" indicates that this letter was misdated and was actually written on Aug. 22, not Aug. 24.

Capt. Edward G. "Ned" Abbott, 2d Mass., older brother of Henry. He was killed at Cedar Mountain, August 9, 1862. *Courtesy USAMHI.*

Boston, Massachusetts, Tuesday, August 26, 1862

My Dear Henry,[28]

I am momentarily expecting your col. to call[29] & take this note, & should have seated myself earlier to write, but I was obliged to go to Cambridge this morning with Sam. I have engaged Professor Lane to hear him recite, & prepare him to enter the soph[omore] class.[30]

I enclose [to] you every thing I can in regard to dear Ned. Grief prevents my writing much about him. I think that I have loved him & the rest of my dear children too much. I have great strength given me to bear the blow. I feel that the dear child is happy—perfectly happy, & that he will be a guardian angel to us all. I often feel his presence. I feel that he loved us too much to be separated from us. And that altho' at this moment he sees the tears streaming from my eyes, that he knows it is for my good that I should be afflicted.

Your dear father bears it with christian fortitude. How happy is the thought to him that he has always done so much to make the dear boy happy on earth. Do you think Ned loved me as much as he did his father? How happy you must feel that he loved you so much. He loved you more than I can tell. I think he will always pray for you & hover around you. He thought more of your good than his own, & would willingly have laid down his life to make you happy. He felt that you loved him. I have heard him say that he thought you felt a great deal for him. It is a great comfort to me to look back upon his life. Every thing to make a parent's heart rejoice. I know I must not repine for him. That I am still blessed with so many good sons. How much bitterer would it be for me to see a son disgrace himself, than to know that he was already dead, having died doing his duty & covered with laurels. God bless & keep you, my dear child.

Your ever loving,
Mother

---

[28]This letter is the only surviving correspondence to Henry from either of his parents, and it is the only letter not written by Henry that has been included in this edition.

[29]Colonel Lee, injured when his horse fell on him during the Battle of Glendale, was in Boston on recruiting duty. He would rejoin the regiment on Sept. 3.

[30]Samuel Abbott enrolled at Harvard University during the fall of 1862.

Camp near Alexandria, Virginia,[31] *September 3, 1862*

My Dear Papa,

Fletch is all right & so am I. I have been considerably worried to think of your anxiety at home while these battles have been going on & both of us up there.

As soon as we got to Alexandria, the men almost dead from being crowded on transport in a way that would have killed brute beasts, after hard marching down the peninsula, we marched outside Alexandria, then the next day 14 miles to more forts, getting in at 12 in the night, the next day as many more, getting in at 5 P.M., through Tenally town in Maryland, [up] the next morning at 3 A.M., marching through Fairfax Court House, getting in at 1 in the morning, being on the marching 22 hours out of the 24, (60 miles in 48 hours), with scanty rations & no sleep, & not finding our division after all, from which we had been detached at Alexandria.

Here we lay in line of battle the next two days, being in reserve at the battle of Chantilly, fought day before yesterday afternoon, losing only one man. The army filed by on each side of us, & our brigade was left in position with nothing in front of us & nothing very near in rear of us. Yesterday at 4 P.M. we marched, being the rear guard of every thing. The enemy took possession of Fairfax half an hour after we left it. Some little time after, Gordon's brigade & some of Banks' artillery marched in from another road & went in rear of us. Gordon was ordered by some fool to go back & burn something or other at Fairfax, which he had just marched through & which the enemy had taken, but very properly didn't carry his exhausted command to destruction.

We got into Alexandria at 1 o'clock the same night, a played out set of shoeless ruffians, having worn our shirts 3 weeks without the chance of washing them. The 2nd camped only a quarter of a mile in rear of us, without our knowing it. The next morning early I set out in search of them & overtook them after running a couple of miles. Think of my feelings. I didn't know whether Fletcher was alive or dead. We had heard dreadful rumors of their being cut to pieces. They haven't been in a battle since that fatal one, though they have had very hard work.

[31]On Aug. 25, the regiment boarded the steamer *Collins* and sailed for Alexandria, Va., arriving on Aug. 28. The following day Abbott was promoted captain of Co. I.

Fletcher is very well & I thought the regiment looked splendidly. It made me feel very sad not to have dear Ned's hand stretched out to me. Fletch is in command of the company & Jim Francis is to have it.[32]

I have had a good many letters about Ned but I can't answer them. To think of the subject unmans me. I have to keep it from my thoughts. Ever since the news came, the regiment has been in the most trying circumstances where it was absolutely necessary to force cheerfulness before the men as well as the officers. A man who didn't would have been a coward & false to his trust. I know I haven't allowed my feelings to interfere with my duties. They say you & mamma felt the shock terribly. I hope you have got over the first acuteness. I wish to God I were at home to talk with you both about it. I got your second letter. I confess I couldn't keep up appearances at first, but it was only for a short time. Write any thing more you can tell me.

Tomorrow at 3 o'clock A.M. we start for chain bridge where the brigade was first ordered & first went. I hope we shall be near the 2nd.

At the great battle we whipped them every where, except under McDowell, where we had a second Bull Run. McClellan came up & drew a brigade across the road & stopped the retreat. Every body thinks Pope is a fool & McDowell a traitor and coward, & they should be kicked out. Sedgwick says that when Sumner came up, Pope actually couldn't tell him where ⅔ of his own forces were & says, as coming from Sumner probably, that Pope is nothing but a "damned blow."

All McClellan's troops were taken from him & sent to the front untill he was left with only 150 men, he the greatest general the country ever produced. Then they got frightened & gave him the fortifications around Washington, then they gave him the Army of Virginia, & he went out & saved it, & now they are, with less reason, more frightened & have given him Halleck's position, who is said to have Stanton's.[33] Every body is overjoyed. We met him [McClellan] riding with one orderly in Alexandria, the first day we got there. He sang out "is this the 20th?" Not the 20th Massachusetts, but is this the 20th.

[32]Capt. James Francis, of Lowell, Mass., assumed command of Edward's Co. A, 2d Mass. on Aug. 10.

[33]Maj. Gen. Henry W. Halleck was appointed general in chief on July 11, 1862. Although McClellan was again in command of the Army of the Potomac after Pope's defeat at Second Bull Run, there was no truth to the rest of this rumor.

I have got 40 recruits & if we rest for a month or two as I expect, I shall work tremendously hard. Thank God, I have had plenty of work since the news. Tell mamma to write. . . .

Your aff. son,
H. L. Abbott[34]

[34]On Sept. 4 the regiment marched to Tenallytown, Md., where it joined the rest of the army on its march to intercept Lee, who had just begun his first invasion of the North. When the regiment reached Frederick, Md., on Sept. 13, Abbott was stricken with typhoid fever and was admitted to the Union hospital, thereby missing the Battle of Antietam. He was soon after sent home to recuperate and was not able to rejoin the army until Nov. 19.

SIX

FREDERICKSBURG:
Nothing but Murder

Near Falmouth, Virginia, November 20, 1862

Dear Papa,

Carry's letter will tell you that I, as well as Holmes,[1] [am] with the regiment all right. They sent us to Warrenton & then back, but 6 miles below Warrenton Junction, while on the road to Alexandria, we heard of Sumner's Corps marching through Warrenton Junction 2 days before, so [we] gave our valises in charge of Rev. Dr. Snob and Toady Fuller[2] of the 16th [Massachusetts], got out of the cars, marched back to Warrenton Junction, set out about 4:30 on the road to Frederick[sburg], marched a few miles & lost our way, the next day 20 miles, & the next 4 or 5 & caught the regi[ment] & have been lying here two days near Falmouth, waiting the capture of Fredericksburg. Our idea is that we are racing with the rebels to get into Richmond first, thus seizing their base, while we change ours to Fort Monroe, with the James for a communication, as Wellington did on the Peninsula,[3] rather a hazardous move, particularly as the rebels are probably already in Richmond, the removal of McClellan[4] having delayed the army just long enough to let the rebels get there.

The removal of McClellan caused as much row as we thought. The men cried & so did McClellan. Officers in high positions were

[1]Captain Holmes had been at home in Boston recuperating from a neck wound suffered at Antietam.

[2]Referring to the Reverend Arthur B. Fuller, chaplain of the 16th Mass., and his son. Although Rev. Fuller resigned from the service on Dec. 10, 1862, he nevertheless offered his services as a volunteer at Fredericksburg, where he was killed on Dec. 11.

[3]Referring to a movement made by the Duke of Wellington during the Peninsular War (1808–14), during which British forces, supported by the revolutionary forces of Spain and Portugal, succeeded in driving Napoleon's French army from the Iberian peninsula.

[4]McClellan had been relieved of command on Nov. 7, turning the Army of the Potomac over to his successor, Maj. Gen. Ambrose Burnside.

only prevented from resigning by a general order from the boss at the War Dept. threatening dishonorable dismissal to all officers who gave McClellan's removal as the reason of their resignation.

The Dutch Emperor who rules over us is worse even than I expected.[5] Something must be done. All the officers have petitioned Revere to come back, but I am afraid he is too sick to think of it for months to come.

Col. Lee (strictly private) is undoubtedly very much shaken in his intellects, at any rate at times. Macy thinks so, so do Alley & [Lt. Herbert C.] Mason. It seems the horrors of Antietam, his previous fatigues & his drinking, completely upset him. After the battle he was completely distraught. He didn't give any orders. He wouldn't do any thing. The next morning he mounted his horse, & without any leave of absence, without letting any body [know] where he was going, he set out alone. Macy, who was bringing up some recruits, met him about ten miles away from the regt. without a cent in his pocket, without any thing to eat or drink, without having changed his clothes for 4 weeks, during all which time he had this horrible diarrhea—just getting ready to turn into a stable for the night. Macy gave him a drink & some money & got him into a house, put him to bed stark naked, & got his wits more settled, & then came on. When the poor old man came back to the regt. they thought he had been on an awful spree, he was so livid & shaky. Macy says he was just like a little child wandering away from home.

One of the col.'s. crazy things while in command of the brigade is rather ludicrous.[6] Somebody came in & told the col. that one of Gorman's aides accused this brigade of running shamefully at Antietam. The col. was raving. He exclaimed Gorman was responsible for his aides. He shall take back the calumny or fight me. Well, poor old Ropes (who was an aide of [the] col.'s.) was in an awful stew. The col. wouldn't listen to any remonstrances, but called for his horse, buckled his sword, to speed to Gorman's. Gorman, of course, denied the whole thing, saying in his own sweet way, "Sooner may the Lord tear my right arm from its socket & beat me about the head with the bloody stump, than allow me or my staff to say aught to tarnish the glory of the noble 3rd brigade." So the thing ended.

[5]Ferdinand Dreher was then temporarily in command of the regiment owing to the absence of Lee, who was on duty at brigade headquarters, and Palfrey, who had been severely wounded at Antietam.

[6]Due to the wounding of Dana at Antietam, Lee assumed temporary command of the brigade on Sept. 18.

Col. William R. Lee. *Courtesy USAMHI.*

144

Capt. Ferdinand Dreher, who survived a ghastly head wound suffered at
Ball's Bluff, only to be mortally wounded at the Battle of Fredericksburg.
Courtesy USAMHI.

Why, there is no doubt about it, papa, his wits are unsettled & will be as long as he stays in the army. He ought to be made to resign. He, I am sorry to say, & Dreher are the laughing stocks of the division. Paul Revere or Frank Bartlett must come out, & that soon. We must have somebody to set things straight, fill up vacancies, & depose these insolent, ignorant, vulgar fellows who are insulting the officers & demoralizing the regt. By the way, Col. Lee actually did send a list of nominations, containing my name, for Billy Milton sealed & mailed it.

The army is about the same, except that the desire to go into winter quarters grows stronger every day, among officers & men. Of the two alternatives, defeat or winter quarters, I think they prefer the latter, though now I am out here I can't form an opinion which it is to be.

I am well, strong, & healthy & eat hearty but don't drink ditto because there is no longer rum. The tea & coffee are excellent, much better than the weak stuff you have at home. I drink a pint of either at each meal & think of the nervous headache it would give you.

Your aff. son,
H. L. Abbott

You needn't write, untill you have plenty of spare time. Ask mamma if she got my two last.

Near Falmouth, Virginia, December 1, 1862

My Dear Mamma,

I forgot . . . in each of my last letters to tell you about Wolf,[7] & so I write this in order that you people at home may no longer remain in ignorance of the fellow's character. Both of my "gentleman soldiers" are now discharged. Balch for physical disability.[8] He is, I imagine, completely used up & never had the constitution for a soldier's life. He was, I think, one of the pluckiest men I ever saw. With more physical strength, a regiment of such men could march right over any two regiments that were ever got together. He marched without a groan or complaint, untill one morning he actually couldn't stand. He took every one of a private's hardships & discomforts without shirking. In fact, with the exception of physical weak-

[7]Pvt. Eric Wulff, Co. I, was discharged on Oct. 16, 1862.
[8]Pvt. Francis V. Balch, Co. I, was discharged on Nov. 10, 1862. He would later become one of Boston's most noted attorneys.

ness, he was a model soldier. Alley[9] tells me that all the men appreciated him fully & knew that he was a gentleman sacrificing his position, so much so that the last day he was with them, every one of them called him Dr.

But now comes the other "gentleman," Wolf. He can't plead ignorance of what a private's life is, especially if, as he claims, he was an officer before, because I warned him before he enlisted & told him he'd better not do it. He is a mere flighty, flashy, foreigner, all in a blaze one moment & then dying out. Instead of buckling manfully to his work, Alley, after long indulgence, was obliged to reprimand him for having the dirtiest gun in the company, & he was actually caught *hiring* another man to do his police work, a court-martial offense. Instead of, like Balch, taking his private's position fairly, he was always trying to intrude himself on officers, & giving the men an idea that although nominally a private, he was, in fact, altogether differently situated from them.

The men contrasted him very unfavorably to Balch. They said here is a man who calls himself a gentleman & is going to win his shoulder straps in a month, who not only doesn't do as well as we do, but actually shirks every possible thing, & tries to back out of the position which he has voluntarily assumed. He borrowed $5 of Ropes' servant, which he has never repaid. Cheating servants is a nice operation for lofty minded gentlemen who scorn commissions & are determined to win their way right straight up from the position of a humble private.

That is cheating on a small scale. What do you think of cheating on a large scale? What do you think of a man who comes clear over here from Sweden to fight his way up from the ranks, win military glory, & battle for the right, &c &c, takes $150 bounty (Balch didn't) & then, after two months' duty, or shirking of duty, gets his discharge because he happens to be a gentleman? He can't suppose that the town of Plymouth meant to pay him $150 or $200 for two months' service. . . . And now, that by the merest favoritism of the Washington government, he has fairly got his discharge, instead of being contented with getting out of the scrape & pocketing the $150 bounty & the money that several officers were fools enough to lend him, he actually has the cheek to send for his final statements in order that he may get his pay. . . . I shall absolutely refuse to give him any descriptive list unless I am compelled to. . . .

[9]Leander Alley was promoted 2d lieutenant of Co. I on Aug. 29, 1862.

Give my love to Col. Lee & tell him how rejoiced we all are to hear that he is home, for we supposed that he was killing himself at Bolivar.[10]

Your aff. son,
H. L. Abbott

Fredericksburg, Virginia,[11] December 14, 1862

My Dear Papa,

We are still in Fredericksburg. . . . The very moment I finished my last letter to mamma we were ordered again to the front.[12] Howard,[13] a most conscientious man, but a very poor general, had heard of batteries stormed & rifle pits taken &c, & without stopping to think . . . he took the weakest brigade in the army, one which besides was considerably demoralized by the fight of the previous day & the shelling they had suffered, to say nothing of the recollection of their awful loss & defeat at Antietam, he took this brigade & ordered it to advance, not altogether, but by regt. after regt. The result was that the 19th [Massachusetts], which first got into position, no sooner reached the brow of the hill than they tumbled right back head over heels into us.

Then came our turn. We had about 200 men. We advanced 2 or 3 rods over the brow of the hill under a murderous fire, without the slightest notion of what was intended to be accomplished. Our men however, though they couldn't be got to advance in double-quick against the rifle pits, which we soon perceived, didn't on the other hand, like the 19th, break & run. They held their position firmly untill Col. Hall,[14] seeing that the pits could only be carried at the run, & that if carried, they were completely enfiladed by a rebel battery on the hill, ordered us to retire, which we did in good order.

---

[10]Lee, who had suffered greatly from exposure to the wet weather following the Battle of Antietam, was then on sick leave in Boston. He was finally forced to resign on Dec. 17. Palfrey was promoted colonel of the regiment on Dec. 18, but wounds suffered at Antietam prevented him from ever rejoining the army. He was discharged for disability on Apr. 13, 1863. Meanwhile, during Palfrey's absence, Governor Andrew named Captain Macy acting colonel, much to the chagrin of Dreher, senior captain of the 20th.

[11]This letter was written the day after the main action at Fredericksburg.

[12]The letter mentioned here never reached home.

[13]Brig. Gen. Oliver O. Howard was now in command of Sedgwick's division, as Sedgwick had been wounded at Antietam.

[14]Norman J. Hall was now commanding the brigade in which the 20th served.

Below the brow of the hill, where the whole brigade lay till 2 next morning, crowds of troops were ordered up, but none found courage even to undertake what the poor little brigade of 1,000 men had been unable to accomplish. At 2 o'clock we were relieved by the regulars who were ordered up as a last resort, since Hall's brigade had failed to take the pits, which they were to storm this morning. However, the generals have changed their minds since, & consider the assault impracticable, so nothing has been done today, except a little shelling—(3 o'clock). Hall stoutly condemned the whole attempt by such a weak, exhausted brigade as simply ridiculous. But Howard is so pious that he thought differently. . . .

Hooker[15] suffered terribly yesterday & accomplished nothing. The enthusiasm of the soldiers has been all gone for a long time. They only fight from discipline & old associations. McClellan is the only man who can revive it. Macy commanded our regiment as well as it could possibly be commanded. This morning, Gen. Howard called him to the front of the regt. & at the same time that he praised the regiment, complimented Macy publicly in the handsomest manner.

The regiment, during the few minutes they were engaged, lost about 60 men & 3 officers. We have now a hundred-odd men & 5 company officers with the regiment. I lost only 4 men, as all but 10 I had sent out under cover to watch our flanks, which were otherwise entirely unprotected. Alley was killed instantaneously by a bullet through the eye. You will know how I feel about his loss when I tell you that for a moment I felt the same pang as when I first heard of our great loss. I don't want to say any thing more about him now, for thinking on such a subject makes a man bluer than he ought to be in the presence of the enemy. I have sent his body home by Sergt. Summerhayes, with orders to call on you for funds, as I have no money. I will settle it from Alley's account. For God's sake, don't let Fletcher get on till after Richmond is taken.[16] I couldn't stand the loss of a third brother, for I regard Alley almost as a brother.

I am in excellent health. My scabbard was smashed by a bullet, but I myself was uninjured. Don't you or mamma worry yourself about our fighting any more. Howard told us we were so used up that we shouldn't fight again except in the direst necessity. Love to all.

Your aff. son,
H. L. Abbott

[15]Joseph Hooker was then commanding the Center Grand Division, Army of the Potomac.
[16]Fletcher, at home on sick leave, was suffering from dysentery.

Fredericksburg, Virginia, December 13, 1862

Dear Madam, [Mrs. Mitchell][17]

Private Josiah F. Murphey, who brings the dead body of your son, will tell you fully all the particulars. I know by judging of my own feelings, how bitterly you will feel his loss. I can say from an intimate acquaintance with him, that he was as brave, resolute, and energetic, and at the same time as tender-hearted a man as I ever knew. When I first heard of his death (I didn't see him fall), I felt the same kind of pang as when I first heard of my brother's death, who was killed at Cedar Mountain. It was only a few nights before his death, that he was telling me about his family, and speaking of you in terms of the strongest affection. Every man in the regiment, from the col. to the men of other companies, respected and admired him as much as any officer that has ever belonged to the regiment. He was a most invaluable officer. A great deal of the superiority of Co. I . . . is due to Lieut. Alley. I shall never cease to think of him with love, to my dying day. I hope after this bloody war is over, I shall live to express to you, personally, what I have been writing in this letter.

I remain, my dear madam,

Yours very respectfully, &c.,
H. L. Abbott
Capt. Co. I

Near Falmouth, Virginia, Wednesday, December 17, 1862

My Dear George [Perry],

I suppose the letters I have written home describing the battles have got there. So I will only say, as a summing up of them, that we took over 320 men [into battle] & lost 165 men & 8 officers.[18] However we are getting back the men in the hospitals, the detailed men & that sort of thing, so that we shall soon have a respectable number again. Holmes & Willard will soon return to duty, too. As it is, we have only 5 officers.

[17]Mrs. Mitchell was the mother of Leander Alley. This letter is not among the collections of the Houghton Library, but is taken from an article published on Dec. 27, 1862, in *The Weekly Mirror*, Nantucket, Mass. Although the letter is dated Dec. 13, and appears here out of sequence, the editor thought it best to insert it after Abbott's letter on the Battle of Fredericksburg.

[18]These figures include losses for the actions of Dec. 11 and 13.

Second Lt. Leander Alley, who was killed at Fredericksburg, December 13, 1862. *Courtesy Nantucket Historical Association.*

Macy & our regiment covered itself with glory & have received no end of compliments. The army generally didn't fight well. The new regiments behaved shamefully, as well as many of the old ones. The whole army is demoralized. The 15th Mass. was seized with a panic at nothing at all & broke & ran like sheep. They have always been considered one of the most trustworthy regiments in the army. Hooker's troops broke & ran. He is played out. Our loss was 10,000. The rebels may have lost 3,000. Burnside, who is a noble man, but not a general, is going to leave the army entirely.[19] He rode through the town the last day without a single cheer. That conscientious donkey, Howard, after keeping our brigade shivering & freezing for an hour yesterday afternoon, listening to a sermon & benediction from him, proposed . . . three cheers for Burnside. Several men in a new regiment, the 127th Penn., gave a mockery of 3 cheers. Not a man in the other regiments opened their mouths, except to mutter three cheers for McClellan. We can never win another victory till he comes back, & even then, not till, after 3 months of winter quarters, he has had time to reorganize the army. Financial troubles & foreign intervention may stop the thing before that time expires, but any other course is certain destruction.

The only two generals left that this brigade believes in are Couch & Hall.[20] We don't know much about the former, except that he protested in the strongest manner against the whole thing. The army went over with the conviction, almost the determination, of getting licked & they have got thoroughly licked. If you people at home are going to allow us to be butchered any longer by Halleck & Stanton, you will find the enemy at your own doors.

Your aff. friend,
H. L. Abbott

Tell the governor that I have sent an order for $75 on him to pay for embalming the body of Alley. I will pay it from Alley's money, as soon as funds come.

I was devlish sorry to hear that Fletch met with an accident. Don't let him come back before something new turns up. Old heads like Johnny Sedgwick know too much to come [back] before McClellan.

[19]Burnside, of course, did not leave the service, but he was given command of the Dept. of the Ohio and later was again in command of the Ninth Army Corps.

[20]Maj. Gen. Darius N. Couch was now in command of the Second Corps.

Maj. Gen. Ambrose E. Burnside. *Courtesy National Archives.*

I forgot to say that we are in our old quarters, with every prospect of remaining.

Near Falmouth, Virginia, December 21, 1862

My Dear George,

While I think of it, tell Carry that [Pvt. James] Blake, the husband of her washwoman, belonging to [Co.] K of this regt., was wounded not dangerously. A very good sort of man, I believe Ropes says.

The piece from the *London Times* about McClellan is particularly approved [of] from the generals downwards, particularly the part which wonders why he chose to obey such a miserable abortion of a government.

Poor old Col. Lee is . . . gone from . . . us. It fairly made my heart ache to see the brave little fellow trying to do duty here. A single week of it would have killed him outright. He is certainly the model of a plucky English officer. When he went away he wouldn't have us officers told of it. He couldn't bear to bid us good bye. He fairly broke down & shed tears when he got into the ambulance which took him away. Holmes has written a very good address to him to express our feelings. I trust it will do something to comfort the gallant little colonel in showing him how much his officers love . . . him.

I wouldn't on any account allow Fletch to come on here before he gets thoroughly well. I have got two or three men dying of the same complaint that he has, because they were obliged to stay here. All officers are very well except Holmes, who still has dysentery badly. Here's one of Sully's[21] stories for you. A runaway soldier coming full tilt from the town is stopped by the guard at the bridge. "For God's sake, don't stop me," the soldier cries, "I'm demoralized as hell."

Hall has told us of the third time that McClellan was prevented from taking Richmond by that cowardly scoundrel Halleck. It seems that McClellan's plan was all settled & arranged to make the greatest battle of the war at Gordonsville [Virginia]. He was to attack Lee with all the reinforcements which he had been so long waiting for & which were to join him at Warrenton, absolutely crushing to pieces the rebel army by his immense superiority in numbers, the rebel general Jackson being still absent in the valley, this being the first time we had ever succeeded in getting between the rebels. Then, following up the broken remnants of Lee's army & taking or watching Richmond with 40,000 men, he was to turn with the remainder of his forces on Jackson & completely surround him with 3 times his numbers. Hall says it was one of the most beautiful plans he ever saw. 3 days before the time fixed for the battle he was removed. Burnside, who knew & approved the plan, felt unable to carry it out himself, & in fact didn't want to try any thing venturesome till he got used at least to handling such a large army, & so moved down to a safe place on this side [of] the river. 13,000 men killed & wounded without a shadow of good resulting therefrom, is the result. Nothing but murder. Good bye.

Your aff. brother,
H. L. Abbott

[21]Brig. Gen. Alfred Sully, former colonel of the 1st Minnesota, was then commanding the First Brigade in Howard's division.

Excuse the want of stamp. Can't get any anywheres.

Falmouth, Virginia, December 21, 1862

My Dear Carry,

I have got yours of the 15th. You at home must have got all mine with full accounts of the fight. The army isn't worth a brass farthing in the way of fighting now. There are hardly any of the old troops left. Our brigade, 5 regts. which each, with the exception of the 20th, came out a thousand strong, now numbers 500 for duty. The strongest peace party is the army. If the small fry at Washington want to hear treason talked, let them come to the army. The rebels assured our flag of truce [party] that had they chosen to destroy the town, they might have ruined our army. And I know that they speak the truth. 3 shells thrown into the town the night we were evacuating would have caused the most frightful loss of life that ever occured since the deluge. I firmly believe that as the rebel Gen. Lee told us, the men who ordered the crossing of the river are responsible to God for murder. I believe that Alley was just as much murdered as if he had been deliberately thrown into the river with a stone tied round his neck. How long you people at home are going to stand it I don't know, but if we again have to turn our backs on the rebel enemy, we shan't stop untill we get to Washington & lay our hands on our true enemies, those blood stained scoundrels in the government. McClellan alone can save the army.

I am glad Fletch has got a staff appointment, but sorry to hear that he is going to report so soon.[22] He certainly can't be well enough for duty. I should think you would keep him a while longer. His accident must have shaken him considerably, in his weak condition, I should imagine. Why doesn't he write? Too much occupied with the women, I presume. I tried to get you some memento of Fredericksburg, but got nothing better than a commonplace edition of Byron. I have got a very good edition of Plutarch's [L]*ives* for the governor. I did get a most beautiful writing desk but it was taken away from my servant. I have two children's books for Frank & Arthur. I went into nearly every house to get some nice little silver thing for mamma & Mary Welch, but was too late. Macy got just the

[22]Fletcher was appointed aide-de-camp to Brig. Gen. William Dwight of the Nineteenth Army Corps, then stationed at New Orleans, La. Fletcher served in that capacity throughout the Battle of Port Hudson but was discharged for disability on Dec. 23, 1863.

thing—a little bed lamp of solid silver. . . . I expect with eagerness an answer to my last letter from Mary Welch.

Your aff. brother,

H. L. Abbott

Near Falmouth, Virginia, December 28, 1862

My Dear Mamma,

I am sorry you missed my first letter, though I am afraid you would hardly [have done] so, for it was tremendously long & very badly written, composed in Fredericksburg just before we went into the second fight.

Poor Alley, you have no idea how I miss him now that I have got back to the old hut where we lived together. Otherwise, I am very well off & in very good condition. The regt. is a new thing altogether in Macy's hands, & we have had a lot of compliments from all the generals; Old Sumner included, though we never cheer him. So, notwithstanding we don't write for the newspapers, as the 19th [Massachusetts] does, we are getting our fair share of fame in the army at any rate.

What an awful greenhorn Burnside is, don't you think so too? His letter is the letter of a high-minded donkey, if it is high-minded at all, which I am beginning to doubt, since I see him maintaining in his testimony that the army was safe in Fredericksburg. Hooker & Franklin[23] told the truth when they said it was perfectly unaccountable why the rebels didn't smash us all into pieces in no time after we got into the town. All the generals lie like dogs, except old bullheaded Sumner, who confesses that there is a good deal of croaking in the army. Do you notice that Burnside proclaims himself a jackass in his report? He says that being informed that the rebels had withdrawn most of their forces further to the right, he intended a surprise by a rapid blow, and yet in the same breath he confesses that it took him 24 hours to effect a landing—more than time enough for the rebels to bring back all the forces which they had withdrawn. He should have given up the thing as a feint & tried it somewhere else, & he knows he should have done so. He was shamefully served, however, by that useless piece of furniture, Halleck, who seems to be

---

[23]Maj. Gen. William B. Franklin was in command of the Left Grand Division, Army of the Potomac.

George N. Macy would eventually become colonel of the 20th Mass. He is shown here in an early wartime photo. He would lose his left hand at Gettysburg. *Courtesy USAMHI.*

good at nothing but equivocating. Pity us sacrificed by a dishonest government and an *honest* general. . . .

Your aff. son,
H. L. Abbott

Near Falmouth, Virginia, January 3, 1863

My Dear Mamma,

Your letter opens with such a charming scene that I wish I were with you. Still, we are having a remarkably comfortable time here now, except in the way of food, in which we are very short. We haven't been able to get any thing of the commissary for 4 days but hard bread and rice. Burnside is a great man to be here 6 weeks and yet, though closer to his base than we have ever been before, he hasn't completed arrangements enough to give the men their full rations & to feed the officers decently. McClellan would have had two lines of railroads & his whole army in tip top condition in half the time. Whereas now, within a few hours of Washington, men are dying of scurvy because they haven't transportation enough to give us potatoes & onions. Some of my men are in a horrible state. They can press their thumb into their legs & leave the dent there exactly as if it were putty. I am in excellent condition. And they say we are to live well, hereafter.

I have just a regular little beauty of a hut & such a charming fireplace, that I really should like to have you see it. The express too, is open. Some boxes have come through & I expect that box of brandy today. This, & giving permission to the sutlers to come up, are the best things Ambrose has yet done. I am very much obliged to you for your promise of a box. I wish you would send, as quick as you can . . . my uniform coat, the pair of army shoes I left at home, the buffalo robe, and my rubber coat which must be at home, since it's not here and I had it with me at Frederick. It was a very thin, light one.

I am sorry to hear Fletcher is going. But glad to hear that it is to New Orleans. I hope to God he will be careful of himself. Poor Tilden has resigned. He is completely used up. He was advised to by Dr. Hayward and Macy as the honorable thing, since he couldn't possibly do a day's duty for at least 9 months. I am afraid Fletcher will have to come back again. I wish I could have been with you on Christmas. However, we shall revivify Christmas when the box comes.

Your aff. son,
H. L. Abbott

Near Falmouth, Virginia, January 8, 1863

Dear Mamma,

The news you give me in your last is the bitterest pill we have had yet. The idea of a foreigner who perhaps has never smelt powder in his life being put over a regiment which has seen as much service as any in the field, and over officers who have earned their promotion by wounds and good services, is too atrocious to be endured.[24] We have just as much right to the promotion which this fellow is going to cheat us out of as John Andrew has to the salary that is paid to him for being governor. I say *we*, for if Col. Palfrey is disabled, as I am sorry to hear the doctors say, Macy would be col., Hallowell lt. col., and Holmes would be the only one between me and a majority. At any rate I should be senior capt. But that isn't of much importance. The great outrage is to Macy and Hallowell. You naturally don't view it with so much indignation as we do. I tell you we are at the boiling point. If this Frenchman has the slightest shame, he would never take it. It makes no difference whether he is a good soldier or a bad one. The principle is just the same. If I didn't think it was cowardly to forsake my men, who can't go, I would resign the minute the fellow showed his face, and be dismissed [from] the service dishonorably if necessary. But I trust we shall be able to get rid of him and not have to resort to that extreme step. You may be sure we shall fight it, and fight it like the—. Why can't somebody at home convey to the man an idea of our sentiments? John Andrew has done this same thing to too many good regiments and ignored them as much as he can, but the idea that the 20th, after all the lives it has lost and all the services it has done, should get such a blow as this, is too hard to be borne.

I really can't answer the rest of your letter. I feel too much excited about this subject.

Your aff. son,
H. L. Abbott

Near Falmouth, Virginia, January 1863

Dear Papa,

I got your letter yesterday & was very much delighted at receiving Brandon's note.[25] But we can't make it out. Did it enclose a photograph to you, or what does it mean? . . .

[24]The identity of the "foreigner" who was considered for command of the 20th cannot be established.

[25]Lt. Lane Brandon, 21st Mississippi, was a classmate of Abbott's at Harvard.

I am trying hard to get across [to the Confederate side of the river] with the next [truce] flag, but of course shan't succeed. I have written a letter [to Brandon] however, which I shall send with Boulinois, who has got the promise of going.

Do you know an Owen McEnarrey of North Chelmsford? I am told he is a man very well off. He had a son in my company whom I had buried in Fredericksburg,[26] & he is very anxious to recover the body & has written . . . several letters. They all do the same, and it is very distressing to have to tell them that the thing is impossible.

Your aff. son,
H. L. Abbott

By the way, will you tell mamma, when she sends the other things I wrote for, to put in my sash, to be sure & get *mine*? It is different in color from common sashes & I think either in my trunk or in the cedar closet with my shoes. I am going to send my photograph which mamma enclosed to me, to Brandon.

Perkins has just got the nomination for the vacancy caused by Beckwith's death, which has just resulted from [a] wound at Fredericksburg.[27]

Near Falmouth, Virginia, January 10, 1863

My Dear Aunt Lizzie,

I have been expecting to hear from you for a long time. I want to know whether you are well and how you are getting on generally this winter. Have you changed your house? and how are all your Lowell friends? . . .

You must have been considerably worried when the rumor came of my wound. I was in fact extremely lucky, not being touched at all except one ball which knocked in my sword scabbard, while every other officer was either regularly wounded, or else got scratched. Henry Ropes, for instance, got one or two bad bruises from spent balls, and, I believe, 8 holes in his clothes without being wounded. The bullets and shells came plenty thick enough.[28] But don't worry about any reports, for they are usually false.

[26]Pvt. Peter McEnarry was killed on Dec. 11.

[27]1st Lt. Robert S. Beckwith, Co. H, was wounded Dec. 13 and died Dec. 31.

[28]Henry Ropes described the intense musketry which the 20th was subjected to at the Battle of Fredericksburg in an unpublished letter to his brother John C. Ropes dated Dec. 20, 1862: "The ground was torn up and it was like the drops of heavy showers striking the ground all around you. I distinctly felt the balls strike my coat, hat, and knapsack. A ball passed over each shoulder, one just touching my whiskers and cutting my knapsack on either side."

Write me and tell me every thing that is worth hearing from Lowell. I have really no news to tell you except that we are, to all intents and purposes, gone into winter quarters and there are no indications of immediate fighting. The president's proclamation is of course received with universal disgust, particularly the part which enjoins officers to see that it is carried out.[29] You may be sure that we shan't see to any thing of the kind, having decidedly too much reverence for the constitution.

Your aff. nephew
H. L. Abbott

Falmouth, Virginia, January 18, 1863

My Dear Mamma,

After finishing my correspondence yesterday (Sunday) I got this morning two letters from you, one of date Nov. 30, containing an account of your going to Lowell on Thanksgiving. . . . The second one dated Jan. 14. I dare say half your letters are missing in the same way this first one has been so long. It was directed simply to Dana's brigade. It is best always to direct to Howard's division, 2nd Army Corps.

It seems we haven't started this morning after all. I suppose the generals told Burny he had better not, the weather is so very cold for these latitudes.[30] I hope the governor didn't say any thing that would lead Mrs. Mitchell to suppose he was not paying for the expenses [for Alley's embalming]. The reason I said to the governor that I should send on the money as soon as Alley's accounts could be settled, was because I wish to pay the expenses myself, and thought if I told the governor to take so much out of my money, he wouldn't do it, whereas if I sent on the sum when we got paid, as from Alley's accounts, it would be all right. I never thought of Mrs. Mitchell writing. . . .

Still, pray let Mrs. Mitchell continue in her error if possible, that the governor is paying, while in reality I shall do it myself & consider it the only consolation I can have. They think every thing of the governor down in Nantucket for his kindness in this matter. I

[29]The Emancipation Proclamation took effect on Jan. 1, 1863. This disturbed many Federal soldiers who believed the issue of the war was the preservation of the Union, not the destruction of slavery.
[30]Burnside was preparing to move up the Rappahannock River to attempt a crossing in order to flank the Confederate army.

shouldn't like to have the thing disturbed. In fact, Alley had no accounts here. His money can only be drawn by his family upon making the proper representations at Washington. I miss him every day. He was a terrible loss to the regt. His family, though once very well off, are now I understand quite poor.

Fletcher is going next week, is he? He must miss the young ladies as much as they miss him. I have written Frank Bartlett,[31] who I have no doubt will soon be a brig[adier general], to look out for him. . . .

[No signature]

Near Falmouth, Virginia, Tuesday, January 19, 1863[32]

Dear Papa,

We have just come from parade where we were assembled to hear an order from Gen. Burnside, in substance as follows. Tomorrow, we shall again meet the foe, in the decisive battle of the war. The comdg. general is assured that the recent brilliant victories of Rosecrans and Foster have drawn off a large part of the rebel force opposite us.[33] He calls upon officers and men to give him their firm & unqualified support in this last great struggle, &c.

Now I am sure of one thing, that our regt. will fight, if without enthusiasm, as bravely as ever. I know it can not disgrace itself. But from visiting other regiments, I can't help concluding that there is serious disaffection through the army, not among the men merely, but just as bad among their officers. I am terribly afraid that the army is going to disgrace itself. I am afraid we shall again see what we had at Bull Run, the spectacle of regiments refusing to go to the front when ordered.

Last night it was announced at parade, I am told, to the 15th Mass., that one of their officers was dishonorably dismissed for tendering his resignation. All the evening the regiments were groaning

[31]W. F. Bartlett, having recovered from the loss of his leg, was promoted colonel of the 49th Mass. on Nov. 12, 1862. His regiment was assigned to the same theater of war as Fletcher Abbott.

[32]Abbott has misdated this letter. It was actually written on Tuesday, Jan. 20. This is evident from his following letter, dated Jan. 22, in which he refers back to the former letter that Abbott says he wrote "day before yesterday." Also, in 1863, Jan. 20 fell on a Tuesday, the day Abbott gives in the letter he misdated the 19th.

[33]Maj. Gen. William S. Rosecrans's Army of the Cumberland defeated Confederate Gen. Braxton Bragg's forces at the Battle of Murfreesboro (Stone's River), Tenn., on Dec. 31, 1862 to Jan. 1, 1863. Maj. Gen. John G. Foster's expedition from New Berne, N.C., succeeded in capturing Kingston, N.C., on Dec. 14, 1862.

Abe Lincoln & cheering Jeff Davis in the most vociferous manner. Nobody has the slightest confidence in Burnside. On the contrary, he is getting to be hated because he has McClellan's place. The announcement we had this morning, under McClellan, would have been received with the most tremendous cheering. . . .

I can't see any hope of victory, unless as Burnside says, the rebels have immensely weakened their forces, a thing which I can't & don't believe. I think if they have only half the force we have, we shall be driven back from those fortifications, whether we try to flank them or not. And if they have as many men as before, I shudder to think of the results. Burnside, either because he is afraid of a clamor being raised about spades, &c, or with an ignorance & carelessness hardly credible, has set the first example in modern times of a general commanding a great army neglecting to secure his base and his communications with fortifications, when there has been plenty of time. If we are desperately beaten (& the fight is going to be, for one side or the other, the most desperate of the war), we have no rallying point, no intrenchments to check the foe, in short, nothing to prevent us being driven pell mell into the Potomac, except the enemy's want of good cavalry & the customary supineness that seems to attend the victorious party in this war. I hope God will give us victory, but I don't believe he will.

If I don't have the luck to come back with the army, good bye to you and all the rest, but if I do, be sure and burn this letter as soon as you hear. Don't show it to any one, in any case, untill you hear. Of course, I shouldn't write that we are going into a great battle & worry you, except that I know you will already be worried by news of the fight going on before this reaches you, & I want to take advantage of the last chance I possibly may have to say good bye to you and all.

Your aff. son,
H. L. Abbott

In case I should not get out of it, I wish you would make over all the money I have saved (I am owed $1,000 by the government & owe a few debts, one to Riddle & several in the regt.) to a fund which is to be raised for the families of Nantucket volunteers killed or disabled in this company.

Camp near Falmouth, Virginia, January 22, 1863

My Dear Papa,

Please burn immediately my last which I wrote day before yesterday, if you haven't burned it already. I ain't afraid of any thing I said in it, for I rather understated, if any thing, the demoralization of the army (and as for talk, what you at home call treason is openly talked by the biggest generals, all the time) but because it is . . . rather a spongy thing to take leave of one's friends unnecessarily. In other words, it has rained like the old Nick ever since Burnside set out on his expedition (we were left to cover the communications) and the whole expedition is now stuck [in the mud] a few miles up the road, so that the common opinion is the thing is at end.

The state of the army is terrible. They will live along quietly as long as you let them alone, but the minute Burnside gave the orders for moving, the explosion took place. The 15th Mass. & Tammany hooted the address on parade, & the former hooted Burnside as he rode past yesterday, hollering in the loudest voices "put him out, put him out." Burnside took no notice of it, but it is the most shocking thing I ever heard of. A piece copied into the *Boston Post* from the *N.Y. Sun*, which you must have read, gives the truest account of the state of the army that could possibly be written, though of course since the intense suffering caused by this advance, things are much worse & almost ready for mutiny. One regiment yesterday threw down its arms & came back. I am terribly afraid the rest are nearly as bad, both officers & men. Thank God we can trust our regiment perfectly!

From a copy of the *Boston Gazette* we see that Palfrey has been made col.—which is almost too good news to be true—Dreher to be lt. col., which is an outrage we won't endure, if it turns out to be true. We have here the certificate on which he was discharged for *mental* & physical disability, & to allow a crazy man to stay at home and draw pay as lt. col. of this regt. while his betters are doing his work is a thing we won't stand. Gov. Andrew will hear from it from this army through the Dept. of War. . . . I shall answer George's letter soon.

Your aff. son,
H. L. Abbott

Cantonment Falmouth, Virginia, January 27, 1863

Dear Papa,

I send by draft on Major Wightman $500, including the amt. of expenses for Alley's embalment, coffin, &c. . . . Then I wish you would take out $10 for Sam as a Christmas present, $5 for Sally, and a dollar for each of the little ones. Now papa, I wish you would really give this to them & not put it in the bank or any thing of that kind, for I promised it for a long time. The government still owes me 3 months' pay, besides $10 extra a month for the time which my commission as capt. covers, for which period I have been paid as 1st lt., in all, nearly $500. I have about $100 on hand after paying all expenses.

I suppose you got my two last. Of course you will know before this reaches you that Hooker is in command,[34] Sumner, Burnside, [and] Franklin, who was the smartest man left, being relieved. Hooker is nothing more than a smart, driving, plucky Yankee, inordinately vain & I imagine from the way he has converted himself to the Administration, entirely unscrupulous. I never will serve under *Fremont* a single second. Neither will any other officer in this army, except the Dutchmen of Sigel's corps.[35]

Sunday we relieved the brigade on duty here & are now cantoned here, in a filthy condition, earnestly engaged in draining the streets, cleaning houses & so on. The Pennsylvanians whom we relieved were beastly wretches. Do see Mr. Joseph Ropes when he gets back.[36] You have no idea what a jolly old bird he is. He is on a regular lark now you know . . . & is immensely entertaining. Besides, he has the highest respect for your politics as well as yourself. He will give you the best possible notion of things here. . . .

We all expect Hooker will soon make his grand failure & patiently wait for it. Our moving to this place on Sunday prevented my usual Sunday letters. But I shall answer soon. Frank's letter was a perfect stunner.

Your aff. son,
H. L. Abbott

[34]Hooker assumed command of the Army of the Potomac on Jan. 25, 1863.
[35]Maj. Gen. Franz Sigel relinquished command of the Eleventh Army Corps, which was composed largely of Germans, in Jan. 1863.
[36]Father of Henry Ropes.

SEVEN

FIGHTING JOE HAS TAKEN US

Cantonment Falmouth, Virginia, February 1, 1863

My Dear Carry,

I reopen my regular Sunday correspondence with a letter to you. We are cantoned in Falmouth occupying deserted houses, i.e. the officers, the men being in sheds which were left in the most filthy condition by the regts. which we relieved. We are getting things gradually into order, though the only way to do it thoroughly would be to drain off the whole town with all inhabitants. . . .

I occupy a room in the house of Mrs. Kelly, together with Mason, Ropes, the Q.M. & Willard,[1] a promoted sergeant. The aristocratic being who condescends to receive our green backs rapidly discovered that we were also aristocrats, & the courtesy is tremendous. She was good enough to tell us that Boston was the most aristocratic city of the North, which was true. She also condescended to tell me that she had met my sisters in Washington, which was not true. In fact, she is so devlish aristocratic that she charges 25 cents a quart for milk, & other things corresponding.

If Mary Welch has something funny to tell me, I am willing to hear it. She has my full consent to write. Her remark to the young English gentleman was of a style she has often made to me, . . . which I have duly reproved, so that she is now in a fair state of discipline & properly submissive.

Your aff. brother,
H. L. Abbott

---

[1]2d Lt. Samuel Willard was made captain of the 54th Mass. Colored Infantry on Apr. 14, 1863.

Cantonment Falmouth, Virginia, February 1, 1863

My Dear Mamma,

I am very glad Mrs. Mitchell is still ignorant. I am very anxious to pay the expenses my self. I have sent home several hundreds of dollars to the governor & desired him to take that out.

The boxes you have sent have been stopped somewhere on account of Burnside's late attempt at a move, but will doubtless get through soon, & then we shall enjoy them.

So Fletcher is gone. The governor's present to him was magnificent. I hope he will have good health, & have no doubt he will, for the staff is decidedly different from the line. We have just had an extremely pleasant visit from Mr. Joseph Ropes. He was exceedingly jolly & except for a bad habit of swearing, a very moral man. He is all right on politics & an admirable observer & describer, so he can give you the best possible account of present things here.

Fighting Joe [Hooker] has taken us. May the Lord deliver us soon, not however into the . . . hands of John C. [Frémont], but into the bosom of the only general & the only honest public man in the country, little Mac (all great men are small of stature, remind the governor, to whom, by the way, I have written 3 letters in the last fortnight). I dare say Hooker, in his anxiety to appear different from the last dozen or so generals that we have had, will imitate McClellan by not attempting the impracticable, & by lying still till it is time for him to be removed.

Very affectionately yours,
H. L. Abbott

Cantonment Falmouth, Virginia, February 1, 1863

My Dear George,

I assure you, in the first place, that the story I told you about the officer who had lost his voice for life is true. Had I told the same about a woman, you would have been justified in doubting the tale, but not this one.

I wish you could come & see us. The next thing to that, however, is to make the acquaintance of Mr. Joseph Ropes who has been on a lark here for the last few days, accompanied by a spoony clerical friend, the Rev. Dr. Means of Roxbury. Mr. Ropes, however, you will find a devlish good fellow. . . .

The president it seems, has prepared a list of officers who are to be dismissed [from] the service for speaking disrespectfully of his jokes.

His military genius, of course, none but the most demoralized man could jeer at, which . . . includes all the officers of the Potomac army, who are as "demoralized as hell" & mean to continue so untill the coronation of the great John C. [Frémont], when they will immediately disband & return to their several homes. Men are deserting by the hundreds. The cavalry patrol yesterday & a day or two previous, arrested 400 who were engaged in building rafts at Acquia Creek in order to cross the yellow Potomac. . . .

I am extremely obliged for your efforts in packing the box which I expect every day, & also for [the] bale of Killikenick,[2] which will be a godsend in this brutal town. If you see Pete Wilkins, ask him why the devil he doesn't write me & give my love to him & the other lame ducks, also to the Commander of the Home Guard, Col. Lee, & let me know how the old boy is.

Your aff. friend,
H. L. Abbott

Falmouth, Virginia, February 8, 1863

Dear Mamma,

Some of my letters must have miscarried. I have written to you, the governor, Carry & George all since the time you give as the date of my last received. I have received yours of the 1st, the only one from the family for a week, the customary one from Carry & George not having arrived.

I am in command of the regt., Macy having started for home on leave of 15 days (I never thought to ask him to stop & see you & I don't suppose he would have had time, if I had), & Holmes being provost marshal. Oh, by jove, you don't know how much I would give to be permanent commander of this regt. & I can hardly imagine greater bliss than to be commander of a regt. in which all the companies were as good as my own. If I should ever get to be commander of this regt., the greatest objection I should have would be in leaving a command so perfect, I was about to say, in every respect, as my company, to take the control of a command where there are many companies so inferior. This isn't vanity, for the merit isn't in me, but in the excellent material of which the company is made up.

I suppose Fletch is by this time in New Orleans. Send me the letters he writes home. I should like to see them exceedingly.

2A very poor type of tobacco.

We daily receive accounts through the *New York Herald*, which by the way isn't, I think, in as great favor now that it has began trimming accounts of the splendid way McClellan . . . is treated. Why did they refuse to offer him the hospitalities of the city? Hooker is doing pretty well, having, I understand, announced himself as the close imitator of Mac. You don't say who Mary Russell is engaged to. Billy Perkins is all right, White having declined the nomination. I have received no boxes, but hope to soon.

Your aff. son,
H. L. Abbott

Falmouth, Virginia, March 5, 1863

Dear Papa,

Will you please draw $100. of my money & send it to Mrs. Wm. Worth, Nantucket. It is for a fund for the families of killed & disabled Nantucket men of my company. Please be very careful to take it from my account, because I wish particularly to make the contribution myself, as my duty, seeing that I can spare it with perfect ease. . . .

We have just received the greatest honor yet. We are one of the regiments selected in gen. orders to have one more officer absent on leave, & one more soldier to the 100 on furlough, for general excellence. The only Mass. regts. out of the whole Potomac army [given this honor] are the 1st, 2nd, & 20th. The rest are the 5th & 10th New York, two famous regiments, 1st Minnesota, 111th Penn., 10th & 19th Maine, & a few other from other states. There [are] a large number, mostly of course from New York & Penn., cut off from leaves & furloughs altogether, on account of general inferiority.

Your aff. son,
H. L. Abbott

Col. Hall has just been here. He says he shall be well enough to come back & take the brigade in 10 days. I hope to heaven he will be here before the campaign opens.

Falmouth, Virginia, March 10, 1863

My Dear George,

Since you won't write, I see that I must, especially as I have been longing to tell you what a prize to the Doctor[3] & myself the tobacco was that you sent me. Where did you get it? It is the best thing I have

---

[3]Referring to Nathan Hayward, surgeon of the 20th.

smoked since the days of Pesique. Infinitely superior to Killikenick. I can tell you too we were getting precious short of the thing & what we did have was ferocious poor quality.

I have been very intimate with the Dr. of late, living in the same room with him, & I like [him] more the more I see of him. I believe he is one of the most thoroughly sincere & honest men I ever knew. We are getting to be great horsemen, riding 2 or 3 hours every morning before duty, but for me that happiness is drawing rapidly to a close, as the time for Macy's return approaches. I suppose you have seen by this time the order which selects us among a few other regiments for additional priviledges in the way of leaves & furloughs. I must give Hooker the credit of saying that this step is the very best for the army that could be taken, by employing the spirit of emulation, the most powerful governing spirit of . . . American troops, a power which Burnside persistently neglected, because he hadn't the pluck to pick out individual regiments for praise or censure, but passed sweeping commendations or condemnations, a course which may be successful once, but soon gets played out. It is a power too which the government has been lately trying to kill, by talking of consolidations.[4]

The [Second] Corps was reviewed the other day by Hooker. He was much better received than Burnside was in his grand review, though the latter had some cheering, while Hooker had none. The latter showed his shrewdness by giving the generals positive orders not to propose cheering, merely to allow the men to cheer, in case it burst out spontaneously, which of course it didn't do. He knew that the ordinary grave & decorous appearance of a review is much better than the forced cheering Burnside had to be content with from a few green regiments. . . .

Very affectionately,
H. L. Abbott

Falmouth, Virginia, March 22, 1863

Dear Papa,

I was very glad to get a letter from you at last, & still more glad to find that you were in . . . New York. I have heard from you since

---

[4]The government had considered merging some of the weaker regiments whose ranks had been thinned due to battle losses and disease in order to create stronger units. This plan, however, was only carried out to a limited degree, as it would have severely dampened troop morale by causing many regiments to lose their identity.

Maj. Gen. Joseph "Fighting Joe" Hooker. *Courtesy National Archives.*

through Murphy.[5] What did you think of him as a specimen of a thoroughbred soldier who has risen from the ranks? If it were not for his Irish characteristics, he would be an uncommonly good officer. He seemed to be strongly impressed from his visit to Boston that it was the thing to belong to the 20th. Macy, too, spoke of you.

I find upon looking over your letter that your usual envy of moderate-sized men breaks out, in spite of yourself. However, some big men have occasionally made their mark, though rarely of course, even as prize fighters. But the more knowledge I get of men here in the army, the more I am convinced that as a rule, they are dreadfully stupid, the reverse being the case with smaller men. Burnside against McClellan for instance. . . .

What do you think [of] the prospects of a campaign? In our corps, half the number, 8,000, are 9 months men.[6] And if we are to keep this line, our only hope of success is what we never had yet, a decisive battle, to take place within one month, & though it only takes a day or two to fight a battle, the preparations for breaking up camp & the requisite maneuvers take a great while longer. If he fails in the decisive battle, Hooker will be everlastingly condemned as the general who undertook a campaign when it was certain that, in less than a month, half his troops would leave him perhaps inextricably entangled by the now superior forces of the enemy. . . . On the other hand, if we are going to the Peninsula, half his force will leave him before he even opens his campaign, & he has got to reorganize his army by drawing away half the troops on the coast. However, I find that I must dry up, so

Your aff. son,
H. L. Abbott

Falmouth, Virginia, March 22, 1863

My Dear Mamma,

Hereafter, by the way, I am going to begin my letters "my dear mother," the former sounds so affected. I am terribly disappointed. I had at last knocked under & made up my mind to go home, & after once coming to that decision, it is a bitter pill to have to give up the prospect, at least for a week. I sent in a leave, but it was rejected by Darius [Gen. Couch], the 15 days allowed for an extra officer being

---

[5]Capt. James Murphy, Co. F, would be severely wounded during the Chancellorsville campaign.

[6]These were men who had enlisted for nine months' service and whose terms were about to expire, thereby thinning the ranks of many units.

out. Dreadful mean of Darius to say no, when it was so easy to [say] yes. However he is a McClellan man, so I shan't give him up yet. Next Saturday, Holmes & I will both put in applications; Kelliher & Hibbard,[7] the two officers who went last, [are] coming back then. . . .

I have bought Macy's horse Jim, used to belong to Palfrey, a good-sized, strong beast, & a pretty good "Critter." I am going to answer Sally's letter immediately. . . . Good bye & look for Holmes & myself at probably Tuesday or Wednesday of next week, as our applications will go in next Saturday.[8]

Your aff. son,
H. L. Abbott

Falmouth, Virginia, April 20, 1863

My Dear Papa,

We got here all right, & though some what worried by reports on the way that the army was moving, we found it stationary still. The rebels know as well as you at home that we are under marching orders with eight days' rations. The roads of course are a subterfuge, & as I can hardly suspect Hooker of the same stupidity as Burnside, I think the thing must be purposely let out to play some game; though it almost seems as if McClellan were the only man able to move us without telling all the world a couple of weeks before hand. You remember the disposition I made previously of my enormous fortune, in case any thing should happen.

I have been getting the [New York] *Worlds* all right. I must agree with you that it is the best paper in the U.S., immeasurably superior to the *Herald.* I wish for the good of the army it were sold here. John Perry is doing admirably.[9] You would suppose he had been out here the whole war. He is the only surgeon we have had that knew any thing since Dr. Hayward.

Your aff. son,
H. L. Abbott
. . . Give my love to all, not excepting Mary Welch, & tell her [so].

---

[7]2d Lt. John Kelliher, Co. F, and 2d Lt. Lansing Hibbard, who was later promoted 1st lieutenant, Co. H. Hibbard was killed at Spotsylvania Court House, May 10, 1864.

[8]Abbott applied for his leave on Mar. 31, for on Mar. 27 Henry's nine-year-old brother Arthur died. The death certificate listed croup as the cause. Abbott returned to the regiment on Apr. 7.

[9]John Perry, cousin of George Perry, arrived in April as assistant surgeon of the regiment.

Falmouth, Virginia, [10] *May 5, 1863*

Dear Papa,

We have done briefly this. We have been over to Fredericksburg again, where we assisted the 6th Corps (Sedgwick) to take the heights, by making a diversion on the right. Our advance was stopped by coming on a canal under the heights, the bridges being broken. We were exposed to a heavy shell fire for a short time, losing a couple dozen men, or 20 [men] & 2 officers, but thanks to Col. Hall, who showed wonderful coolness & self possession, where many a man in an open space under a heavy fire would have lost his head & destroyed us. He rapidly deployed his brigade, which was advancing in one long column, & advancing a couple of rods, got [to] a stone wall where we lay safe & comfortable, the shells piling over us, untill we saw the 7th [Massachusetts], 10th [Massachusetts], [11] & a few other regiments take the heights by storm. Notwithstanding there were very few [Confederates] behind the pits & only a scattering fire, they wavered several times. Once we gave up hope, the rebels on the other hand cheering all along the line & taunting us with numerous derisive questions, but Sedgwick supported the storming party so admirably, & the defense was really so weak, our artillery engaging theirs on at least equal terms, that soon we gained the pits. The cheering was then on our side, & as the Jhonnies in the pits before us put off, we certainly would have given them a roust, if it hadn't been for the cursed canal. As it was, we had to double-quick clear round to the place where the assaulting column had got up, and then double-quick up the heights, & then deploying, sweep across the plateau, our skirmishers driving the rebels like sheep.

When we got to the top, we found the works of the meanest description. Nothing whatever but rifle pits for the infantry, which you know are trenches a few feet deep, with the earth thrown out in front, & which are in fact better suited for an infantry fire, particularly down a slope, than the most elaborate intrenchments. For the artillery, there were epaulements which covered the pieces well

[10]On Apr. 27, Hooker set out with the bulk of the army to cross the Rappahannock and Rapidan rivers in order to outflank the Confederate army. This move led to the Battle of Chancellorsville, fought May 1–6, 1863. Sedgwick, commanding the Sixth Corps, was left behind with the remainder of the army (including Gibbon's division of the Second Corps, to which the 20th belonged) to make a demonstration against Fredericksburg itself. He attacked and carried Marye's Heights on May 3.

[11]These regiments belonged to the Sixth Corps.

enough, but didn't pretend to be works. It was evident they depended on the position & not on the works. It is certainly, both for artillery & infantry fire, the best position that can be imagined, being just the right slope & having spurs which run out from the hills & enfilade a great part of the slope.

Here Sedgwick, leaving us, shoved his column, covered by skirmishers, straight along to join Hooker on the right; we descended into the town, being selected to do provost duty there as the brigade which captured the town before, this time (I forgot to say) it having been abandoned without defense. We quartered luxuriantly on the platform of the railroad station, until, next morning, we were alarmed by a couple companies of the 62nd New York (6th Corps) arriving in, who said they had been left out on picket towards the left when Sedgwick kept on, & that the enemy were advancing from the left, along the ridge, in force, a thing which seemed incredible to us, Col. Hall included, since we could not imagine that we, one weak brigade, not 1,200 strong . . . had been sent down in the town, unless Sedgwick had either kept the heights with some forces of his own, or was aware that there were no rebels on the left of the heights, he having broken through the center of the ridge & turned the right.

However we had hardly time to get our forces posted, forming one thin line of skirmishers round the town, . . . & without men enough to have any *reserve*, before the rebels appeared, rapidly moving along the ridge from the left. When the rebels got to the position which we stormed the day before (Sunday), they advanced down towards us in a heavy column, but seeing the display of our forces, they retired again & deployed behind the pits, sending out skirmishers to feel ours. When they got very near, my company, which was deployed at intervals of 10 paces, about 25 feet, my men, having retained their fire until they were very close, lying on their bellies, suddenly opened, knocked over a lot of them & sent the rest rapidly back to their pits; the Tammany [regiment] meantime, were posted behind my men as supports, having most of them run in [from their picket posts] without firing a shot, so strong was the tendency to a panic at the rebels having so unexpectedly occupied the heights, in such large force, when it wasn't supposed there was a Jhonny within 6 miles, & when we were so small & isolated.

All day there was skirmishing & the heat was terrible, but our salvation was that the rebels had to send all their artillery & much of their infantry over to the right, where toward night there was a severe fight, our men trying to take in reverse the heights which they had taken in front the day before, being badly repulsed & driven very close to the river.[12] It was very discouraging to have the rebels . . . jeering at us from these heights again, but all day & the following night we entrenched ourselves, digging pits along the edge of the town, barricading the streets & loop-holing the houses. I believe we should have given the rebels fits, unless they could have got artillery, which I suppose they would. At any rate, this morning we were ordered to retire, which we did under a heavy fog, pretty well played out, & here we are at Falmouth again in our old quarters. Without having had any fighting to do, our regiment has kept a good front under trying circumstances & has won a new name, "Hall's Regulars."

Who made the blunder of leaving the heights open, I don't know; I am very unwilling to believe it was Sedgwick's fault, since I think so much of him & since his dispositions to take the heights were so admirably conceived & carried out. Who ever is to blame has, I am convinced, injured our affairs exceedingly. As far as the main fighting on the right, the reports are contradictory. One thing I am sure of, we have not been successful. At the most we have held our own. And this is all, because the 11th Corps, Sigel's Dutchmen, broke and run, all of them, at the first shot, as I always knew they would, losing 16 pieces [of artillery]. Hooker exposed himself recklessly in trying to rally them, but the rebels were brought up suddenly & repulsed with heavy loss, by our corps, which with the exception of our division, had gone up to the right. Our corps saved the army. I wish to God we had been with them. At present accounts, our whole line is entrenched & covered with abattis, & Hooker is supported by the whole army except the 11th Corps, in [inkblot] ruination. . . .

I have just heard from the best sources that the whole army is on the retreat. Many a man here would give up his life to hear that the news is false but there can be no doubt about it. It is horrible awful. Every man in Sigel's Corps ought to be hauled off the face of the Earth. I am afraid we shall never lift our heads out of this terrible infamy. Hooker has done gallantly, according to his ideas, & I feel less inclined to hit him now than ever, but I must say that it seemed from the first very strange, dividing our forces into . . . two equal parts, one of which was held at bay for the first 7 days, by the heights

---

[12]Referring to the action at Salem Church.

Maj. Gen. John Sedgwick, whom Abbott regarded as a personal friend. He would be killed by a Rebel sharpshooter on May 9, 1864, at the Battle of Spotsylvania Court House. *Courtesy USAMHI.*

of Fredericksburg. He seems to have thought he had only about 40,000 against him.[13] Give my love to all.

Your aff. son,
H. L. Abbott

Whatever you think at home, papa, remember that our feeling here is only to call back McClellan, recruit, & *wipe out this disgrace*. That is the uppermost thought. We can never sit down under this humiliation.

Falmouth, Virginia, May 7(?), 1863

My Dear Mamma,

I suppose you know by this we have suffered another repulse, & what appeared to be an error in dividing the army into halves has really turned out so, & not to be strategy, as every one had to think at first. Hooker thought he had only 40,000 men to bag, & kept tempting the rebels to bring on more because he thought they wouldn't be glory enough. I hear the administration will give the whole thing out to be merely a demonstration, which however will hardly tally with the losses & the first Washington accounts of brilliant victories &c. . . . I should think the whole nation would cry out for McClellan.

In confidence we are going to cross again tomorrow, either owing to Hooker's insatiable vanity, or the presence & orders of those two old "caterpillars on the commonwealth," Lincoln & Halleck.[14] If we do we shall certainly go to pot, but I think the present tremendous rain will block that game.

I wrote yesterday a long letter to the governor. Keep shady about this letter, or it might cost me [my] commission, as I suppose the despotism at Washington will be making as many victims as after the last wholesale butchery of this poor army. Sedgwick, the wisest man left in this army, will be the first victim. He declared when the movement began that he had never known but one man fit to command us, Mac. of course.

It certainly seems as if it were impossible for abolitionists to stop lying & doing all they can to injure this army. There is Johnny Andrew, after all his promises, outraging the regiment by these new appointments. Sheppard,[15] of course, we expected meanness from,

---

[13]Total Confederate effectives numbered about 60,000 as opposed to Hooker's 133,868 men.

[14]Henry W. Halleck was then general in chief of the Union Army.

[15]Allen Shepard had been promoted major of the regiment on May 1.

as he is merely a low, cheating, shop keeper, & if he ever comes out here, we will fix him easily. But from Paul Revere,[16] I did expect . . . the ordinary honesty of a gentleman. Instead of that however, after never being in the regiment but 6 months . . . never having commanded it in a battle, being more ignorant than any non-commissioned officer in my company of drill & the most ordinary internal arrangements of a regiment, besides being of an impracticable peevish disposition which makes mountains out of molehills & renders him totally unfit to command men & to adapt himself to the numerous worries & small vexations of a regiment in the field, having resigned out of the regiment at a most trying moment because he disliked Palfrey & got an uncommonly good staff berth with increase of rank & pay, having believed & declared that he had left the regiment for good, Paul Revere, I say, . . . finding his place on the staff is filled, goes mousing round the imbeciles at Washington until he gets them to declare that the . . . regiment is still his & that Macy's appointment is illegal[17] . . . & instead of resting content even with that, he writes a letter to Macy, telling him that he should dislike very much to oust *so esteemed a friend*, & accordingly, he will kindly allow Macy to retain his place, while he himself will take the colonelcy.

I tell you he has no more right to it than any civilian there in Boston & that if he sticks to this nasty little technical subterfuge that a gentleman would be ashamed to mention, after getting the letter I have written him expressing the feelings [of] the officers, he will be declared unfit . . . to associate with gentlemen, all but the barest official intercourse will be refused him, & . . . he will be left . . . to howl & snarl out ridiculous orders until he gets publicly kicked out for shameful ignorance & inefficiency. . . .

By rights, Macy is col., Holmes lt. col. and myself major, & we will never cease the fight until we get our rights. Oh it makes one terribly bitter, after fighting & working and suffering until you get close to the prize, to have it snatched from you by men whom you despise. I should like to have it in my power to do a great mischief to these fellows, with that miserable old lying, bloated, bragger of the State House [Gov. Andrew] at the head of them.

Your aff. son,
H. L. Abbott

[16]Promoted colonel of the regiment on Apr. 14.

[17]Macy was promoted lieutenant colonel on May 1, following the death of Ferdinand Dreher, who, after much suffering, had finally succumbed to wounds received at the Battle of Fredericksburg.

Col. Paul J. Revere (grandson and namesake of the patriot) was mortally wounded at Gettysburg, July 2, 1863. He died three days later. *Courtesy USAMHI.*

Falmouth, Virginia, May 17, 1863

My Dear Mamma,

You don't know how much pleased I am to find that you understand so thoroughly the merits of the case in the recent promotions. There are so very few persons in civil life that can appreciate the feelings of this regiment, that it overjoys me to find you and papa & the rest all right on the goose. I knew you would be.

I am exceedingly glad you have got the governor off on a journey. I am sure he needs it enough. Where shall you go this summer? You will have a stunning time with such a party. I wish I were to be with you, I can assure you; it makes me almost sick of the service to have a man lead the army who has shown himself so incompetent as Hooker. His recent ridiculous order written by Dan Butterfield,[18] disgusts every body. He says in that, that it is unnecessary to mention the cause of the failure, every one in the army knows it, &c. But it wasn't the disgraceful flight of those miserable Dutchmen, who every body knew would run away. It was the incompetency of the general who could only get one half his men into action. Smalley,[19] the abolition panegyrist of Hooker after the battle of Antietam, stated the other day at Gen. Couch's table that he had asked the opinion of every corps commander in the army, & with *one* exception, they all stated in the most unequivocal manner, that they had lost all confidence in Fighting Joe. At Gen. Couch's & Gen. Sedgwick's & Gen. [John] Gibbon's hdqrts.,[20] the only hdqrts. I go to, they cry out openly for McClellan.

Then besides the curse over the army in general, our regiment gets it in particular. I can't meet Revere without feeling sorer & sorer, although the conviction has become general here that his motives are honorable. I can only believe that his feelings have got the better of his judgement. By the way, you must remember that Holmes is a particular friend of mine & not blackguard him. He spoke to me openly about the question whether he should waive his claims to promotion for me, & I advised him not to do it by any means.[21]

[18]Maj. Gen. Daniel Butterfield was Hooker's chief of staff.

[19]George W. Smalley (1833–1916) was a war correspondent for the *New York Tribune*.

[20]Gibbon had taken command of the Second Division, Second Corps, when Howard was promoted to command of the Eleventh Corps.

[21]Holmes was then at home recuperating from a wound in the heel which he received on May 3 during the attack on Marye's Heights. Because of his condition, Holmes had offered to waive promotion as lieutenant colonel so that Abbott might get the position. Abbott, however, refused to accept the offer.

Such a course would give an entirely erroneous opinion as to his competency, for he is a very good officer.

When Revere first came out, I felt terribly tempted to cut off my nose to spite my face, but I flatter myself that I have not imitated him in allowing my feelings to get the better of my judgement. I believe firmly we shall weather him, & also the cripples, who have declared open war against Macy & myself, headed by Putnam,[22] who considers Macy & myself as bloodthirsty, inhumane, & several more. We are certainly more bloodthirsty than he, in the sense that we have done considerably more to slay our fellow mortals than he, but towards himself I fancy we have shown great generosity in allowing him to stay as long as he has, & only expostulating him when we found he had designs for the colonelcy. I believe we shall get our rights sometime, & I am going to wait for it. Hurrah for the time when Macy shall wear the eagle, Holmes the silver leaf & myself the gold leaf.

Tell papa that the [New York] World is now, since I have brought it into notice, universally read by the fellows and considered by every body the only paper in the U. States. Not only its articles on McClellan & Hooker, but its political articles go to the right spot.

That infernally bloated aristocrat & bore Mrs. Kelly is at me again. I send enclosed a list of things she wants Carry to get, also $35 which I don't suppose will be half enough. In that case she promises, & I think she may be trusted, to send the rest, upon finding so. She expects Ropes to bring the bundles. I presume it will be too heavy & you had better put it on the express directed to me. You will find in, I think the cedar closet, 3 thin pairs [of] boots; please ask Ropes, if he has room to bring on, not the thinnest pair, but the larger of the two thicker pairs.

I am much obliged to you for promising to send the map. Tell Mary Welch that her picture is beautiful except the nose is thicker than the most delicate original, also, that Herbert Mason, having accidentally obtained a sight of the picture, promised not to tell, if I would only let him look at it whenever he wanted to; terms of course which I promptly refused. John [Perry] says he hasn't heard from George since he came. I got a long letter from Brandon. I am hunting up a cousin of his, who was brought over here with a leg off.

Your aff. son,
H. L. Abbott

[22]Capt. John C. Putnam, having lost an arm at Ball's Bluff, was discharged for disability on Sept. 8, 1863.

Falmouth, Virginia, May 18, 1863

My Dear Oliver [Holmes],

I was devlish glad to get a letter from you. Let me congratulate you upon your wound, now that I know that it is no worse. It will keep through the summer & you will be well in time for the reopening campaign in autumn. I remember looking down the line and seeing you limping, telling Macy that you were hit. We were told you were going to lose your foot & you may be sure there was no end of feeling for you.

I can almost wish I were with you. I feel so sick of Hooker as a commander in general & Revere in particular, though to do the latter justice, he hasn't commanded a single parade or drill since he came to the regiment just a week ago. I am bound to believe after [the] argument we had with him, that he is moved by the most honorable motives, because he says so himself; but it is only another proof to me that the most honorable man may allow his feelings completely to get the better of his judgement, & that brains are necessary as well as instincts, to be really honorable. I think it a defect in Revere's brain that won't allow him to change an opinion once entertained. . . . The cripples are also furious. I expect, if I ever get home, to be attacked by a legion of one-armed fiends. Beware of Putnam the Bummer.

The remorsed Hallowell[23] is also in a phrenzy of virtuous & magnanimous indignation, & has written me a letter that I should have expected from any abolitionist except him. . . . I thought at first that he must have been joking, a take off on Putnam's letter, but since I have made up my mind that he was drunk, as the letter is dated from the Parker House. . . .[24] Take care of yourself & don't be impudent.

Your aff. friend,
H. L. Abbott

[23]Capt. Norwood P. Hallowell accepted a commission as lieutenant colonel of the 54th Mass. Colored Infantry on Apr. 11.

[24]The Parker House was a noted Boston hotel and restaurant, where the city's upper crust frequently wined and dined.

EIGHT

GETTYSBURG:
Worth All Our Defeats

Near Gettysburg,[1] *July 6, 1863*

My Dear Papa,

When our great victory was just over the exultation of victory was so great that one didn't think of our fearful losses, but now I can't help feeling a great weight at my heart. Poor Henry Ropes was one of the dearest friends I ever had or expect to have.[2] He was one of the purest-minded, noblest, most generous men I ever knew. His loss is terrible. His men actually wept when they showed me his body, even under the tremendous cannonade, a time when most soldiers see their comrades dying around them with indifference. Col. Hall, I believe, means to mention him in his report. He says that of every body in the army, Henry was the only one he knew that was fighting simply from patriotism, & that he would himself almost have given his life to have had Ropes live to see the splendid victory he always earnestly hoped for. I can't cease to think of him, whenever I am alone, which is pretty frequent now that we have only 3 [officers] left.

All our pique against Revere too had long ceased, since we saw him on the march struggling so nobly with his physical weakness, & he is regretted as such a man should be.[3] Then there is poor Macy

---

[1]The Army of the Potomac began moving northward on June 5 to intercept Lee's second invasion of the North. This letter was written three days after the resulting Battle of Gettysburg.

[2]Henry Ropes was killed during the cannonade of July 3 while the 20th was awaiting the Confederate attack. It seems that a New York battery about fifteen feet in rear of the line had been shelling the Confederates by firing over the heads of the Union troops. Ropes, who had been sitting under a tree reading Dickens, was struck in the back by a fragment of a shell that exploded immediately upon leaving the muzzle of one of the pieces. After uttering "I am killed," the gallant soldier fell over and died almost instantly.

[3]Revere was mortally wounded by a shell fragment on July 2. He died three days later.

Letter of H. L. Abbott to his father, written from the Gettysburg battlefield, July 6, 1863. *Courtesy Houghton Library, Harvard University.*

with a hand gone. Herbert Mason hit too, with Ropes my most intimate friend here, & one of the finest & bravest officers that ever fought in this war. Just as he was going off from the hospital, with a consideration that wounded men going home rarely feel for those left, he sent me his brandy, tobacco, &c, a perfect godsend at the time. Patten[4] too, who is going to be mentioned by Col. Hall for the gallantry with which he held his outpost, when the skirmishers on both flanks had run, & our whole force in the direst confusion had gone over him.

Indeed with only two officers besides myself remaining, I can't help feeling a little spooney when I am thinking, & you know I am not at all a lachrymose individual in general. However I think we can run the machine.[5] Our losses are—of 13 officers, 3 killed, 7 wounded. Of 231 enlisted men, 30 killed, 84 wounded, 3 missing, total 117, with officers, aggregate 127.

I haven't time to give you an account as I have to write to Mr. Ropes & John Revere, also to Paine's father. (Paine was one of the finest officers I have ever seen, though only 17 years of age.)[6]

The enemy, after a morning of quiet on our part of the line (a little to the right of the left center) began the most terrific cannonade, with a converging fire of 150 pieces, that I have ever heard in my life & kept it up for 2 hours, almost entirely disabling our batteries, killing & wounding over half the officers & men [of the artillery] & silencing most of the guns. The thin line of our division against which it was directed was very well shielded by a little rut they lay in & in front of our brigade by a little pit, just one foot deep & one foot high, thrown up hastily by one shovel, but principally by the fact that it is very difficult to hit a single line of troops, so that the enemy chiefly threw over us with the intention of disabling the batteries & the reserves which they supposed to be massed in the rear of the batteries, in the depression of the hill.

In the former object they were successful, in the latter they were better than successful. The one brigade brought up in support had to be retired 2 miles, & no other reserves could be brought up, for any massing of troops . . . under that fire would have proved their own

---

[4]Capt. Henry L. Patten, Co. D, was promoted major of the regiment following Abbott's death, but died on Sept. 10, 1864, from wounds received at Deep Bottom, Va., on Aug. 14, 1864.

[5]Since all of his senior officers had either been killed or wounded, Abbott assumed temporary command of the regiment, a post he would retain until his death.

[6]Sumner Paine, who joined the regiment in April as Abbott's 2d lieutenant, was killed on July 3.

Lt. Henry Ropes, one of Abbott's dearest friends, survived several bloody battles, only to be killed by a blast from a Union cannon at Gettysburg, July 3, 1863. *Courtesy USAMHI.*

destruction, without their being any service to us. No infantry in the world could have been massed under that fire for half an hour.

The rebels thus left us entirely unsupported & advanced with perfect confidence after ceasing their artillery—our artillery being so knocked up that only one or two shots were fired into them, which, however, were very well aimed, & we could see [the shots] tumble over squads in the rebel lines. Had our batteries been intact, the rebels would never have got up to our musketry, for they were obliged to come out of the woods & advance from a half to ¾ of a mile over an open field & in plain sight. A magnificent sight it was too. Two brigades in two lines, their skirmishers driving in ours.

The moment I saw them I knew we should give them Fredericksburg. So did every body. We let the regiment in front of us get within 100 feet of us, & then bowled them over like nine pins, picking out the colors first. In two minutes there were only groups of two or three men running round wildly, like chickens with their heads off. We were cheering like mad, when Macy directed my attention to a spot 3 or 4 rods on our right where there were no pits, only a rail fence, Baxter's Pennsylvania men had most disgracefully broken,[7] & the rebels were within our line. The order was immediately given to fall back far enough to form another line & prevent us [from] being flanked. Without however waiting for that, the danger was so imminent that I had rushed my company immediately up to the gap, & the regiment & the rest of the brigade, being there some before & the rest as quick as they could. The rail fence checked the main advance of the enemy & they stood, both sides pegging away into each other.

The rows of dead after the battle I found to be within 15 and 20 feet apart, as near hand to hand fighting as I ever care to see. The rebels behaved with as much pluck as any men in the world could; they stood there, against the fence, until they were nearly all shot down. The rebels' batteries, seeing how the thing was going, pitched shell into us all the time, with great disregard of their own friends who were so disagreeably near us. Gen. [Alexander S.] Webb, who commands the Philadelphia Brigade, in his official report has given Hall's brigade the credit of saving the day, after his own men had run away. A miserable rowdy named [Brig. Gen. Alexander] Hays, comdg. the 3rd Div. of our corps, who was not engaged at all in the musketry fire, claims I believe, all the credit of the thing. So look out for false stories in the papers. Don't confound this fellow with

[7]Col. Dewitt C. Baxter commanded the 72d Penn.

[Brig. Gen. William] Hays, comdg. the corps, who is said to be a good officer, & who got up just after the fight, [Maj. Gen. Winfield S.] Hancock, commanding the corps & Gibbon comdg. the Div., a splendid officer, being both wounded. . . .

The field was mostly open where we were with scarcely a perceptible rise, commanded by the rebel side; on the center a little wooded, still better commanded by the rebel side; on the right, I am told, wooded & rocky, both parties contending for the slopes towards us. . . . Moreover, our line of retreat was so narrow that it was easy, if our left was turned, to cut us off from it. Had the rebels driven in our left (they twice tried it & I have told you how near they came to it) it would have been all up with us.

The advantages of our position were that the comdg. general could over look almost the whole line, a rare thing in this country, & that moving on the chord of the circle while the enemy moved on the arc, we could reinforce any part of the line from any other part much quicker than they could, an advantage which Meade availed himself of admirably in the first day's rebel attack,[8] but which their shell fire prevented him from doing in the second day's [July 3].

In person, Meade is a tall, thin, lantern-jawed, respectable [man], wearing spectacles, looking a good sort of a family doctor. Uncle John Sedgwick, as have most other of our good officers, long ago told us that McClellan was the first choice, Franklin the 2nd, & Meade the 3rd. An extremely good officer you see, with no vanity or nonsense of any kind, knowing just exactly what he could do & what he couldn't. Our troops were so elated by the removal of Hooker, both generals, line officers & men, & by the feeling that they were on their own soil, that perhaps they deserve fully as much credit as the generalship of Meade. I don't know, however I am afraid Meade would hardly have conducted an invasion into Va. as well.

I find I am getting a good deal longer than I meant to be, so I will conclude with asking you to thank mamma for the things she sent. Mrs. Kelly was delighted & the tobacco for me came just when I was starting on the march without any. You can imagine what a godsend it was.

I suppose you have all been suffering a great deal of anxiety, but how thankful you must be now that certainty doesn't bring you

[8]Maj. Gen. George G. Meade replaced Hooker as commander of the Army of the Potomac on June 27. Here Abbott refers to the action of July 2, which was the second day of the battle but the first day the 20th saw action.

Maj. Gen. George G. Meade. *Courtesy USAMHI.*

the same grief that the Ropes family have. God grant we may have no bad news from Fletcher.

My love of course to all the family including George [Perry] & Mary Welch. . . .

Your aff. son,

H. L. Abbott

Warrenton Junction, Virginia, July 27, 1863

My Dear Papa,

I have gotten two of your letters together . . . & as we are lying by a day I seize the opportunity to write.

Shepherd has gone home on the conscription detail & has promised to go into the invalid corps immediately. I agree [with] you in every bit of what you say about the mob and the conscription act.[9] I have all along believed that the courts must pronounce it illegal & consequently have never indulged as others do in dreams of seeing these poor old battered regiments filled. The loathing you express for those miserable reptiles, I have always expressed here openly, & while Col. Hall & Gen. Gibbon & Hancock were here there was no danger, but now they have got a fellow named Smith to command the brig., which by the way only has 450 muskets in it.

An administration tool, named Harrows [Brig. Gen. William Harrow], a western col. promoted for a bloodless skirmish out west ostensibly, but really for cursing rebels, is here in command of the division, having been assigned to a vacant brig. & taking the division, after Gibbon went, as the only general officer in it. He toadies the men & calls them boys. He had some trouble with me & I was the means of getting him snubbed handsomely by the corps commander Hays (who by the way is an old woman but a gentleman.) He avenged himself by putting me in arrest for sending a sick man ahead of the regiment, when we were coming back through Manassas Gap. There were no ambulances & the soldier must have been gobbled, if I hadn't taken the responsibility of sending him ahead, though of course I violated the law that no soldier should leave the regiment except to be put in the ambulances. Harrows could have found plenty of comdg. officers who allowed dozens of their men to straggle *to the rear*, but he gained his object in insulting me.

[9]On Mar. 3, 1863, the first effective draft act in U.S. history was signed into law by President Lincoln. This action brought about a number of riots, the worst of which occurred in New York City, July 13–15, 1863.

However, before night, he was forced to release me & to write a letter that amounted to an apology wherein discipline was spelt *diss* & double negatives were plenty. I think we shall get rid of him soon. . . .

Col. Hall, who I very much fear has the consumption, has two months' leave & is going through Boston. I know that if you can see him, you will show him all the attention possible, for he has been to us . . . the kindest superior, as well as the greatest and ablest we have ever had. He had been very ill the whole campaign, & I am afraid will hardly pull through, at least so as to be in the field again.

I don't think I have ever before been glad to hear that you were going into politics but now I agree with you that it is your duty. The vilest rowdies in New York have shown the fruit of Lincoln's teachings, & if resistance to tyranny is to come only from them, why then despotism will surely triumph as preferable to anarchy. I agree with you fully that the next election alone can save the country. I wish to God it could come now. They still have time to destroy us. Wouldn't it be glorious for you to get it next time, & for the people to overthrow these weak, cowardly rulers all in a lump[?] Hurrah for the time when we shall have our heels on their necks, particularly in Massachusetts. Tell them of the Copperhead regiment that lost over one half of the enlisted men, & 10 out of 13 officers. Not an abolitionist in it, with the exception of one officer. Uncle John Sedgwick says he is a Copperhead too.

About Meade I hardly know enough to form an immediate opinion. I can hardly tell yet whether he *is* Wellingtonian or simply apes it. But I do know that he fought the battle with 70,000 against 100,000.[10] (By the way, your summing up of the battle and its results is just what all sensible men out here think), that it would have been madness to attack the tete de pont of the rebels, as besides the intrenchments the positions of Gettysburg would have been precisely reversed. . . .[11] I certainly feel great confidence in him as do most others, though no enthusiasm. He hasn't had a cheer, so far as I can learn.

I don't think we shall fight soon, as with our reinforcements we have only some 60,000 men. Our corps has only 4500 muskets, & there are only 7 other corps. It is hard work to make it come higher

[10]Actually, the Union troops numbered approximately eighty-five thousand to the Confederates' sixty-five thousand.

[11]Meade had fallen under criticism for not attacking the Confederates' fortified bridgehead on the Potomac during their retreat from Gettysburg.

than 50,000 infantry & artillery & perhaps the cavalry corps will make another 10,000. Col. Hall can tell you, unless he thinks it wrong to say out of the army. The men in the ranks believe we have 20,000 men in our corps, as far as I can learn from some intelligent men. I shall write to Riddle as soon as I can, also another letter to Mrs. Paine.

Your aff. son,
H. L. Abbott

Don't stay and gloom at the Parker's House all the time, or you won't have all your energy for the slaughter of the loyalists. . . .

Near Warrenton Junction, Virginia, July 27, 1863

My Dear Mamma,

I haven't yet thanked you for your kind offers to come on for me in case I should be ill & for writing me so often since the battle while I have replied so rarely. But I do now most sincerely. And what I know will please you more, I tell you that I am in the most stunning condition. Campaigning in this country is nothing to the Peninsula, & now that I am mounted, it is a mere joke.

Be very sure & tell me in every letter all you can hear of Herbert Mason's condition. Your last letter saying he was out of danger was the best news we have had for a long time. We were beginning to get terribly anxious for him.

John Ropes writes me that they are most grateful to you & papa for the kindness you have showed them since Henry's death. I have written to him another letter & am trying to find Henry's sword. I feel extremely sorry about it, for I took the greatest pains to send it home. I am in hopes it may turn up yet.

You oughtn't . . . let the governor gloom away there at the Parker House. By the way, if you have a chance, show all the attention you can to Col. Hall. He has, I fear, the consumption, & is going through Boston to the mountains. He suffered very much during the campaign, but bore up through every thing, battle & all, with as much self control as I have witnessed. One of his last orders on the field caused the annihilation of a rebel brigade advancing on our left. After the battle was over he was so much exhausted that he couldn't stand up.

Hasn't Mary Welch got my letter? I wrote her long ago, telling all I know. I have no doubt she misses poor Tom very much, but I fancy she is mistaken in supposing herself in love with him. . . . I have written John Revere, the same time I wrote to Ropes. Do you know whether he got the letter? I have also written Aunt Elizabeth & Riddle. How is old John [Perry]?[12] Every body out here is anxious to know, & if I didn't know that he hated letters, I should write him. Let any body who does tell him that Bessie is all right, & is comparatively well taken care of. . . . If he wants to sell her, I may be able to sell her, though not for the price he gave.

Tell Sam I am very much obliged for [the] cap & patent sun . . . protector. . . . I am delighted to hear that he has got into the sophomore class. Did he get any conditions? I trust he won't make as big a fool of himself as I did when I was a sophomore.

I am glad to hear that you are getting your picture taken. I hope it does do you justice, for there is nothing more disagreeable than to have a poor likeness about. It is as ridiculous a thing as sour sugar, or sweet lemons. . . .

Your aff. son,
H. L. Abbott

Warrenton Junction, Virginia, July 28, 1863

My Dear Oliver [Holmes],

You know I am not much of a hand at the emotions, but I was inexpressibly gladdened and at the same time saddened at getting your letter last night. I believe your letter made me feel blue not merely because it called up Ropes & Mason & you & myself as we used to be at Falmouth, but because any thing which breathes such sincere friendship makes me soberer than usual. Henry Ropes' loss I felt as I should a brother. Such a pure hearted, generous and brave a gentleman I shall never meet again. I think Col. Hall was exactly right in saying Henry had the real flame of patriotism & not the newspaper stuff that makes most of us fight. Think how he would have gloried if he had lived to see that victory.

I wish you could have been with us. By jove, it was worth all our defeats. You don't know what I would give for a long talk with you & I'll bet I would have my share of it, too.

I think the army has great confidence in Meade. I hear no disparaging stories such as circulated about Hooker. That yarn about the council of war had just enough truth in it to be a damned lie. I have been hesitating some time about asking you to write a 20th song, Col. Hall, brig. colors (which are red, white & blue), Ropes & the

---

[12]Perry severely injured a leg during a riding accident just prior to the Gettysburg campaign.

Capt. Oliver Wendell Holmes, Jr., future associate justice of the U.S. Supreme Court, was perhaps the closest friend of Henry L. Abbott. He would be wounded three times during the war. *Courtesy USAMHI.*

other dead. Something which would make a man thrill you know. But I suppose you have still too much of the lassitude of an invalid. I know what that is, & so I shan't be angry if this isn't answered within 30 days, but beyond that time beware!

"No more at present from your"

Affectionate friend,
H. L. Abbott

Near Warrenton Junction, Virginia, July 28, 1863

My Dear Aunt Eliz.,

I have only time to send you a word, to send you greeting after my late escape, when so many whose loss is hard to bear, went down.

There is but little left of the poor old 20th and all my dearest friends were killed or wounded. The carnage was terrible, but I don't think we shall have another immediately. We are lying quietly for 2 or 3 days near Warrenton Junction, so invested by guerillas that it is unsafe to travel without an escort even to the station, a distance of barely 2 miles. Lots of men were gobbled up on the march here, within half a mile of the column, by these fellows who live round here.

It is a very desolate country, not a thing to be had for love or money, the people squalid & the houses contemptible. Very different from Maryland, where we had the fat of the land. Give my love to all my friends & believe in your aff. nephew,

H. L. Abbott

Near Morrisville, Virginia, August 7, 1863

My Dear Papa,

I enclose a check for $160, the amt. I send from my pay.

You have no idea how much delighted I was to get another letter from you. I hadn't at all expected an answer, because I know how much a person who has to write a lot of business letters hates to waste his leisure writing what could be said in so much shorter time & . . . because I know you like to get letters, but not to be haunted by the spectre of answering them. And I don't want you to. Don't do it at all with the idea that I shall expect it. If you are glad to get my letters that will be quite enough.

I opened yesterday & read some ten *New York Worlds* which had come on the march when I had no time to read them & which I had preserved until yesterday, the first moment I had fairly got ahead of the business on hand. Out of one of them dropped a picture of little

Arthur. It is really beautiful & I feel your kindness in sending it to me. Poor little fellow, one can't help feeling sad to look at it, though it is so pleasant to have it.

I also got the *Vox Populi*[13] with verses about Ned by young Greenholgh. And I noticed in the paper an obituary over some man of his company who went out with him, almost the last one of the original left, following his old commander to the grave.

The day after the battle of Gettysburg, I went to the hospital of the 12th Corps & saw some of Ned's old sergeants, who were lying there wounded.[14] It brought up before me Ned & his company as I last saw them in winter quarters at Frederick, so strongly as to be almost too much for me.

The 2nd I hear has gone to New York. I sincerely hope that they won't be mixed up in any of those rows. It is very unfashionable to say so in the army, for such is military training that the very same men who damn all abolitionists, & all the ruling party, join in the same cry about the actual delight they would feel in charging the mob [of draft rioters], after a volley of musketry, to see how they would go down. It isn't, of course, the desire to suppress the mob merely, in which every body agrees, but it is the intense delight professed at the chance of opposing their organized skill & strength against the anarchy of the mob, & seeing how quickly the side of order would prevail. It is a professional feeling. . . . However there is nothing I should dread so much as any of this business of shooting Northerners when there are so many chances of getting one's belly full down here.

We breathed freely when we heard at last from mamma that Herbert Mason was out of danger. Poor fellow, he must suffer terribly. It was very kind indeed of you to take my letter to Herbert; I didn't know his address & don't now & so am going to send to you to send to him a box of photographs belonging to him which he may want at home, & certainly can't want out here, retaining one for myself.

I have written the governor [of Massachusetts] in reference to promotions, saying which was all that an inferior could, that I made my nominations on the basis of Macy being made col. & Holmes lt. col.[15] By the way, papa, Holmes is one of the best friends I have. & I assure you I should a thousand times rather see him in the place his

---

[13] A Lowell newspaper.

[14] The 2d Mass. was now a part of the Twelfth Corps.

[15] Though not included in this book, Abbott's letter to Governor Andrew, dated Aug. 6, 1863, is among the *Executive Dept. Letters* (vol. XXIII, no. 106) at the Massachusetts State House Archives, Boston.

rank entitles him to have, than to have him offer it [to] me, for of course I should only return it to him.

If you should see H. Mason, tell him that I have recommended Milton, who is coming back, [Thomas] McKay & [William H.] Walker for captains, Perkins having voluntarily waived promotion in order to keep the adjutancy, & Riddle having promised to withdraw his commission, & Schmidt having resigned.

Harrow is the name of the brute, but he has since been awfully gracious to me, though I can never make up my mind to take my hat off to such a fellow, the usual salute to a general officer.

Col. Hall from all I hear, will never come back, & I am afraid has a short lease of life. He has borne his sufferings as nobly as any man that ever lived.

I hope you will get Fletcher home soon. I don't know how he will ever cease his extravagancy. I am afraid he is one of those who will get along, without stopping it. Still I don't think he will ever go to ruin by any means; he has at bottom a large fund of good sense & great sagacity. I believe [he] will pull through all right. He didn't have college, you must remember, to sow his wild oats in & his style is certainly much less objectionable than that of some others. . . .

Your aff. son,
H. L. Abbott

Near Morrisville, Virginia, August 7, 1863

My Dear Mamma,

I was delighted to hear by your letter that Herbert Mason was all out of danger. I had heard very disagreeable rumors about him & we were all exceedingly anxious. I am very much obliged to you & the governor & Carry for taking so much pains to find out & report about him. Tell him from me & he will know that it is no blowing, that after he was wounded the regiment behaved so nobly & that most of the dead were taken from the place where the rebels burst in. I'll have a long talk some time with him & tell him all about it.

Poor Shaw.[16] He was too good a fellow to be sacrificed for an experiment, & an experiment I think that has demonstrated niggers won't

---

[16]Robert Gould Shaw, recently promoted colonel of the 54th Mass. Colored Infantry, was killed on July 18 in an ill-fated attack on Battery Wagner, Morris Island, S.C. Though the 54th, which led the assault, managed to make it to the fort, they were cut to pieces while attempting to hold their position. A Rebel defender wrote that Shaw was "as brave a colonel as ever lived," and stated that his men were "as fine-looking a set as I ever saw."

fight as they ought. For I am satisfied they went back on their officers at the first shot. Their losses were so great because they couldn't [advance] in time. Though their losses are terribly exaggerated, as they naturally would be down there where they are green at fighting. [17]

We are lying here very idle, very hot in a large, open & grass [covered] plain, not a tree here, but delightful on account of the grass. Peninsula mud at first & blinding sand afterwards, make this style of campaigning seem like an everlasting picnic. We shall probably be here some time, though we may move to Falmouth. Certainly, if we stay here, our railroad will be bothered unless our cavalry is very active.

Remember me to all my friends at Princeton & give my love to the family.

Your aff. son,
H. L. Abbott

Morrisville, Virginia, August 17, 1863

My Dear Papa,

I have got the stockings, stamps & sponge which last is such a magnificent article that it excites the admiration of all the neighborhood. I take by means of it, a regular shower bath every morning. I am much obliged to you for taking the photographs over to Herbert Mason. I feel your kindness in taking so much trouble when you are so busy. . . . Did you see Herbert? I am told that nobody is admitted. What a terrible prospect that hip disease is. It means, I suppose, a life long lameness, a thousand times worse than if he were to lose his leg. Poor old fellow, he must suffer terribly, particularly in hot weather. I am glad to hear from you that he is cheerful, for he is naturally rather inclined to worry & I was afraid he might get low spirited & so do himself injury.

Dear old Ned, I wish he could have lived. I can't think now of him lying on that field, unable to speak, & turning his eyes to the soldier that spoke to him, without being a good deal unmanned. He could now be col. of the 2nd & would have had a chance to show, in a larger sphere than he had, those abilities to command men, to overcome obstacles, [and] that tremendous . . . force and will, which I believe he possessed in a more extraordinary degree than any other

[17]Abbott's view of black troops was shared by many Northerners. As it turned out, however, the 54th Mass., as well as many other black units, performed nobly under fire.

Capt. Herbert C. Mason (on crutches) and Capt. Henry L. Patten (seated). Both officers were wounded at the Battle of Gettysburg. Mason's wounds would force him to resign from the service in March 1864. Patten would return to the army, only to be mortally wounded at the Battle of Deep Bottom in August 1864. *Courtesy USAMHI.*

man I have ever met. But as you say, I suppose it is all for the best. At any rate that is the only consolation.

As for Holmes senior, I agree with you fully, that he is a miserable little mannekin, dried up morally & physically, & there is certainly nothing more aggravating than to have such a little fool make orations & talk about traitors & the "man who quarrels with the pilot when the ship is in danger" &c, &c. But for all that, his son is a good fellow & remember is 6 feet high.

I am delighted to think Fletcher is coming. Think of two majors in the family, for I think I shall get to a majority sooner or later, if I don't get bowled out of course.[18] I have never yet thanked you for buying the degree which enables me to sign myself

Your aff. son,
H. L. Abbott, A.M.[19]

Near Morrisville, Virginia, August 20, 1863

My Dear Old Oliver,

Let me congratulate you 10,000 0000 times on your promotion.[20] But don't hurry out. We don't expect you for two months yet. Ain't it bully to be lt. col.? Do you feel proud? Will you speak to a poor devil of a capt.? I expect whenever Shepherd resigns to get the majority, at least I don't see how it can well be otherwise. But I am in no hurry, because I can't get mustered. You can be mustered as soon as Macy is, & I think he can be as soon as he gets out here, whether the regiment has the requisite number, 800, or not, on account of his being so well known.

Pray write & tell me how your foot is; you said nothing about it in your last. I myself am getting over a rather bad cold, so you must excuse me for not writing a longer letter.

Your aff. friend,
H. L. Abbott

[18]There was some talk of Fletcher being promoted to major, although it never came about. Still suffering from chronic diarrhea, Fletcher was then preparing to return home on furlough.

[19]From 1642 to 1869, the master of arts degree was awarded to Harvard graduates three years after the date of their bachelor's degree. In order to receive the advanced degree, however, the alumnus was expected to stay out of trouble and pay a nominal fee.

[20]Though commissioned lieutenant colonel, Holmes would never be mustered at that rank. When he finally returned to the army in Jan. 1864, he was placed on detached duty and assigned to the staff of Brig. Gen. Horatio Wright, commander of the First Division, Sixth Corps.

464 *men* borne on the rolls, or absent. You could be mustered as lt. col. immediately were it vacant.

Near Morrisville, Virginia, August 27, 1863

My Dear Papa,

I have been quite ill for the last week or two. I am just getting energy enough again to answer the letters which have accumulated. . . . You can hardly imagine how much we were transported by finding that Macy & Holmes had got their dues. That nasty little cur of a Riddle, who has been spreading about reports to Macy's discredit in the late action, also started the story that a regular officer was going to be put in [as colonel].

By the way, I wish you would refuse to receive Riddle any more. I have always known him to be a disgusting toady, & I think that since he has uttered these terrible calumnies against Macy, prudence alone demands that he be kicked out of the society of decent men. I am going to have him & Putnam transferred immediately to the invalid corps. They have long ago forfeited every title to consideration, & there is no reason why they should encumber us any longer when there is a corps got up for men in their condition, on purpose to remove the burden from regiments in the field. Shepherd's papers have gone up & I expect pretty soon to get the majority.

Fletch is a long time about getting home. But now that he has got through so much, I have no fears. He will land on his feet certainly. Just think of Major Fletch Abbott! His harum-scarum humour & wit seem to have been as fully appreciated as in the 2nd in days gone by. . . . He can't but miss Ned & more unconsciously I expect, than to his own knowledge. There is a support gone & nothing to take its place. . . .

I had almost forgotten to say that we have some 180 substitutes, a very decent lot of men, though some rogues. Riddle has no more to do with picking them out than the man in the moon.

Your aff. son,
H. L. Abbott

Near Morrisville, Virginia, August 27, 1863

My Dear Mamma,

I have just written the governor & find that I am still weak & leaning over gives me a crick in the neck, so this letter will be a short one. I am just getting over an attack of my last year's fever but

I knew it this time & headed it off. Thank God! During the heat of the day, the fever [is] some what distressing as well as sleeplessness at night, but I am now well-over it, with only the loss of superfluous fat, which you know I possessed in abundance.

Pray tell Mr. Spooner that I can't thank him enough for his kindness & thoughtfulness in the matter of the claret. It would be particularly grateful just now, when a fellow is run down, but there is no express, though there will be soon, I think.

There is positively nothing to say. I send a picture of Dr. Hayward for my collection kept by Carry.

Tell George I have been sick ever since getting his letter but shall now answer it very soon. The old fellow must keep his spirits up.

Your aff. son,
H. L. Abbott

Dr. Nathan Hayward, surgeon of the 20th Mass. *Courtesy USAMHI.*

NINE

JUST WHERE I OUGHT TO BE

Mitchell's Station, Virginia,[1] *September 4, 1863*

My Dear Father,

   . . . I suppose all letter writing is particularly odious to you now, that is, unless you have got over your influenza. I know, now that I have business to attend to, how provoking it is to be kept ill, particularly with so disagreeable a thing as influenza. It seems to be as contagious as the dysentery is here. These deuced cold nights pull down the men considerably, though the officers escape [by] sleeping so much warmer.

   We are very comfortable here indeed. But it is extremely annoying to have one half your men on picket, & one half just off, so that you have nobody to drill, especially when it is so needed by these conscripts. These fellows have been deserting terribly, particularly the Dutch & French. Out of 200 drafted men for this regiment, 180 came here, 30 have deserted & 40 have gone to the hospitals, ill of diseases which they had when they came on. . . .

   This drafting business is, every where through out the army without an exception, so far as I can learn, acknowledged to be a most lamentable failure. Though all the men obtained are in reality $200 volunteers, the circumstances attending have left them without any of the pride, self respect & honor which even the worst of the volunteers felt at being elevated by the press and the nation . . . into an heroic volunteer for the defence of his fatherland.

   Desertion in the field & worst of all, desertion to the enemy, was almost unknown before this jumble of French, Italians, Germans, & in some cases, *Chinese* came to us. Now the orders are never to put a conscript on outpost without an old man in his company. Very bad

---

[1]Located on the Orange and Alexandria Railroad, between the Rappahannock and Rapidan rivers. The Confederates were then encamped near Orange Court House, south of the Rapidan.

to have one half your army guarding the other half, but very admirable for the veteran party, since it puts him right on his taps. I think upon the whole, our new men will fight decently, unless we should get "flanked", since discipline is socked into them from the old soldiers as well as the officers.

There seems to be no chance of the army leaving here, until Lee is reinforced & attacks or we do so. . . .

Your aff. son,
H. L. Abbott

By the way, weren't you, as mamma suggests, a little premature in buying those [shoulder] straps, for which I am ever so much obliged to you? The commission doesn't come while others are issued to all the other regiments. I have begun to give it up.

Mitchell's Station, Virginia, September 4, 1863

My Dear Mother,

I hope by this time you are entirely over the illness you had. What with Carry & the governor down with the influenza, & yourself recovering from your illness, I should think you were having a rough time of it. Though it is painful to the governor, I should think it might be beneficial in making him give up the oppression of his business a while.

What do you get an ugly picture for? It seems to me the only object of a picture is as a likeness. If it is not a likeness, you might as well invest in a portrait of Queen Bess or any body else.

Tell Grafton & Holker I shall expect a letter as soon as they learn to write at their new school. I have not heard from you how the spot where Ned fell is marked. I have avoided going over there until I could find the spot.[2]

This Stone who sold the house at Grantville to the governor is [an acquaintance] of Perkins. He says the house is a most picturesque old place, a sort of an English appearing pile, if he remembers the right one.[3]

We are still at our old place, down under the guns of the enemy. Each man having only one night in. Very rough, considering that it deprives us of nearly all chance to drill our new men.

[2] Abbott was then encamped just five miles from the Cedar Mountain battlefield.
[3] Abbott's father had recently purchased a summer cottage in New Hampshire.

Most amusing scenes occur here on the picket line. When we first came, we relieved some foolish cavalry, who had been shooting away at the rebel pickets constantly, notwithstanding the latter desired the old fashioned plan of civilities. But when we came down, we obstinately refused to return a shot, though the rebs made it very hot for several days, wounding several officers & men of the division, two or three of the latter from our regiment. Finally however, they stopt too, & the [Rapidan] river, only ankle deep in many places, a merely conventional barrier, was soon crossed. In fact, they have all along had posts on our side.

Now things have come to such a pitch that it is hard to say whether they are most ludicrous or disgraceful. Of course, the orders are very strict to prevent all intercourse, & it is the duty of the officer of the day to enforce these orders. You see the officer of the day riding at full tilt on a group of our men & rebs playing cards. The party scatters, & the of. of the day chases the fleeing rebs with his drawn sword, while occasionally some that escape his eyes stay on this side & laugh at his efforts.

The confusion of pickets was awful. Ours was the only regiment that obeyed orders & kept them back. The other day, it is said, the rebs on this side, who had been permitted notwithstanding orders to come over & get some pumpkins out of a garden occupied by our posts, refused to obey our officer of the day when told to leave, on the grounds that they couldn't recognize an officer of the day without his sash. . . . In fact, ferocious as the quarrelers at home are, Sumner et. [al.], the fighters out here fraternize frightfully. Desertions on both sides are consequently numerous. Day before yesterday, when the officer of the day rode at a group of Jhonnies & Yankees, one of the latter bolted with the rebs to the other side, & when he was about to come back, the officer of the day coming up, he hung back, & finally refused to come at all, for fear of being punished. . . .

Deserters are shot every Friday, 5 or ten at a time, & I trust the evil will soon be cured, though privately I think Lincoln is responsible to God for the deaths of many poor men, since, until the matter was taken out of his hands entirely by congress, he persistently pardoned every case of death for desertion until the crime came to be thought trivial. Answer all this nonsense whenever you have time. I shall write Fletch soon.

Your aff. son,
H. L. Abbott

Bloomfield, Virginia,[4] *September 5, 1863*

My Dear Papa,

I got your letter yesterday. I wish I could come home. While I was under the weather it was a terribly strong temptation to take a leave, which I could easily have got. But it was absolutely necessary for me to stay. I had 4 company officers who each had 90 men under his charge, ⅔ of them being conscripts, & each officer . . . having all the organization of 2 & some of them 3 companies. Add to that, that we have only 4 sergeants left from the battle, & 7 corporals & no material to make new ones of, until these conscripts get drilled. So you see the difficulties. The men were numerous, most of them ignorant, the non-com. officers absurdly scarce, & the officers so few that they can't help getting bewildered among so many companies & forgetting more or less what they ought to do, when besides they have to perform the extra duties of guard, picket, & even courts martial. The comdg. officer of the whole has consequently to keep his attention continually on the pack, & oversee every thing. Otherwise, the pressure being so much greater than any officer ought to have, . . . every thing would go to the devil. . . .

Notwithstanding the horrible stories told by Riddle, . . . the conscripts of our regiment are better than the men that originally made this regiment, & the 19th [Massachusetts] conscripts are of the same class as ours. We have put the screws to them like the devil. We have lost some 6 or 7 by desertion, but I think we shall make excellent soldiers out of them in time, though I think it will be a great while before men who have sold themselves into slavery can be made to have the honorable & manly instincts that prevailed or were easily stimulated in the volunteer.

If it was impossible for me to leave when I was ill, it is still more so now, because I am well, which is proved by the fact of my going in command of the regiment to Banks' ford [on the Rapidan], a distance of 17 miles. We came back yesterday, starting at 6 P.M. & getting in at 2 A.M. Night marches are very fatiguing, even when you are mounted, & you may be sure that a man who can stand them is a well man.

I agree with you fully in what you say about charity, & I also think as a rule that it is foolish to make a man an enemy, simply because he is your friend's enemy. But in Riddle's case, it is different. In calumniating Macy, I think he has passed the bounds, & no

[4]Abbott added a footnote to this letter indicating that Bloomfield, Va., and Mitchell's Station were the same place.

mercy should be shown [to] so contemptible [a] fellow—however you know best about it. But in reference to his love for me, I really think from indications from other quarters, slight to be sure, is more an affectation, in order to carry favor with you. I don't know though positively.

Fletch I am going to write to. I am delighted to hear that both Bartlett[5] & [Brig. Gen. William] Dwight praise him in such high terms. How foolish of the boy to worry about his not being educated &c. Why, Fletch is a genius I really think. At least I never knew a man who had a brighter wit, or a keener insight into human character. And though he doesn't always act on it, he certainly has an intuitive perception of what is right & doesn't have to reason to it.

I am delighted to hear you have got back & are going to have Col. Hall to dinner. But we are all wild here at hearing that the col. expects to come back after his [leave] is up. We had given him up for good, & with the exception of Mallon,[6] we have had such a set of half-made idiots that we sigh more than ever for the col. Our present [brigade] commander is a rowdy with a dyed mustache whose great act is to tell vulgar stories & to rough the 20th as much as possible. He is Lt. Col. Wass of the 19th Mass. He is devlish green and devlish saucy.

P.S.

I reopen my letter to tell you that, thankful as I am to you for looking after my interests as you always have & offering to get the [position of] lt. col. in Bartlett's regiment for me, nothing would induce me to leave this regiment. After fighting through every battle with Ropes & Mason & the rest, & all of us agreeing to stick together, I should think it cowardly to leave now when I escaped, & both of them got it badly. I feel that I belong to the regiment, & as God has spared my life so long through great dangers, I trust he will [if I remain] with the regt., as I am the only officer here that came out with it.

[5]In spite of the loss of his leg during the Peninsular campaign, W. F. Bartlett accepted command of the 49th Mass. and was wounded in the hand and arm while leading that unit against Port Hudson, La., May 27, 1863. Upon recovering from that wound, Bartlett took command of the 57th Mass. and was again wounded during the Battle of the Wilderness, when he was struck in the head by a spent ball. Upon resuming active service, Bartlett was captured during the siege of Petersburg, July 30, 1864. Having been exchanged after three months in Libby Prison, he was promoted brigadier general and assumed command of the First Division, Ninth Corps. He died Dec. 17, 1876, at the age of 36.

[6]Col. James E. Mallon, 42d N.Y.

I am just as grateful to you, for suggesting the change, & the stay at home would be most pleasant, if it were not impossible.

H. L. A.

Bloomfield, Virginia, September 5, 1863

My Dearest H., [Holmes]

I have to make the same excuse to you as to every body else, for neglecting your letter so long. I have had one of those nasty little . . . fevers which prostrate a man like the devil without being of themselves any thing great.

You don't know how thoroughly I appreciate your generosity, my dear old boy, in that matter of the promotions. But I am infinitely gladder that the governor showed a spark of good sense, & did not allow your generosity to rob you of your hard earned laurels. I should have felt like a fool for ever after if any thing of the kind had been done.

My governor wrote me before I got your letter how shabily you were treated in being refused further extension [of sick leave] in Boston & sent on to Washington. The outrage of refusing a gentleman thrice wounded an extension absolutely necessary, stirred even his venerable bosom to the utterance of some very strong language. But I never thought the order was meant for any body but skalywags & I don't think the [War] Dept. should attempt to enforce it, except in cases brought to notice from the regiment.[7] However, as Halleck settled it favorably, it is now all right. But they certainly ought to take into consideration the worrying & harassing a fellow [goes through] who has been out & got hit where they don't dare to go.

I went over to see C. Whittier the other day at the presentation.[8] He had been so ill of the dysentery that Craw told me he had a devlish narrow squeak for his life at one time. He had got mostly over it but was terribly thin. John was there with clean clothes on & frightened to death at the part he had to perform.[9] After the rum got well going however, he recovered himself & asked affectionately after

[7]Apparently the War Department had issued an order stating that any officer absent from his command for longer than some specified period was subject to dismissal from the service. The editor has been unable to locate the original order.

[8]Whittier had been serving on Sedgwick's staff since the Battle of Antietam. On Aug. 27, officers who had formerly served under Sedgwick in the Second Corps presented him with a thoroughbred black stallion called "Handsome Joe."

[9]Abbott probably refers to John Perry, who had recently returned to the regiment after partially recovering from his leg injury.

you, expressing the opinion that you could easily floor Charley under his present circumstances.

It made me think of our visit last year & our [march] across the country, fearing guerillas & sleeping in the crawling hut of a friend and a brother. That was after all a devlish pleasant journey to look back on. I have felt a sort of brotherhood ever since. However that sort of talk is spooney & I must stop to go out on ten miles of picket line which accounts for the horrible hurry I write in, instead of my usual accurate penmanship.

Your aff. friend,

H. L. Abbott

Don't forget the song. Something like that mention of an officer killed in Mexico in *Benny Haven's*, I have always thought extremely touching, nobly warm of course. Pray try & do something of that sort.

Bloomfield, Virginia, September 6, 1863

My Dear Mamma,

In the first place, I must explain that Bloomfield is the same place that I formerly called Morrisville. But as Bloomfield has only one house which the inhabitants had deserted & which is occupied as division hdqrts., we were a long time in discovering that we were even cantoned in the midst of a village.

I can't thank you enough, mamma, for so kindly offering to come & see [me], but I assure you that although the stay-at-home "ma baby" feelings of old days was strong within me when I lay under this beastly sun (now at last departed leaving it very cold) yet now I am perfectly well. This morning I have ridden 10 miles on the over extended picket lines as officer of the day & this afternoon I shall again ride 10 miles. So you see I can't be very idle. We are greatly delighted to hear that Herbert Mason is doing so well. I am going to write him immediately. Poor old Mr. Mason must have suffered terribly from anxiety.

Col. Hall is very kind in what he says of the 20th & of myself.[10] And he was the first commander who saw that our discipline & our set of officers made us immensely better in camp & in the fight than the 19th [Massachusetts] who drilled more showily than we. And we are wild with delight to hear that the col. is coming back. We shall again have some one whom we can respect, instead of the half educated style of men that have commanded the brig. lately.

[10]Referring to Hall's report on Gettysburg.

I trust Holmes won't leave on any account & I have no idea that he will not get well enough to come back. He is a devlish fine fellow & a devlish brave officer & I tell you that the fearful slaughter has brought us down so low that we have fifteen vacancies, our non-com. officers are killed & disabled & we have no material left to make even non-com. officers out of. We can't recruit from civil life, because all the young men's mammas are afraid to let them come into this regiment.

Miss Nelly Perkins, whom you speak of, though I have hardly spoken to her since she was a girl, I have always thought would make a remarkably sensible, honest & warmhearted woman, much more agreeable than the majority of women who are prettier.

Sam will make up his condition all right. Let me know how he gets along in college & tell him to write to me when he gets hard up & has run on the governor rather too strong.

I am glad you have got back to Boston. How is the house in the country? What is Fletch doing? The young ladies as usual? I suppose by this time he knows accurately all the changes in the hours of the young ladies' school since he has gone. . . .

Your aff. son,
H. L. Abbott
Capt. comdg. 20th Mass.

Bloomfield, Virginia, September 6, 1863

My Dear Fletch,

I am devlish glad to hear that you have got home. I suppose your time is pretty well taken up with your numerous friends, male & female, particularly the latter, but I hope you will have time to answer this letter.

I was greatly delighted to hear that Frank Bartlett & Gen. Dwight agreed in praising you so highly. The governor says too that if Dwight is made major gen. & gets a corps, you as senior aide will get a majority. I shall get one probably about the same time, & there will be two majors in the family, & dear old Ned might have been col. & possibly brig. gen. had he lived. But there is no use thinking of that. He is better off as he is.

I hear you are going to New York to see the 2nd.[11] You will probably be as much surprised to see how few of the faces you know as

---

[11]The 2d Mass. was then in New York City to quell any further uprising by draft rioters.

212

one of the old officers of the 20th would, were he to visit us. We have only about 25 of the men who came out with us.

We have just got 200 conscripts, but have lost about 12. We expect to catch them & have them shot. An old deserter from this regiment, who left at just about this place when we were along here a year ago, we had [shot] at the same [time] with a deserter from the Sharpshooters . . . who are at present attached to the regiment. The fellow was a substitute and being sent out to the 19th [Massachusetts] was immediately recognized & tried. These men were shot in presence of the conscripts & yet a dozen of them have deserted notwithstanding the example.

We are devlish hard up for officers. Hardly a regiment in the division has more than 7 officers since the details for conscripts have left. The highest officer for duty most of the time since the battle of Gettysburg, has been a captain in this brigade & [our brigade has] been commanded until lately by a col. from another brig.

By the way, Fletcher, I am exceedingly grieved that you have fallen off from your faith in McClellan. Gen. Dwight's opinion is undoubtedly entitled to great respect in most military matters, but you must remember that it is a failing in all the Dwights to be anti-McClellan men. Such men as Franklin, Porter, Sedgwick, [and] Meade have always been strong McClellan men, & they are certainly among the best officers we have in the country. The great cry against McClellan's slowness arose from the too great impatience of men who forgot that Rome wasn't built in a day, & also the fact that McClellan was invading the most difficult country in the world, with an army only equal to the army of the country invaded, whereas all the rules say that a general invading should have at least one half more than the army he is attacking, to counterbalance the disadvantages of the invasion. However, they forget how McClellan was . . . cheated of his men by the War Dept. However there is hardly room to discuss the subject here, and I trust your own good sense, when you think of the thing a second time, will lead you back to your original views.

I am very glad to hear that your disease is better, though sorry that it is not completely eradicated. You can't be too careful. It is a horrible thing to get fixed on you. Make your stay [at home] as long as you can.

I enclose some photographs which I wish you would give to Carry to put in my collection.

Your aff. brother,
H. L. Abbott

Lt. Fletcher M. Abbott, 2d Mass., younger brother of Henry. *Courtesy USAMHI.*

Near Raccoon Ford, Virginia, September 18, 1863

My Dear Father,

You see I have given up "Papa." It sounds too young in formal writing, but you may be sure that it isn't because my feelings are any more formal.

I was delighted to get your letter. I am glad you are going to take Holmes under your wing. His father of course one can't help despising. But Oliver Junior, though you have an instinctive dislike to his speculative nature, is infinitely more manly than the little conceited doctor. I am very confident that he is worthy of your friendship, because a man here in the hardships & dangers of the field can easily detect what is base in a man's character, & it is particularly trying to Holmes, who is a student rather than a man of action.

But since I have seen him intimately, he has always been most cool, cheerful, & self sacrificing. And I think his action in regard to my commission is simply, entirely, a gratuitous act of generosity that would not be seen in any other regiment. He is considered in the army a remarkably brave & well instructed officer, who has stuck to his work, though wounded often enough to discourage any but an honorable gentleman.

Now Fletch & George Perry talk about him in a way that pains me very much. It will certainly get to him, & coming from my family will seem to be but a poor return for his voluntary attempt at self sacrifice. Of course, also it is very hard to hear one's friends blackguarded, even if done with the best intentions to yourself. . . .

Between you & me, that is, not to be ventilated too openly as coming from me, Murphy, though capable of being a good officer & having served with distinction, is, at bottom, *untrustworthy* & has long been anxious to quit the service. He was only too glad to get the chance of resigning in Washington. . . .[12]

Riddle, Putnam & Messer have been mustered out for absence over six months from their appropriate duties, by order [of the] War Dept. They have long gloried & claimed their full rights in the matter of promotions & so on, forgetting the sword that hung over their necks. The thread is cut at last & I think righteously. I suppose they will go into the place provided for them, the Invalid Corps. . . .

I wish you would tell me what you think of this proclamation & whether congress can delegate its power of suspending the Writ to the judgement of the executive, & whether it was meant to give the

[12]Capt. James Murphy was discharged for disability on Aug. 28, 1863.

power of suspending [the writ] over the peaceful parts of the country as well as the warlike.[13] It seems to me that if these [are] all answered yes, that until congress rescinds the late act, the president, without the people having any legal means to prevent it, is only prevented from exercising a Russian despotism by the fear he may have of shocking too much the sense of decency of the whole world, & the pride & self respect of a great people.

It is only necessary to arrest a citizen, no matter who, & by asserting that he is held for the offence of abetting the rebellion, to keep him safely until the end of the war, unless congress interferes. But any man who stirs it in Congress may be treated in the same manner. . . .

The question of the legality of the law can not be tested, & since any man can easily be charged with one of the numerous offences enumerated, the proclamation virtually puts the whole North under martial law. The extent to which the government may go will only be limited by [the president's] fear of public opinion, & since he has a large party who follow every stride with applause of the principle so long as the example is a Democrat, I don't see to what lengths he may not go. I should like to know very much your opinion.

We are lying here on a vast picket line, on the Rapidan between Raccoon Ford and the [Orange & Alexandria] railroad. It seems to have been some of Halleck's strategy to prevent Lee [from] reinforcing [Braxton] Bragg. But as it turns out we are stopped short & can't cross, because the enemy hold the hills opposite with all arms. We can't turn the position without entirely uncovering the railroad, unless, of course, we have so immensely larger a force than Lee that we can afford to divide, & while one portion holds the front, another column dislodges them by coming in on their right rear. This of course is improbable.

But the rebs on the other hand can easily turn our flank by going round our right, since they can base, if necessary, through the gaps into the [Shenandoah] Valley. In our present position, it is impossible to calculate the force of the rebels, except by spies. 30,000 men could frighten us as effectually as Lee's whole army. We shall soon fall back, & perhaps without having accomplished our object, though I can hardly think it will be Meade's fault. . . .

[13]On Sept. 15, President Lincoln extended the suspension of the writ of habeas corpus throughout the nation, so that anyone suspected of any crime, civil or military, could be arrested and held without being formally charged for an unlimited period of time. Previously, suspension of the writ was only directed toward those suspected of treason.

We have been in sight all this time of Cedar Mountain. Part of our corps, at a distance of several miles, rests upon it. If possible by any means, I shall go to the battle field. It has made me feel more sad than a man ought to be in the presence of the enemy, & I have tried to counteract the feeling, but whenever I see the mountain, it is impossible not to think of that terrible time.

I have with me all the printed accounts [of the Battle of Cedar Mountain] yet still I am afraid that I should be unable to find the place, even if I get a chance to go, which I am afraid is small, since we are merely a picket support & kept close to our places.

Your aff. son,
H. L. Abbott

On the Rapidan River, Virginia, September 21, 1863

My Dear Mother,

I have written Fletch to tell him how sorry I feel that he & I should think so differently about Riddle & Putnam on the one hand, & Macy & Holmes on the other, but I trust I have so worded it that there is nothing to hurt his feelings in the way I express my differ-ence of opinion, for rather than that I would let the whole thing go, particularly as his zeal is in great measure stirred by what he consid-ers my grievances.

I am very glad that you remind me of what Riddle did for me when I was ill at Frederick City. I am so much incensed at Riddle's last infamous act that I confess I am in danger of forgetting those things for which he is entitled to be remembered.

I went over day before yesterday to Cedar Mt. battle field, in com-pany with Capt. Wood of Gen. Gibbon's staff, who got to the field shortly after the battle & was able to point out to me the exact spot where Gordon's brigade was massacred. It had been shown to him at the time by some of the Wisconsin officers. I should recognize it by Mr. Dean's account in the Lowell paper, which I have here, even without Wood.

Of the man who ordered the battle generally & the advance of Gordon's brig. in particular, it is enough to say that he is fully as infamous as Burnside after his Fredericksburg assault.

The general position of the rebels with their right resting on the impregnable Cedar Mountain, & their lines running along other ridges & woods, it is enough to say that their position is strong by nature, at any rate for a good sized army, & if beaten, the more they are driven back, the nearer they come to the mountains in the rear which,

having a converging fire & covered by batteries, would turn the worst
rout into a complete victory. Indeed, victory for the assailants was
extremely improbable, & if gained, must be barren of results. . . .

Ned came through the wood, skirmishing the way for the regiment. The regiment halts at the edge of the wood, & Ned advances
through the field, where he is met by a heavy fire from the front and
the bushes on his right, driving him back with tremendous loss, & it
is back on the edge of the wood that he is at last hit.

When I look at the place, I think he was murdered. How could an
officer cross this open field rising towards the rebels & with his right
entirely uncovered . . . offering the strongest temptation to the
rebels to creep across through the bushes & entirely out flank him.
Think of that noble life lost by the heartless vanity of a politician
who wishes to have the newspapers say that he advanced &c. . . .

Of course, Wood could not show me the spot where Ned lay. But
only the line of the brigade. I fancied a great many places. Ask
Fletch what that enclosure made by laying rails together is. It is near
I should think the right of the regiment, & whether there is any way
of telling the spot. . . .

I think Fletcher should by all means get mustered out of his regiment & commissioned by the U. States if in any way possible. At
present, he is liable at any moment to be sent back under officers
who used to be enlisted men when he was there. Think of him under
the orders of a Lowell overseer or something of that kind. . . .

How I wish I were sitting by you at that coal fire you speak of. You
musn't bring up those pictures of home, because though I am naturally of a warlike & ferocious, & not of a domestic turn, it makes me
for a moment forget that I am really just where I ought to be.

Your aff. son,
H. L. Abbott

On the Rapidan River, Virginia, September 22, 1863

My Dear Holmes,

I hasten to write to you, not to answer that miserable little scrap
of paper of yours, but to ask if the report is true that I have heard,
that you mean to quit the service. For God's sake, my dear fellow,
don't think of it, if it can be possibly avoided.

No matter if you have to stay at home six months longer, if you
will then be well, stick to it. I want to ask you, in the earnestest
manner possible, not for a moment to be influenced by any idea that
in staying at home while you are unable to come out, you are keep-

ing others out. All that is damned nonsense. I tell you we can't afford to lose you. No matter whether your wound is going to be a great while longer or not, if there is a prospect of its getting well, you must stay on the rolls & come when you can.

I tell you, my dear Oliver, that when we heard that rumor that you talked of leaving us, we all felt alike. Any oversensitiveness, if that is it, which would make you think that you had stayed too long, is simply ridiculous. Any good officer might stay twice as long. And in your case, twice wounded before & each time back so promptly & in nearly all our battles, when most officers wouldn't have been back in time for any of them, in your case there are the strongest demands for consideration to the longest extent.

Don't be frightened by any sixty day order & be assured that it will be long in the future before you hear any complaints from a single officer in the regiment, & complaints, you know, always begin long before justice demands.

If any impudent stay-at-home wide-awake asks you when you are coming back, punch his head. They are beneath notice of any other kind. Take my advice, Oliver, & remember it is the request of all.

Let me know how your heel is. God knows that if any man has a right to stay at home as long as he likes, you are the man, & so don't hurry a moment before you ought to come out, though I should like to see you immensely. I have lots to say & if you haven't, you won't be the Holmes of old.

Your aff. friend,
H. L. Abbott

On the Rapidan River, Virginia, September 24, 1863

My Dear Father,

I got your letter tonight. I am so strongly impressed with the truth of every word you say about public matters that I can't help feeling devlish gloomy about the future.

There seems to be an awful feeling of indifference that will make it only too easy for somebody to usurp power in the course of events. Any army of aliens & conscripts can certainly be used to do any thing they are bidden. I don't see how there can be any reply to your arguments about the proclamation & your distinction between a government of men & of laws. But the trouble is [that] the large party of Abolitionists don't attempt to answer the arguments. They seem really indifferent to the danger & utterly unable to appreciate the results of the present system. Thank God, however, that in this regiment they are all unanimous[ly] on the right side. The few abolitionists in the army call this the copperhead regt. However, I must stop this, as I only wish to inclose a check.

The newspapers are kept from the army as if we were such cowards as the Washington people, but what little we glean indicates that [a portion of] the Army of Virginia has got hold of Rosecrans & licked him.[14] We can only hope that the inferiority of the rest of the rebel western army will give Rosecrans the superiority. Whenever *Lee's* army meets the army of Rose., they will surely lick them, because our two armies here in Va. know what real fighting is & the western armies never have.

After a solemn silence we have suddenly . . . struck up a great tooting of drums & horns, whether to bluff the rebels or because they have disappeared from out front, I don't know.

I suppose you at home have got, by this time, my letters stating my visit to Cedar Mt., & also the case of Riddle & Putnam.

When I was on the field where the 2nd fought, it seemed as if I could see Ned alive, looking as he did on the becan-club regatta, & then as he fell after the race was over. With Fletcher's aid, we can find the exact spot, which alone I fancied in a dozen places.

Your aff. son,
H. L. Abbott

Near Mitchell's Station, Virginia, September 28, 1863

My Dear Sam,

I was devlish glad to get your letter. I hope you will keep up the correspondence & let me know what sort of a time you are having in Cambridge.[15] You are evidently doing very well now, both in regard to your duties and your pleasures. But for God's sake be careful & don't get immoderate. When you are tempted to do any thing very dangerous, just remember that the family at home will be the chief sufferers, if you should come to grief.

Above all Sam, though there is no great harm in patronizing freshmen, smoking their cigars and drinking their wine moderately when they offer them to you, don't ever insult or abuse a gentleman, & much less a scrub, because he is a freshman. It is neither manly nor is generous to rough a man whose hands are tied.

[14]Lee had sent Gen. James Longstreet's First Corps to support Bragg in repelling Rosecrans's Army of the Cumberland. They did so at Chickamauga, Ga., Sept. 19–20, 1863.
[15]Samuel Abbott had just begun his sophomore year at Harvard.

And remember Sam, that it will always be a damned sight better to keep on the rolls a good scholar. You can do twice as much with impunity, to say nothing of the great advantage in disciplining your mind in the course which will be necessary after you leave college. I ran down & lost any chance of standing well & I found out my error & for the last two years in college, I never missed a lesson, & though I never could gain any standing on the rank list, I found it a great advantage when I began to study in earnest after leaving college.

Read a good deal Sam, whatever you like best. It is the best chance you will ever have. Above all, don't be as silly as I was to think it pretty to be hard, until as I did, you get going too far to stop. There is nothing very wicked about hazing the faculty, but getting drunk, gambling & whoring are bad. Of course getting drunk is entirely different from drinking, & now that you are growing you must look for your growing or it will be stopped.

You needn't be frightened by this lecture. I shan't write you any more, only write to you as I would to Fletch or any one. But be sure & let me know when you get into any scrape which needs either money or advice. I have plenty of either at your service.

Your class I should think is a great class like '60. Imitate it [in] every thing but its vices. You have a bully little chum. Give my love to him, & tell him to see that both of you take care of your respective muscles & keep out of mischief.

Your aff. brother,
H. L. Abbott

We are still on the Rapidan & shall probably move to the rear in a few days. I send you Sam a picture I have just had taken. You can imagine me just off a hard night's duty as officer of the day, riding for hours along the picket line, over rocks & brooks.

Blackburn's Ford, Virginia,[16] *October 17, 1863*

My Dear Father,

I seize the first chance of writing you, though you all doubtless know the news by this time. The mails are now closed, though we are so near Washington, owing to the stupid postal arrangement of

---

[16]The Army of the Potomac was then encamped in the vicinity of Centreville, Va., near Bull Run. On Oct. 14, Gen. A. P. Hill's Confederate Third Corps attacked the Union Second Corps, temporarily commanded by Maj. Gen. G. K. Warren, near Bristoe Station. Though Hill lost in excess of 1,300 men, Union casualties were relatively light.

Henry L. Abbott in an undated photograph. *Courtesy USAMHI.*

this division. Still I got your letter on the march, & one from Carry; you can imagine how glad I was. They are peculiarly pleasant in hard times. Since I last wrote I have suffered terribly from the loss of two friends, one very dear indeed. Before the war, one could scarcely feel the same for a companion, untried as those friends since made have been by the scorching ordeal of this war, which discloses all the noblest qualities of the noblest men.

You have of course heard how Capt. McKay was assassinated by a conscript named McClusky, who shot him in cold blood in the night as McKay was standing near the fire.[17] The fellow knelt behind a tree & took deliberate aim. He has managed to escape, but $2,000 reward has been offered, $1,000 by the officers of the regiment, $500 by the officers of the brig., and $500 by the men of the regiment, who felt the thing deeply, for McKay, though a very strict disciplinarian, was just the man to win the love of his soldiers. He was a devlish fine officer and I felt his loss terribly, particularly from the manner of his death.

You know, I suppose, by this time, how our corps was assailed on the march. We were in simple column of march, & the attack was entirely unexpected. Our position was speedily taken by merely halting, fronting, & lying down behind the embankment of the railroad which ran parallel to our road. We repulsed easily the rebels who came up in their usual style, 3 lines, and though our own loss was insignificant in numbers, 3 lines of their dead covered the field. The Sharpshooters attached to this regiment, who are a splendid set of men, were thrown out as skirmishers after the repulse of the rebels, & took two pieces of a rebel battery & brought them in, a very audacious and skilful thing.

It was here, just after rallying a company of his regiment which broke, that Col. Mallon was killed. Ever since the battle of Gettysburg & particularly since he commanded the brigade, we have been on the most intimate terms. I loved him almost as a brother, & while his eyes were glazing & he could no longer see me, he told me of his

[17]Thomas McKay was murdered the night of Oct. 5. The soldier named McClusky, whom Abbott originally thought guilty of the crime, was later found to be innocent. Although Abbott mentions nothing of it in his letters, the actual murderer was a snubbed suitor of McKay's fiancée who had enlisted in a New York regiment brigaded with the 20th for the sole purpose of killing McKay. Although he was eventually apprehended, tried, convicted, and sentenced to be hanged, the assassin was ordered to be released on a legal technicality before the sentence could be carried out. For the full story of this bizarre case, see Perry, *Letters from a Surgeon of the Civil War*, 80–98.

friendship. He was going towards me to speak to me when he was hit.[18] It was a terrible blow, but it seems almost as if one were destined to be calloused by these repeated losses of the best and noblest. He was a magnificent officer and a great loss to the brig.

The army is now occupying the circle round Washington & we are near the left at Blackburn's Ford, where the First Mass. fought the day before Bull Run. From what I can learn, Meade's management has been very skilful. The rebels have disappeared from our front, whether for Maryland or not is uncertain. They may occupy the Shenandoah & send expeditions into Maryland, but I can't hope for any thing so good as another invasion. I think Lee has done about all he calculated on in forcing us back, after Rosecrans' retreat in the West, thus setting the Confederacy right before the world, though every military man knows that we are a thousand times better off any time since Lee was in Pennsylvania.

The whole army, though it has suffered a good deal, is in the highest spirits of any time since McClellan left us, not only at getting nearer the soft bread, but from the feeling that they are well handled & can lick the rebels. The conscripts behaved unexpectedly well. They had got pretty well disciplined. I shall answer the other letters as soon as I get time.

Your affectionate son,
H. L. Abbott

I have been mustered as major.[19]

Blackburn's Ford, Virginia, October 18, 1863

My Dear Oliver,

I suppose you have already heard the full particulars of poor McKay's murder. It was a horrible affair. The murderer, who was in

[18]Mallon, who had become concerned for Abbott's safety, went to tell him not to needlessly expose himself to the enemy's fire. John Perry later recalled warning Mallon not to attempt to talk to Abbott: "I begged him not to, saying that he would surely be shot, but he answered, 'No, I cannot stand the suspense, and it will take but a moment,' whereupon he rose, and was instantly shot through the abdomen.

"I dragged him to a little muddy stream,—the only place of safety,—where the poor fellow lay with the water almost running down his throat. He lived until the fight was almost over, and finally expired in my arms. He was just married." Perry, *Letters from a Surgeon of the Civil War*, 112–13.

[19]Abbott was mustered as major on Oct. 10, with the commission to date from May 1, 1863.

all probability a conscript named McClusky, an ill looking fellow & a deserter from [Gen. J. E. B.] Stuart's rebel cavalry, knelt down behind a tree, & took deliberate aim at Tom as he stood in the light of the fire. It was about 10 o'clock at night & Tom was standing behind his company tents, having just sent to their tents some men who had been noisy from drinking. There was however no disturbance & the shot was entirely unexpected. I was asleep at the time, but Patten & the Dr. [John Perry], who were sitting by the fire, rushed down when the shot was fired & Tom cried out. Too late however. Tom never spoke another word.

I had the regiment turned out under arms & we found every man with a clean gun except one, who said he had left his gun standing against a tree when he went to sleep & when the regiment was turned out he couldn't find it. It was impossible to suspect the man. The missing gun was found lying behind the tree where it had been fired, foul & with the cap exploded. As soon as it was light I examined every man on oath with one hand on the corpse, but could find out nothing. The next day this McClusky deserted, & I have since received information whose author I can't just now disclose, that he was the man who fired the shot. The only cause any one can imagine is that McClusky did [it] in revenge, because he had been once or twice driven up on the march by McKay.

The men raised $500 to be paid to any one giving information which should lead to the detection of the murderer. The other officers of the brigade [offered] $500 more, and our officers $1,000. John Perry and myself took $250 apiece with the idea that you & Macy & Mason would each take $100 . . . so that each individual contribution would be $100. The young officers, though anxious to subscribe like us, we would not allow to put down over $20 apiece. The money will not have to be forthcoming until the desired information is given.

The affair was a terrible thing. I don't remember having suffered so much for a great while. I will tell you more some time.

You have doubtless heard how easily the 2nd Corps repulsed the attack of [A. P.] Hill's column on the march. The conscripts behaved unexpectedly well, as most of the cowards & villains have by this time deserted. I will tell you all about this some time when we are together. It was different in circumstances from any thing we have ever had before. Poor Mallon's death was a very severe blow. I had learned to feel for him as for the others whom I call brothers.

I haven't time to tell you how much I am delighted at your decision to stick to the old mother.[20] I believe you have done not only
what is agreeable to yourself & us, but what is thoroughly right and
proper. . . . Write me soon.

Your aff.
H. L. Abbott

Don't, even if well enough, come out until Macy is mustered because
until that happy event, you can't be mustered. I have just heard that
Macy is at the station with a new lieutenant.

---

[20]Holmes had been contemplating the possibility of accepting a commission in one
of the Mass. Colored Infantry regiments, but he finally decided to stay with the 20th.

TEN

GOD WILL BRING US OUT OF IT

Near Warrenton, Virginia, November 1, 1863

My Dear Father,

I got your short note, enclosing the stamps, for which I am very much obliged. We have all been reading your speech with the greatest delight; it was vilely reported in the other papers, but in the [extract] which you sent, I suppose it was as correct as any of yours could be taken down.[1]

It seems to me that any waverer . . . would have to be a democrat upon hearing that statement of democracy. I believe ⅔ of the people in Massachusetts today would accept the whole of that speech as true, if they hadn't been poisoned so long that they can no longer appreciate statements, which showing equal truth in any thing but politics, would convince immediately.

What you say about the soldiers' pay is strikingly true, & besides leading to perhaps a better condition of things, is a shot right into the enemy's camp. They can't deny the fact of course & if they attempt to palliate it, they lose even the vestige of the confidence of the soldiers, which they toady for so hard.

If the money had been given to the old veterans, instead of used in buying recruits, it would have elevated the soldier into the importance which is given by a handsome wages; it would have made him happy & contented, instead of feeling all the time rankled with injustice and the idea that the government were making a *bargain* out of him. Legally they knew the government was all right, but morally the injustice of paying the peoples' money to greenhorns, while they who had done so much went unrewarded, was . . . I believe, the greatest shock to the feeling of patriotism or whatever you choose to call it, the feeling in each man that he was doing a big thing & was

---

[1]Josiah Abbott was then campaigning against incumbent Charles Sumner for a seat in the U.S. Senate. Abbott was defeated.

a sort of hero, the greatest shock to this was given by the systematic way in which the government has refused to recognize the services of the old soldiers as long as they hold them fast in the service. I find I have [been] blowing pretty much what you said & of course not expressing it half so well, so I will cut it short.

I hope I shall get a chance to take Thanksgiving dinner or at any rate Christmas dinner with you.

Your aff. son,
H. L. Abbott

Near Brandy Station, Virginia, November 13, 1863

My Dear Father,

I got your letter of the 6th several days ago, but now have the first chance to answer it, owing to business of one kind or another.

The picture you draw of the condition of the country is terrible, & I can't help believing that it is true. But I do believe that God will bring us out of it. At least that is the only way one can see out of it, that He will rescue us as he did the English people in the reign of James II, by restoring the nation to its common sense.

It seems to me that the nation, from a state of routine & the most peaceful kind of peace, has passed into such an entirely anomalous condition of circumstances . . . where all that was once most strange, most horrible, & entirely out of their conception, such a series of wonders, coming so thick & fast, that they have lost all power of properly estimating them. They are struck blind. The accumulation of horrors has deprived them of the power of discriminating between the evils which they are obliged to bear, & those which they may stop by their own free will. They are like the inhabitants of a plague-stricken city, devoted to nothing but selfishness, too little generosity to care for their fellows when suffering, & too little reflection to see, too heedless & reckless to note, that the danger is contagious, & the stroke which brings down another may just as well reach themselves.

In fact, I believe that all they want is to keep straight on, & let those whose duty it is to manage the war do it their own way, so long as they themselves are not interfered with, no matter if a few of their fellow citizens are crushed under the wheels. They hate to be asked to open their eyes & look at the reality, rather than stave off all connected with it as long as they can. But you know it was pretty much so before the revolutions which overthrew Charles I, James II, & later before the revolution of the Tory party which, for the first 14 years of this century, tyrannized over England as the administration does over us. . . .

I find I have been writing a great deal, & what must seem very crude. I didn't mean to make a discourse of it, but reading your letter set me going & I have wearied you longer than I meant, though you must remember that I haven't the power of writing so much in so small a space as you. Mournful as your letter is, you don't know how proud I feel to hear from you your confidential opinions on such subjects; & your time is so scanty & so precious that I hope I know how to value such letters.

How can they get the recruits we need so terribly? The draft I am afraid took, as substitutes, nearly all willing to volunteer, though the heavier bounties & greater exertions may bring out as many more. But as you say, the injustice to the old soldiers in the field is terrible. If greenbacks are so plenty, why not bounty those who have been out here all the time, as well as those to come? This meanness has certainly hurt the cause of recruiting as much as any thing, as meanness and injustice do in every case.

We are on the move again by day after tomorrow, Monday, probably, & unless we can fight them near the Rapidan, a bootless journey. Reports are, that they have wisely left the Rapidan altogether, knowing that the army of detachments we have to leave as we advance—for every foot of the railroad has to be *constantly* guarded—& the approaching wet season, will baffle us much better than a battle, in which I am confident we should lick them.

Please excuse the length of the letter. I won't do so again.

Your aff. son,
H. L. Abbott

Near Brandy Station, Virginia, November 15, 1863

My Dear Father,

The bearer, [Capt.] Wm. Walker of our regiment, was an intimate friend of Capt. McKay, who was murdered, & comes from the same town. Of course he is as deeply interested as I am, he couldn't be more so, in detecting the murderer. Will you please listen to the account he gives you of what circumstances we know & what proofs, & let him know whether there is any case in the civil courts, & whether you can see any clue.

In haste,
H. L. Abbott

Near Brandy Station, Virginia, November 18, 1863

My Dear Fletch,

First let me again remind you that you owe me a letter, & how! I mean that you have forgotten to send the bill & that George owes me a letter, of which please remind him.

We are to march again tomorrow probably, the railroad being completed to the Rappahannock & being intact on this side to the Rapidan, from which river deserting darkies say the rebs have retreated, possibly to take a position from which they can advance on either the Fredericksburg or the Gordonsville route, according as they find our intention, possibly to go & lick Burnside,[2] possibly the Peninsula . . . as if the latter [Benjamin Butler] are really advancing.[3] The Beast would certainly be in his natural element if he gets into the mud of the Chickahominy.

Miss Lizzie Lee knows a great many secrets, doesn't she? Who told her I was in love with the most loveable Mary Welch? I am sure I never did. Let me advise you Fletch, not to be so foolish as to think of offering yourself, because you might wake out of the dream in a month or two to find it was only a temporary smash after all. I am always afraid of that in my own case. At any rate, I am glad, from what I hear, that there is no danger of it being the young Horton female. I always knew that was a slight flirtation which wouldn't last long, because the whole of the Horton tribe are of such a description, that you would soon find them out. . . .

I sympathize with you sincerely in having to give up your commission, and yet, much as I lament, your constitution has got such a shock, I can't help feeling relieved from a great deal of anxiety to find that you are out of the army. Why not try a voyage round the world, as the governor advises? I believe it would be the greatest possible benefit to you in every way. It is better than resting. You could do every thing to set up your health, for the danger of such a shock as it has received can't be too highly estimated.

What was the printed handbill against Sam, & why don't the young rascal write to me? I hardly know how he is getting on. Tell

---

[2]Burnside, then commanding the Army of the Ohio, was under siege in Knoxville, Tenn., as Confederate troops under General Longstreet surrounded the city.

[3]Maj. Gen. Butler had just been given command of the Department of Virginia and North Carolina, with headquarters at Fort Monroe, Va.

Grafton that the next letter I write him will be in a separate envelope, & give my love to all the young ones.

Your aff. brother,

H. L. Abbott

Near Brandy Station, Virginia, November 22, 1863

My Dear Aunt,

Notwithstanding you owe me a letter, I am going to show that I
am not proud by writing again before you have answered. I haven't
heard from you for so long except indirectly, that I [am] anxious to
know from yourself how you are getting on, what you are doing, how
your Lowell friends are.

I had a letter from [illegible first name] Beard tonight. He tells me
that the [textile] mills have stopped & nevertheless that Lowell is
very gay. How is this? I thought the mills never stopped except in
very hard times.[4] I can't understand why people appreciate so little
the awful danger there is of a regular smash up. Pray God, we may
weather it but it seems to me inevitable.

It will be a consolation to you to know, I suppose, that there is
very little prospect of more fighting here for this army this season,
though I confess I regret it very much. I can't sit down contented
after the awful losses of Gettysburg & nothing more accomplished. It
seems too hard that the mud should come now that the army is in
such excellent fighting trim.

We expect soon to go into winter quarters at Fredericksburg or
Falmouth, as that is the only possible safe line, except of course the
defenses of Washington, which would be disgracefully safe & of
course not to be thought of.

Excuse this hurried scrawl & give me in return a good long letter
with news of all my Lowell friends to whom much love.

Your aff. nephew,

H. L. Abbott

Near Brandy Station, Virginia, November 1863[5]

My Dear Oliver,

I have just got yours of the 11th. Gen. Webb's request to the Adjutant General that Macy might be mustered was refused, but he has

---

[4]Many eastern textile mills were forced to stop operations, at least temporarily,
during the latter part of the war due to the unavailability of cotton.

[5]The original of this letter to Holmes was misdated as Nov. 28, for it is clear that
it could not possibly have been written then since the regiment broke camp on Nov.

sent up a second request stronger than the first.[6] There is, however, little hope I understand, of any formal request sent through army channels being granted.

Now Macy of course can't go in himself for using political influence on his account. There are too many [such] cases . . . here in the division. Hudson,[7] for instance, the other day was mustered as colonel, after having been cashiered for drunkenness on duty, being notoriously a bad character, & his regiment having about half the number of men for duty that we have, [and] twice as many officers & one field officer besides himself. But Macy's services, character, & sacrifices are not sufficient recommendation.

Moreover, you know you can't be mustered, of course, until he is, & although . . . you will, when you come out here, have the position of lt. col. in the regiment, as far as all rights & priviledges in the regiment are concerned, you will have to be borne on the rolls as capt., & legally considered as such, which, of course, would be more or less disagreeable. So if you can put your own case through politically, as is right enough for you, & as a necessary condition Macy's, I advise you to do so, by all manner of means. And don't let the grass grow under your feet.

Speaking of the latter, I am devlish sorry to hear your heel is no better. I knew from home that it was still open. Why the deuce aren't you more careful? You will be maimed for life if you don't look sharp.

In reply to your inquiries, you don't want any shelter tent. In your case, I shouldn't buy a horse. Better than the trouble, expense & risk of bringing the animal out, is the risk of getting one here, as you can get a good one any day for $170 or $200. Bring a good groom by all means, if you can get one that doesn't drink, & really loves horses. They are coming down on having servants from the ranks like the devil. I pay this next pay day, or rather lose, $50 for mine, 2 months.

We are very well off for comforts, except *soap* & *tobacco*. Your great coat was sent back in the surplus baggage the other day, in very excellent condition, looking full as well as when bought by the hero

---

26 when the Mine Run campaign began. In all likelihood it was written between Nov. 23 and 26.

[6]Brig. Gen. Alexander S. Webb was then in command of the brigade to which the 20th belonged. Also, it seems that Macy had recently returned to the regiment with the hope of being mustered as colonel. Although that event would not occur until May 5, 1864, Macy nevertheless stayed with the 20th until mid-January 1864, when he was granted another sick leave.

[7]Col. Henry W. Hudson, 82d N.Y.

of Ball's Bluff. So you don't want a new one. I advise you to get a pair of boots, coming clear over the knee like mine, at Rice's. Price steep, $25, but cheap for the article.

We shall look for you with eager eyes the first of January. Don't be alarmed when we move. It is only to go into winter quarters at Fredericksburg or Falmouth. . . .

Every body sends warmest love.

Your aff. friend,
H. L. Abbott

The first page of the following letter is missing, but it clearly was addressed to one of Henry's parents in November, 1863.

. . . Palfrey has sent on a magnificent contribution of raisins, &c, to give the men a Thanksgiving dinner in winter quarters, which I faintly hope I shall eat at home myself, but I am afraid not.

Has Fletcher got his resignation accepted yet? I don't imagine there will be any great trouble about it. But I should like to know that it was settled. Poor fellow, I am considerably alarmed about him. He will have to be terribly careful of himself. Col. [Francis E.] Heath of the 19th [Maine] has at last resigned for the same cause. He tried every thing, but had to resign at last. Make [Fletcher] look out for himself.

Your aff. son,
H. L. Abbott

Near Brandy Station, Virginia,[8] *December 3, 1863*

My Dear Father,

As you probably know, there has been no engagement of a general character. We skirmished & lost 2 or 3 men, but no officers. We are back in our old camp near Brandy Station—having arrived here after a terrible march of 24 hours . . . having suffered a great-deal from the extreme cold. We are now all right however. I haven't time to write a letter, but shall next Sunday, my regular time, you know.

Your aff. son,
H. L. Abbott

[8]On Nov. 26 the Army of the Potomac crossed the Rapidan River in an attempt to outflank Lee's army and attack it from the south. However, after an examination was made of the nearly impregnable Confederate entrenchments, the Union attack was cancelled. During the night of Dec. 1, Meade's army quietly slipped back across the river and moved back into its old camps. The Mine Run campaign thus ended with nothing accomplished.

Brandy Station, Virginia, December 6, 1863

My Dear Father,

First of all I want to thank you for your tobacco. I think it is most kind of you, considering especially your personal prejudice on the subject. But if you selected it yourself, I am afraid you must have overcome that repugnance . . . for nobody could select such tobacco who didn't know all about it. It has given me a great deal of comfort on this march.

& what do you think of this last expedition? If it was meant for an advance to Richmond it was a failure, as it most probably was. But if it was merely a diversion, I suppose it was as successful as necessary without losing more than the diversion was worth. Impracticable as one can't help considering it, it was I confess a disappointment to wind up with nothing done, after so many longings. I don't know yet whether the non-occurrence of the fight was the fault of Warren's backwardness, or Meade's deliberate conclusion, & in such ignorance, it is hardly fair to form an opinion.

When I think of the 28,000 men, under Warren, formed in two long lines, the men so determined that only the strictest orders prevented them from cheering when Webb, going to each regiment, told them that we had got to go into those works, & that every man must make up his mind either to be killed, [or] to go into those entrenchments, I think we must have been successful in taking the first line. We must have got in somewhere. But then the 2nd line! These are not the Western rebels, who fire a volley & run because the line is somewhere pierced, but they are men who will fight desperately. The reserves, in good order, would have met our broken & tumultuous throng. . . .

Perhaps we should have been successful. A man of genius alone could tell. An assault would certainly [have] been contrary to the methodical rules of war, inasmuch as it would have been an advance in full sight [of the enemy] for one half a mile, against a sufficiently formidable line, & probably two lines, of works, heavily manned & defended by a large number of guns, both men & guns entirely sheltered from our artillery, & the assailed men of the same race . . . have shown before, at Fredericksburg, that a little earth more than counterbalances our personal superiority.

The chances [were] apparently against us. None but a man of genius would have a right to violate the ordinary rules. He alone could say that now was the one time out of ten which was the exception to the rule. Napoleon could tell intuitively, but I think Warren just as likely to strike the wrong one as the happy, & nobody should blame him for refusing to violate the laws of war.

But I think he is to blame for not attacking the same after-noon, . . . when our regiment, at double-quick, drove the rebel pickets into their works, giving the reserve time to fire only one vol-ley at us, & without firing a shot ourselves. Then, if a line of battle, with reserves, had followed as rapidly as possible, I feel sure we should have gone over their works easily & broken their right. I be-lieve Hancock would have done [so], but Warren, though devlish fond of distinction & notoriety, hasn't a dash of genius, & on the other hand isn't a fool, but a well educated engineer, who can appre-ciate only the physical advantages & disadvantages & position, & not at all the moral superiority of men who have made up their minds individually to die, but not to run.

We were so much wrought up that, after waiting from midnight until 8 o'clock, the hour at which we were told the assault was to begin, without fires & without talk, walking up & down to keep from freezing (it was a regular winter night), it was with a real feeling of disappointment, momentary with most, of course, that we were reprieved. Macy & I, going up from the ravine which concealed our troops to look at the work at daylight, computed that 2 officers and 30 per-cent of the men would come out of the scrimmage all right. We were behind a Pennsylvania regiment whose place we should very soon have taken.

It is very certain that if our army had been repulsed, the calamity would have been almost certain ruin. The wounded, frozen to death on the field, at least ½ the army killed, wounded, or missing, the poor, miserable remnant would have gone staggering back, utterly destitute of spirit, their confidence in their leader gone, in fact, a thousand times worse than after Fredericksburg. I hope Meade won't be removed, for if the battle wasn't fought it was Warren's fault; & as for the retreat, that was precisely as necessary as food is to the exis-tence of life.

Still, I can't help feeling great disappointment that we didn't do any thing. I am afraid when I look back & see what a long letter I have written, that I have bored you a great deal more than I have any right to, but it is because I want you to see fully the disadvan-tages that we labored under &, at the same time, I can't help feeling that we ought to have charged, and it is a great relief to talk about it. If I could only see Gen. Sedgwick, I should know all the facts precisely, for he always tells us every thing, & he knows every thing.

I am afraid I shan't be able to [go] home [for] Christmas after all, but there are suspicions that they will start us off again. At any rate, we shan't be safe in going home until January.

Your aff. son,
H. L. Abbott

Brandy Station, Virginia, December 6, 1863

My Dear Mamma,

I am very much afraid I shan't get home to you on Christmas. At present appearances, I don't think it would be safe to leave the army before January, for of course it would be inexpressibly mean to lose a fight while philandering home in perfect health, particularly after sticking out here so long. It will be a great disappointment, but I think it will be the last Christmas in the army.

The next time you see Herbert Mason, you tell him that I am awfully mad at his not answering my last, also for being so down in the mouth. Tell him I think it is because he has forgotten to be a copperhead & I expect soon to hear of him following in the train of Charles Sumner. I thought he had more pluck than to be demoralized by stay-at-home people as soon as he left this army of noble copperheads.

So Sam has had his class supper. I hope he didn't get tight & that, if he did, he suffered enough after it to warn him for the future. I owe him a letter.

We have had a hard time on this last march. We marched from 8 o'clock one night until 8 o'clock the next night, 24 hours, making about 12 miles with a halt of 2 hours only. Warren & French[9] were so played out that they left the management of the march to the staff, & they left it to any body who chose to take it, so we would march about 5 rods & then halt 30 seconds & so on; no man could sit down for fear of freezing, & it was really fatiguing. We had only 4 or 5 men hit. I'll come Christmas if I can, but don't expect me.[10]

Your aff. son,
H. L. Abbott

[9]Maj. Gen. William H. French was then in command of the Third Corps.

[10]On Dec. 10, Abbott applied for and was granted a fifteen-day leave to visit Boston. While there, however, he was afflicted with chronic diarrhea and was granted a twenty-day extension to date from Dec. 24. Both he and Holmes had rejoined the army by mid-January.

ELEVEN

VICTORIOUS AT LAST

Near Stevensburg, Virginia,[1] *February 8, 1864*

My Dear Mamma,

We are back in our old camp again, all right. We were not engaged at all, but wonderful to relate were very much in the reserve & had a chance to look on & see the whole thing. The first crossing by Capt. Seabrook, who jumped his horse in & rushed across [the river] followed by a hundred men, was quite plucky.[2]

It was a very small affair as far as fighting was concerned. We lost only a couple hundred men I believe, & a few officers. I am always glad to be out of these things. It doesn't pay to lose a valuable officer & a dozen good soldiers in a paltry skirmish. Our skirmish lines went up to the works very gallantly, & I have no doubt that if it had been thought worth while, we might have captured a good many infantry & several pieces.

One regiment (a rare thing to say of any in this army now) behaved disgracefully—the "Garibaldi Guard," a beastly set of Dutch boors, Maccaronis, & Frogratecs, in short the rag tag & bobtail of all creation, little short beastly fellows with big beards & more stupid than it is possible for an American who has never seen them to conceive of. It is a rule in this army that the more foreign a regiment is, the more cowardly it is. A Dutch regiment is bad enough, but when you come to Frenchmen & Italians, you get men absolutely incapable of showing any pluck at all. . . .

[1]On Feb. 6, the Second Corps crossed the Rapidan in order to stage a demonstration against a segment of Lee's army. This movement was designed to prevent Lee from detaching a portion of his troops to the vicinity of Richmond, where Butler was planning a raid to free Union prisoners held in the Confederate capital. Butler's plan failed, and by the morning of Feb. 8 the Second Corps was back in its camps.

[2]Seabrook was an officer in Hays's division of the Second Corps and one of the first men to cross the river.

I got your letter last night & very pleasant it was, in our then rather cheerless state. I am very sorry to hear the governor has a boil in such a disagreeable place. Thank heaven that I don't resemble him in that particular, the having of boils, if I do in any others. I am afraid that not only he, but yourself are rather run down. How is this, you having another cold? This is the second time you have been ill since I went away. You must look out for yourself mamma. You & the governor being in the same box, you ought to take him on more junkettings like that to New York.

Carry must be launching into quite a sea of gayety. I am glad to hear it. It will do George as well as herself good.[3] I am very sorry she is going to a party given to that lying old ass Burnside, even if it is not in his name. . . .

Your aff. son,
H. L. Abbott

Near Stevensburg, Virginia, March 6, 1864

My Dear Father,

I am delighted to hear from you again, especially that you are in New York, because it is an evidence that, if I may "say it reverently," you are getting a little more sensible and are no longer bent on killing yourself with hard work. I don't believe any man in his sound senses ever kept up his business so unremittingly as you have. . . .

And you must be an awful bean to satisfy if you are not contented . . . with what you have accomplished. How many men, I should like to know, have reached the top of their professions, in a city famed for superiority in yours, at your age? And of course, you had much rather be a man like yourself, with such a position & a character as firmly established & much respected by everybody who knows it as the Duke of Wellington's, than have simply written a lot of books like Story.[4]

Really, you make me very indignant at such an uncalled-for attack on my father. You might now . . . go on the bench at the first chance & take only a moderate amount of work for the rest of your life. And the fact that you don't feel like working immoderately any longer is a very healthy sign. Why should you work hard any longer?

[3]George Perry and Caroline Abbott had just become formally engaged.
[4]Joseph Story (1779–1845) was one of the country's most renowned jurists. He served on the U.S. Supreme Court from 1812–45 and authored several books concerning U.S. law.

You have been doing so ever since you left college, & now you can, with a quiet conscience, knock off all except enough to keep you from idleness. There is one thing, at any rate, that I have quite made up my mind to, & that is that you go abroad with me when I go after the war.

Sam, I suppose, has got to run through his puppyhood. We have all had, or are still having it, & Sam's certainly takes as unobjectionable a style as any, don't you think so? I fully concur now in the opinion you used to express to me that all college boys are regular fools of one sort or another & they can't help themselves.

You don't say how much you subscribed for the 20th recruiting fund, but I know it must have been a handsome sum. We need it badly. I hope you have seen Gen. Gibbon. I know you will like him. Will you send me Sheldon's edition of McClellan's report?[5] I have read the one copy of it, but they say it is mutilated & it hasn't the maps. But even that is enough to show McClellan's . . . sagacity & foresight, both political & military, wonderful comprehensiveness, energy, tenacity & directness of purpose, & above all his *pluck*, never to be ruffled by any danger or suffering, even when every body else knocked under.

It does seem to me that Lee deserves to be ranked with the very first military geniuses, except that I don't as yet see any absolute proof that he is a good tactician, that is, can fight a battle better than many other generals, & still it is almost impossible to believe that he should be very deficient in this one military quality, when he possesses every other so wonderfully. What do you think of it?

Your aff. son,
H. L. Abbott

Near Stevensburg, Virginia, March 6, 1864

My Dear Mother,

I am immensely delighted that you carried out your threat of taking the governor to New York again. As he says you do what you choose with him, I trust you will take him frequently & not let him work hard any longer, for it is all nonsense he isn't obliged to. But please don't talk in that horrid way of leaving Boston. I should feel like cutting loose from my native country & moving to a foreign

[5]George B. McClellan, *Report on the Organization and Campaigns of the Army of the Potomac* (New York: Sheldon and Co., 1864).

country. It would be terribly bad too for one's relation to go from city to city in that way. People would say it was the Jimmy Ayres style.

Now that you are better, & I have no doubt you needed the excursion as much as the governor, I hope you will carry out your intentions of doing the handsome thing by Macy. Have all the 20th officers, Macy, Perkins, Walker, [Lt. James H.] Spencer to dinner, won't you? . . .

Remember the governor says you control him, so you and he can go to the fair. I suppose you could have made him come out to the army if you had come, but this is really no place for ladies. Where is Fletcher going into business & why doesn't he write me occasionally? Ever so much obliged for the mustard. John Perry brought a bottle, but we can't have too much of it, it is so good. Don't forget to write as often as you can.

Your aff. son,
H. L. Abbott

Near Stevensburg, Virginia, March 13, 1864

My Dear Mother,

Yours is the only letter received from home this week. You don't seem to have got my last 2 or 3. I am sorry to hear Carry is still unwell. She is having rather a long pull of it. What you say of George I should naturally be inclined to believe in. But John [Perry] seems a good deal alarmed about him & says that he & Marsh[6] felt it their duty to tell him plainly that he wouldn't live two years if he didn't give up all business. Now John you know is pretty sensible. They say George has tubercles already formed. Give my love to him & tell him I haven't written him for fear he would, while ill, be rather bored by it, but that if he would like to hear from me I will write him, without expecting an answer.

I went over yesterday to see John Sedgwick, who talked his democracy very openly & made some hard hits at John Ropes in a quiet way.[7] Mason & Ropes are both here, both well & I hope enjoying themselves. It is an awful loss to bear, parting with Mason, but Dr. Hayward considers it as perfectly absurd to think for a moment of him staying. [Henry] Ropes & Mason both gone from the regiment is a terrible blow.

[6]Dr. Marshall Perry, father of George and uncle of John Perry.
[7]John Codman Ropes, brother of Henry Ropes, was a noted military historian and author of several books on the Civil War.

240

Uncle John [Sedgwick] said he was very favorably impressed with Grant, for when he last saw him . . . he was drunken & dirty to the last extreme.[8] This was in the Mexican War, & afterwards he had to resign on account of delirium tremens, & used to beg a quarter of a friend, boring them to death. He is to accompany us on the Spring Campaign for a while & then go to the other armies.

Your aff. son,
H. L. Abbott

Near Stevensburg, Virginia, March 27, 1864

My Dear Mother,

I am overjoyed to hear George is so well, & I very much suspect that your impressions in regard to his illness & the frights of his relations are correct. I have had a letter from him which I shall answer speedily, & I never knew him to write so cheerfully since I have been away. The constant exercise must be doing him a heap of good.

How unlucky you all are, another sickness all round. I should think you yourself would be pretty well run down, what with your second illness & the trouble of taking care of all the rest. George says Carry frightened you all to death by word she had the diptheria. What a terribly careless girl she is. How has the governor been? . . .

Nelly Perkins, you see, has completely verified my predictions with regards to her. I am glad to hear it. Is Sam still attracted in that direction or has he roved off somewhere else? Isn't Fletcher ever going into business? I am afraid he will be spoiled & he is too good a boy for that.

We are soon going to start on the coming campaign. We shall have by long odds the greatest battle ever fought in this continent. Every battle grows worse and as this corps lost 45 percent at Gettysburg, it will probably lose 50 percent this time, that is about 15,000. It makes me sad to look on this gallant regiment which I am instructing and disciplining for slaughter, to think that probably 250 or 300 of the 400 which go in, will get bowled out.

It was very patriotic of the governor to come down so handsomely in [the] recruiting fund. It is only what every body [who] knew him

---

[8]On Mar. 9, Grant was promoted general in chief with the rank of lieutenant general. On Mar. 10, he arrived at Brandy Station, Va., the headquarters of the Army of the Potomac, and determined to accompany that army during the spring campaign.

would expect. We shall miss Mason terribly. I don't know any body that I should miss more, unless it were the Dr. [Hayward] and John [Perry].

Your aff. son,
H. L. Abbott

How is Miss Sally & the young ones?

Near Stevensburg, Virginia, April 4, 1864

My Dear Mother,

There isn't the slightest necessity for you to apologize for not writing oftener. I know what a tremendous lot of work you have on hand, & I feel only too glad to get letters as often as I do. I wish I were going to join you in the house at Grantville. Still, though I am cut off [from] that source of happiness, I think the prospect out here is very pleasant.

From what I can learn, I feel pretty sure we shall be victorious at last. I have no idea that Grant is a genius. In fact I am very sure that he is not. But still if he has only as much shrewdness & character as he is supposed to have, with the immense resources which he can command, I feel that it is pretty safe.

We have been having fearfully bad weather of late, of which I am very glad, for as long as the rebels can't move any more than ourselves, I had much rather wait for May before doing any thing. I shan't be at all surprised at another invasion of the North by Lee, unless our army is overwhelmingly superior in numbers as to compell them to keep on the defensive.

How are all your colds, the same question which I remember asking in my last? I hope I shan't be able to in the next. It seems to be a fearfully bad season every where. Our men are sicklier than they have been for two months.

Tell Mary Welch I shall answer her letter immediately, if you see her, & that I have complied religiously with her request. You haven't had Macy to dinner yet? I wish you would if you can get time. But I know how much you have to do & I can hardly expect you will.

I am going to buy a magnificent animal, blooded, with tremendous long legs & a beautiful chest, for something like $250. Poor old Jim has got so old that I feel it will be almost a cruelty to try him on the next campaign, & yet his spirit isn't broken at all. He still tears along, though his knees are so weak that he is apt to stumble & nick the skin off. Now if I send him home, will the governor keep him on the Grantville place? I wouldn't sell him any more than I would sell one of the old scarred veterans of the regiment. Let me know.

Your aff. son,
H. L. Abbott

Near Stevensburg, Virginia, April 4, 1864

My Dear George,

I was never more delighted in my life than to find from your letter that you were feeling so well. I don't remember ever getting a letter from you so cheerfully written as this. Let me thank you for the poetry also, which was heard with great merriment by the crowd.

The last two weeks have been great weather for campaigning. A constant succession of rain & snow. And very lucky for us, for our army isn't yet what it should be. Many well-informed officers talk about the size of the army as 150,000. Meade, I am told in good authority, says we shan't have a fight this side of Richmond because we shall have such an overwhelming force that Lee will have to leave. But for my part, I can't see where in hell all this great army has sprung from. In December we hadn't more than 70,000. We have only got 8,000 recruits. We have also had several thousands of heavy artillerymen. But our corps, the biggest in the army, only numbers at the outside 25,000 men for duty × by 3 = 75,000. 150,000 − 75,000 = 75,000, which where have they come from? I should feel rather [more] alarmed than otherwise to take such a mass of raw troops into battle. However I have omitted 25,000 cavalry & light artillery, which still leaves a deficit of 50,000 to be accounted for.[9]

I suspect myself we shall have the biggest fight the world ever saw. Meade of course will be merely chief of staff to Grant, but as the former has shown himself quick witted, skilful, a good combiner & maneuverer & is unquestionably a clever man intellectually, while the latter has got force, decision &c, [and] the character which isn't afraid to take the responsibility to the utmost, the union of the two

[9]On Mar. 23, the five corps of the army were consolidated into three: the Second Corps, under Hancock; the Fifth Corps, under Warren; and the Sixth Corps, under Sedgwick. Thus, Abbott estimated the strength of the army by multiplying the strength of his corps by three. The total strength of the army at the opening of the spring campaign would be 99,438. However, when added to the 19,331 men of Burnside's Ninth Corps, which, though not officially a part of Meade's army, would accompany it during the campaign, the total force would equal 118,769 men.

may be the next thing to having a man of real genius at the head; in short it may be as happy as the combination of Blucher & Gneisenau.[10] Moreover, Grant has unlimited power, & has shrewdness enough to see what he is about. The proper theory with regard to things here in Virginia, ever since McClellan unfolded it, has been perfectly understood by every body in this army above a corporal. The surprising thing is to see a general who knows it & has also the power to execute it.

This regiment, I expect, will take the field with 400 muskets and 15 company officers, the largest number since the days of the Peninsula. I went over to see [Brig. Gen. Francis C.] Barlow the other day who has the 1st division of this corps. He struck me very favorably indeed. But just think of our getting Gibbon back again.[11] With Webb for brigade commander, Gibbon for division & Hancock for corps, we have got a team that can't be beat. Poor Hall I understand is completely invalided. He was a great loss.

I think your idea of getting a house of your own is immensely better than paying the enormous rents in Boston. I hope you will be successful. Now be sure George & don't get lazy about your exercise. Keep it up one year & you will be as healthy a man as you could possibly wish.

Just think how I have been disappointed about my [illegible word] *Consulate & Empire*. When you were ill, I supposed I could get it in Washington as I wrote you, but after repeated efforts by the sutler [I] find that barbarous town hasn't [got] it. So I enclose $10, with the prayer that you will send me a copy with the speed of the wind. I am actually dying for reading matter. Try Burnbam's second hand bookseller's shop & if you can't get it in paper, get it in as many volumes as possible & send them by express, directed to me, & if you can smuggle in the Duchess D' Abantes' *Memoir of Napoleon*, I will after reading return it in the best possible condition.[12]

. . . Holmes has gone on Gen. [Horatio] Wright's staff, comdg. a division in the 6th Corps. I miss him exceedingly. We heard the most alarming rumors of Frank Bartlett's new affliction, but ever so much delighted to find that it is nothing serious.

[10]August Wilhelm Gneisenau (1760–1831) was chief of staff to the Prussian field marshal Gebhard von Blucher (1742–1819) at the Battle of Waterloo.
[11]Gibbon had been on leave, recovering from a shoulder wound received at Gettysburg.
[12]Referring to Laure Junot Abrantés, *Memoirs of Napoleon, His Court and His Family* (New York: Appleton, 1864).

I am exceedingly sorry to hear Carry is ill as well as my mother. She must be very careless indeed. I suppose however it is nothing serious, as I hear she is going to a ball. . . . It is a good [thing] George, for you and Carry to go out. You both need it. It will set [you] up in health I believe much more than to lead a regular routine sort of life. . . .

[No signature]

Camp Near Stevensburg, Virginia, April 13, 1864

My Dear Father,

I have today bought a horse for $200. Not having the money on hand, I took $220 belonging to a reenlisted veteran & gave him an order on you, which will you please cash out of my funds & send the receipt to me?

It was an awful hard pull to come down to so much, but old Jim I felt it would be cruel to put him through another campaign. His legs have got so weak that he interferes constantly & stumbles, though his spirit is just as proud as ever. The horse I have bought is exceedingly graceful, a beautiful shape, fleet & perfectly sound, 8 years old, . . . being a family horse of an officer named Hait, a New York gentleman who has been sent from the staff by the late consolidation. I am thought to have made a wonderful bargain. . . .

We are sending our baggage to the rear & are having reviews whenever there is a fair day, preparatory to a move. Grant has no particular influence on the army one way or another, notwithstanding what you see in the papers.

Your aff. son,
H. L. Abbott

Near Stevensburg, Virginia, April 15, 1864

My Dear Mamma,

I have received yours of the eleventh. I believe I have answered every one at home since they have written, except you. It is again raining, though we have had an intermission of a couple of days in which we managed to have the greatest review of the corps. Our divis[ion] was reviewed by Hancock; Meade, Sedgwick & a host of inferior lights were over to see it.

We knocked all the other 3 divisions of the corps into pie. This regiment led the column, & with glittering brass, polished belts, shining faces, white gloves & trefoils to contrast, well set up, hair &

beard close cut & clothes clean, but above all marching in lines absolutely perfect, the rear rank moving snug on the front rank and
like Siamese twins, it could not be surpassed. All the generals were
in raptures over the regiment & in fact their marching fairly surprised me. But they were on their taps, because I told them before
starting that there was one other regiment which could march better
than they. They all admired it so much that they had the regiment
up to drill at Gibbon's [headquarters] before them all, after the review, when we showed them something none of them had ever seen
before, breaking ranks to go through each tactical change, every
man on his own hook. . . .

Well, the regiment behaved so finely that it reflected its glory on
me as its commander, & Gibbon sent for me into his tent, where
[there] were nothing but general officers, & I was presented to Meade
& 7 or 8 others, who all spoke in the most flattering manner of the
20th. At the corps review, I believe they are going to trot us out for
Grant, who has just got back. I had quite a talk with Meade, who
said among other things that Uncle Abe was very tender hearted
about shooting a deserter, but that he was perfectly willing to sacrifice a thousand brave men in a useless fight. . . .

I find I have written more about regimental & personal matters
than I can hope you will read with interest, & left myself very
little room to speak of family matters, on which I had considerable
to say. Much obliged for those photographs. Can't you send me one
of those earliest with blouse & bunch of cigars, it is asked for.
Are you all well yet? Nearly every body here is a little under the
weather.

You have got another horse, I see, in place of the pony. It can't
come up to mine, which is a blooded animal & superb. I shall keep
Jim also for the present here. . . .

Tell George that John is ill, a trifling spring sickness that he will
get over in a few days. We have all been bolting quinine at a great
rate.

Your aff. son,
H. L. Abbott

There is a rumour that all letters *from* the army are to be stopped
after Monday. Won't Fletch hunt up that brown round hat of
mine & send it on by *mail* (the express will be stopped.) I have got to
have one for the campaign. Please send me one (1) pair ladies kids,
size 7¾. I borrowed & used up a pair of [Capt. Arthur] Curtis' at
the ball.

Near Stevensburg, Virginia, April 24, 1864

My Dear Carry,

The newspapers say that the mails have been stopped from the army, & so before I revel in the luxury of . . . receiving hosts of letters without answering, I have seized the opportunity offered by Capt. Walker's kindness, who is going home discharged for disability by reason of wounds in the legs, both at Antietam & Gettysburg, to write a letter home, & as I wrote the mum the last, this one I address to you.

In the first place, has the governor got the draft on him payable to Mrs. Keefe? In the second place he will receive some $360 belonging to Private Thomas Rourke, Co. H, 20th Mass., to be deposited in the savings bank so that it can be drawn when necessary by Mrs. Rourke, Sullivan St. South Boston, wife of the aforesaid Thomas. I knew he wouldn't begrudge letting one of his people attend to this, as it couldn't be sent home in the usual way.

I think you have hit the expression of the governor's photograph exactly, though withal a rather good humored objurgation. How soon do you go to Grantville? I hope I shall be home to your marriage next Autumn.

We have got a large number of German recruits, I suppose you know, who can't talk a word of English, enough to muster all our officers & we shall take the field. . . .

Unfortunately, the remainder of this letter—the last that Abbott ever wrote—is missing. Twelve days later, May 6, 1864, Henry Livermore Abbott died, a casualty of the Battle of the Wilderness. It was his brother Frank's twelfth birthday.

CONCLUSION

THE WILDERNESS AND THE END

On May 4, 1864 (just ten days after writing his last letter home), Abbott began his final campaign as Meade's army, accompanied by newly appointed General-in-Chief Ulysses S. Grant, slowly wended its way southward along the dusty roads that led to the lower cross-ings of the Rapidan. In the early hours of May 5, the Federal host collided with Lee's troops in a region of dense second-growth timber, known appropriately as the Wilderness, thus initiating one of the bloodiest and most confusing battles of the war.

At the time the fighting erupted, however, Abbott's regiment, along with the rest of General Winfield S. Hancock's Second Corps, was nearly five miles south of the scene of action, having led the Federal march in its drive to cut Lee off from Richmond. It was nearly 12 P.M. when Hancock at last received orders instructing him to halt his command and informing him of the desperate situation to the north. The left wing of the Federal army was in trouble; General George W. Getty's Sixth Corps division, fighting in the woods west of the Brock Road (the main north-south artery that led through the Wilderness), was hard-pressed by A. P. Hill's corps which was moving eastward down the Orange Plank Road. If Hill's troops reached the point where the Plank Road intersected the Brock Road, Meade's army would be cut in half and in danger of being cut up. Getty needed help, needed it quickly, and it was up to Hancock to provide it.

The Brock Road was a congested mass of men, wagons, and horses as Hancock's men marched toward the scene of action. And while the van of the Second Corps reached the threatened sector shortly before 2:00 P.M., the 20th, marching in the center of the column, did not arrive on the field until nearly 5:00 P.M. The regiment's arrival, however, could not have come at a more opportune time. General Gershom Mott's division, fighting in the woods south of the Plank Road, had just been routed, and the 20th was immediately

249

rushed into the woods to plug the gap. The fighting here was desperate as Abbott and his men met the rebel onslaught head-on, finally driving it back into the woods from whence it came.[1] Throughout the remainder of the day the regiment nobly held its ground while bullets whistled angrily through the air, clipping off branches, spattering into trees, and occasionally striking flesh and bone.

Shortly after sunset, the roar of musketry diminished to the sharp crackle of picket firing, and the day's fighting at last came to an end. The men of the 20th were dog-tired; their faces were blackened with gunpowder and their teeth and jaws ached from tearing open countless paper cartridges. Thus, when the regiment was finally relieved of its position in the front line, the men gladly trudged to the rear to try and get some rest. And that night, Colonel George Macy, having finally recovered from the shock of losing a hand at Gettysburg, rejoined the army and relieved Abbott as commander of the 20th. Although Abbott was certainly glad to see his friend back on active duty, he must also have felt deep regret in surrendering command of the regiment he had led for the past ten months.

On the morning of May 6, the fighting on the Union left resumed as Hancock's assault force, commanded by General David B. Birney, renewed its attack on Hill's corps. Initially, Birney's attack was a tremendous success. Hill's troops were routed and Lee's army was nearly cut in half. Fortunately for the Confederates, however, General James Longstreet's corps arrived on the field at the crucial moment, delivered a crushing counterattack against the advancing Federals, and so turned the tide of battle in favor of the Southerners. It was at this crucial juncture in the fighting that the 20th entered the battle. The Bay Staters had spent the first few hours of May 6 waiting anxiously in reserve east of the Brock Road, and they were eager to get on with the bloody business at hand. Colonel Theodore Lyman, of Meade's staff, had been observing the fighting on Hancock's front that morning, and watched with admiration as the 20th marched into battle. "It was about seven o'clock, I think, that Webb's brigade marched along the Brock Road," Lyman recalled, "and, wheeling onto the pike, advanced to the support of Birney. Among them was the 20th Massachusetts. Abbot smiled and waved his sword towards me, as he rode by, and I called out to him wishing him good luck."

---

[1]Robert Garth Scott, *Into the Wilderness with the Army of the Potomac* (Bloomington: Indiana University Press, 1988), 83–85.

The sight of Abbott cheerfully leading his men into battle would remain with Lyman for the rest of his life, and he would forever remember him as "a man who could ride into the fight with a smile on his face."[2]

Marching up the Plank Road toward the scene of action, the 20th was detached from the rest of Webb's brigade and ordered to deploy into line across the road. Firing from behind a barricade of felled trees, Abbott and his men bitterly contested Longstreet's advance until about 8:30 A.M., when an ominous lull fell over the field. And while the bluecoats were no doubt satisfied at having held their position against the vicious Rebel counterattack, the worst was yet to come, for during the brief respite in the fighting, Longstreet detached a four-brigade flanking force to locate and attack the extreme left wing of Hancock's line, while the remainder of the gray troops assailed the front of the Union position. Promptly at 11:30 A.M. the signal was given, and the Rebel troops surged forward. Longstreet's flank force moved northward through the brush and struck Hancock's left without warning, rolling it up— in the words of Hancock himself—"like a wet blanket."[3] Caught in a murderous crossfire from the Rebels in their front and on their flank, the stunned Yankee troops found it impossible to hold their ground and soon began to pour out of the woods by the thousands.

Meanwhile, Hancock and his staff were riding up and down the crumbling line desperately trying to rally the men and form a new line of defense along the Brock Road. Yet to do so took time—and time, unfortunately, was one commodity the Federals had precious little of. By noon, the only Union troops still holding their ground were those stationed on Hancock's right in the immediate vicinity of the Plank Road, and among them was Abbott and the 20th. General James Wadsworth, commanding the troops on Hancock's right, sensed the gravity of the situation immediately. With the Confederates pressing his front and flank, Wadsworth realized that he could not hope to hold his ground much longer. The only way to stave off the Rebel advance, he believed, was to attack it head-on, and for that task he turned to the 20th.

[2]George R. Agassiz, ed., *Meade's Headquarters, 1863–1865: Letters of Colonel Theodore Lyman from the Wilderness to Appomattox* (Boston: Atlantic Monthly Press, 1922), 94–95.
[3]Scott, *Into the Wilderness*, 160.

Wadsworth's plan was, indeed, a desperate one. And when he informed Colonel Macy of his decision, Macy protested in the most vehement manner, telling Wadsworth that such an attack would be little more than mass suicide. Wadsworth, however, insisted that the attack was necessary and made some statement impugning Macy's courage, saying that if Macy would not order the charge he would do so himself.[4] So, realizing that he could not ask the 20th to do what he would not willingly do himself, Wadsworth rode to the front of the regiment, drew his sword, and called on the Bay Staters to follow him. Leaping his horse over the breastworks, the general charged headlong into a torrent of musketry. Ever true to its nature, the 20th—with Macy and Abbott leading the way—gave a cheer and followed Wadsworth toward what most knew to be certain death.

Just as Macy had predicted, the 20th's charge up the Plank Road met with disaster just seconds after it was launched. The first fiery blast of Rebel gunfire wiped out nearly a third of the regiment. General Wadsworth was lying in the road, mortally wounded with a bullet in his brain. Macy himself had been shot in the foot and was forced to go to the rear. As a result, Major Abbott was once again in command of the 20th. In order to escape further destruction, Abbott ordered the men to lie down and continue firing from a prone position, while he himself remained erect, calmly walking up and down the line without the slightest regard for his own safety.

It was by now nearly 12:30 P.M. In the woods to the left there was a great crashing as the Rebel flank force neared the Plank Road, their bullets already beginning to enfilade the 20th's position. Up ahead, Longstreet's main line, momentarily stunned by the regiment's attack, was once again advancing up the road. And still the 20th hung on, defending an indefensible position and spilling its life's-blood to buy time for Hancock to reform the rest of his troops in the rear. Yet even in the midst of this confusion, many of Abbott's men found themselves gaping in awed wonder at their commander, who paced back and forth along the line with Rebel bullets literally ripping the edges of his clothing. Captain Gustave Magnitsky summed up the feeling of the entire regiment when he later remarked: "My God . . . I was proud of him as back and forth he slowly walked before us."[5]

[4]Henry Greenleaf Pearson, *James S. Wadsworth of Genesee: Brevet Major General of United States Volunteers* (New York: Charles Scribner's Sons, 1913), 283–84; Scott, *Into the Wilderness*, 150–55.

[5]Scott, *Into the Wilderness*, 155.

As Longstreet's line pressed on, the Rebel troops—now firing at almost point-blank range—delivered their destructive volleys with ever increasing fury. No one, of course, could remain unharmed for long amidst the storm of lead that was ripping through the 20th's ranks. One of the bullets struck Abbott in the abdomen, knocking him to the ground mortally wounded. As one might well have imagined, Abbott's fall signalled the collapse of the regiment's line of defense, and the Bay Staters steadily retired back to the Brock Road defenses, which by now had been made secure. Using a blanket for a stretcher, three of Abbott's men carried their beloved major two miles to the rear to the Second Corps hospital.[6]

Inside the hospital tent the regiment's surgeon, Nathan Hayward, examined Abbott's wound and sadly shook his head: There was no hope; Abbott was going to die. Barely able to speak, Abbott said that he knew the end was near and calmly made his last requests. All of his money, he said, should be given for the relief of the widows and orphans of his fallen men, and he asked that his parents be told that his last thoughts were of them. He then asked to be left alone so he could think.[7] A few hours later, Colonel Lyman, the same officer who had proudly watched Abbott ride into battle that very morning, rode back to visit his dying comrade, later recalling the scene in a letter to his wife: "Abbot lay on a stretcher, quietly breathing his last—his eyes were fixed and the ashen color of death was on his face. Nearby lay his Colonel, Macy, shot in the foot. I raised Macy and helped him to the side of Abbot, and we stood there till he died."[8]

John Perry, assistant surgeon of the 20th, was stunned at the news of Abbott's death, as was the rest of the regiment. He later wrote: "Harry Abbott was an ideal man; an ideal officer, reverenced by his friends and deeply respected by all who knew him. What will become of the Twentieth without him I cannot imagine; for he was its life, its discipline, and its success."[9] Others in the army also offered high praise for the fallen hero. General Alexander Webb wrote in his official report:

> Maj. Henry L. Abbott, Twentieth Massachusetts Volunteers, died from his wounds received in the advance of his regiment. He lived but a short time after being wounded. It will be found very difficult to replace him. No truer soldier was in my command. His reputation as

[6]*Lowell Daily Citizen and News,* May 30, 1864.
[7]Palfrey, *In Memoriam,* 20.
[8]Agassiz, *Meade's Headquarters,* 97.
[9]Perry, *Letters from a Surgeon of the Civil War,* 171–72.

an officer stood far beyond the usual eulogies pronounced on our dead officers. I feel that his merit was so peculiar and his worth so well known to all the officers of the corps and to the general commanding that it is not necessary for me to attempt to do him justice. My brigade lost in him its best officer.[10]

Generals Hancock and Gibbon spoke similarly of Abbott in their reports, and it is recorded in the regiment's official history that "General Meade had become well acquainted with his merits, and intended soon to offer him a position of importance on his staff and a higher rank. The news of his death reached headquarters while the battle was in progress, and General Meade spoke feelingly of it to General Grant while the two were sitting on a log together."[11] As a final tribute, Abbott was posthumously promoted brevet brigadier general "for gallant and meritorious services at the battle of the Wilderness."[12]

Shortly after his death, Abbott's body was taken by ambulance to Fredericksburg for embalming. It was then shipped home to Boston where, on May 15, funeral services were held at Emmanuel Episcopal Church. As the Boston Transcript reported: "The edifice was crowded with the relatives and friends of the young soldier, many of whom had gathered only two years before, to witness the last sad rites over the remains of his elder brother. . . . Among those present was His Excellency Governor Andrew with his aides, and many distinguished gentlemen."[13] Colonel Macy, recovering from the wound he had received alongside Abbott in the Wilderness, was there too; Colonels Lee and Palfrey, along with several other former officers of the 20th, served as pallbearers. Atop the coffin, which was draped with wreaths of flowers, were Abbott's hat, sword, and sash; "sans peur et sans reproche" was inscribed on a metal plate affixed to the coffin's lid.[14]

Immediately following the Boston services, Abbott's body, accompanied by friends and family members, was sent by rail to Lowell, where the young hero would be buried alongside his beloved older brother Ned and younger brother Arthur. As the funeral train chugged into the Merrimack Street depot, hissing steam and sounding its mournful whistle, it was greeted by tolling bells and flags

---

[10]Report of Brig. Gen. Alexander S. Webb, Official Records, ser. 1, vol. 36, pt. 2:438–39.

[11]Bruce, Twentieth Massachusetts, 356.

[12]Abbott's service record, National Archives.

[13]Boston Daily Evening Transcript, May 16, 1864.

[14]Palfrey, In Memoriam, 29.

flown at half-mast as the city paid homage to its fallen son. With a contingent of the 6th Massachusetts Infantry for an escort, the somber procession quietly made its way toward the cemetery as hundreds of spectators lined the route looking on in silent reverence. Indeed, the number of mourners was such that the *Boston Transcript* estimated them to be in the "thousands," and stated that "rarely has such a large assembly been gathered in the streets of Lowell upon any occasion."[15] The *Lowell Daily Citizen and News* reported: "On arriving at the place of burial, the band played a dirge, funeral services were performed, . . . and the body was lowered into the grave, the military firing the customary three volleys over the last resting place of the departed."[16]

Those who had the great fortune to know Abbott and to serve alongside him would never forget the sublime courage and moral discipline he exhibited both on and off the field of battle. In his famous Memorial Day address of 1884, Oliver Wendell Holmes, Jr., remembered Abbott, his longtime friend:

> There is one who on this day is always present on my mind. . . .
> I saw him in camp, on the march, in action. I crossed debatable land
> with him in every kind of duty, and never in all the time that I knew
> him did I see him fail to choose that alternative of conduct which was
> most disagreeable to himself. He was a Puritan in all his virtues, without the Puritan austerity; for, when duty was at an end, he who had
> been the master and the leader became the chosen companion in every pleasure that a man might enjoy. . . . He was little more than a
> boy, but the grizzled corps commanders knew and admired him; and
> for us, who not only admired, but loved, his death seemed to end a
> portion of our life also. [17]

[15]*Boston Daily Evening Transcript*, May 16, 1864.
[16]*Lowell Daily Citizen and News*, May 16, 1864.
[17]Howe, *Touched with Fire*, 40–41 n. 5.

Grave of Henry L. Abbott, Lowell, Mass. *Photo by Ron Carlson.*

BIBLIOGRAPHIC ESSAY

Those wishing to do further reading on Henry L. Abbott and the 20th Massachusetts would do well to begin with Thomas H. Wentworth, ed., *Harvard Memorial Biographies*, 2 vols. (Cambridge: Sever and Francis, 1866). That work contains biographical sketches of all the Harvard graduates who sacrificed their lives to the Union cause, including many members of the 20th Massachusetts. Francis W. Palfrey's sketch of Abbott in volume two of that work is essentially a reprinting of his *In Memoriam: Henry L. Abbott* (Boston: Privately printed, 1864), which was published on the occasion of Abbott's death. Volume two also contains a brief biography of Henry's elder brother, Edward. Also of interest is Thomas E. Rice, "The Bright and Particular Star," *Civil War Times Illustrated* (May 1987).

For the 20th Massachusetts in particular, there is Lt. Col. George A. Bruce, *The Twentieth Regiment of Massachusetts Volunteer Infantry, 1861–1865* (Boston: Houghton, Mifflin and Co., 1906. Reprint. Baltimore: Butternut and Blue, 1988). Bruce's book, which is the official history of the regiment, provides much important basic information on the unit that can be found nowhere else, including casualty lists for most of the battles the 20th fought in, as well as a complete roster of officers and men who served in the regiment.

Nevertheless, *The Twentieth Regiment* is lacking in many crucial areas. To begin with, most regimental histories were written by men who had served with the unit in question, or at least by one who was well acquainted with that unit. Yet Bruce, though a veteran of the Army of the Potomac, did not belong to the 20th Massachusetts; in fact, he never even *saw* the 20th during the course of the war, which he apologetically admits in the book's introduction. As a result, the history lacks the reminiscent flavor that characterizes similar works.

Bruce, however, cannot be held responsible for this, since the task of writing the 20th's history was more or less dumped in his lap. John C. Ropes, a noted military historian of the period, and brother of the 20th's Henry Ropes, was originally chosen as the regiment's historian but regretfully had to abandon the project due to the "pressure of business and the completion of other literary works." Capt. Edward B. Robins, who joined the regiment in the autumn of 1864, was chosen as Ropes's successor, but dropped the project after completing the first two chapters. Bruce then reluctantly accepted the job of completing the work.

Even though Bruce was not a member of the 20th, he could have captured a bit of the flavor of a primary account had he been able to incorporate letters and diaries into his book. At the time he wrote, however, few such accounts were at his disposal (although today an abundance of this material exists in Boston area libraries). Thus, *The Twentieth Regiment* seems incomplete, and many of the unit's battles are sketchily and inaccurately depicted. The accounts of the battles of Antietam and Fredericksburg, for instance, lack the detail that could have been provided from primary sources; and the portrayal of the regiment's role in the Battle of the Wilderness is full of inaccuracies. A new history of the 20th Massachusetts is sorely needed.

Other books relating to the regiment are: Mark DeWolfe Howe, *Justice Oliver Wendell Holmes, Vol. 1: The Shaping Years, 1841–1870* (Cambridge: Belknap Press of Harvard University, 1957), and, with Howe as editor, *Touched with Fire: Civil War Letters and Diary of Oliver Wendell Holmes, Jr.* (Cambridge: Harvard University Press, 1946); Martha Derby Perry, comp., *Letters from a Surgeon of the Civil War* (Boston: Little, Brown and Co., 1906); and John C. Gray and John C. Ropes, *War Letters 1862–1865 of John Chipman Gray and John Codman Ropes* (Boston: Houghton, Mifflin, 1927).

Of a more general nature is George R. Agassiz, ed., *Meade's Headquarters, 1863–1865: Letters of Colonel Theodore Lyman from the Wilderness to Appomattox* (Boston: Atlantic Monthly Press, 1922). Lyman was an acquaintance of Abbott's who served on Meade's staff. For battles that the 20th participated in, one might wish to consult the following: Kim Bernard Holien, *Battle at Ball's Bluff* (Alexandria, Va.: Moss Publications, 1985); Stephen W. Sears, *George B. McClellan: The Young Napoleon* (New York: Ticknor & Fields, 1988), and *Landscape Turned Red: The Battle of Antietam* (New Haven: Ticknor & Fields, 1983); Edwin B. Coddington, *The Gettysburg Campaign: A Study in Command* (New York: Charles Scribner's Sons, 1984); and Robert Garth Scott, *Into the Wilderness with the Army of the Potomac* (Bloomington: Indiana University Press, 1988).

Most of the above works are easily accessible through libraries and bookstores. For rare and unpublished studies, please refer to the footnotes in the introduction to this book.

INDEX

FALLEN LEAVES

was composed in 11-point Goudy Oldstyle leaded one point
on a Xyvision system with Linotron 202 output
by BookMasters, Inc.;
printed by sheet-fed offset on 55-pound Glatfelter Natural stock,
an acid-free sheet bulking at 360 pages per inch,
Smyth sewn and bound over .088" binders boards
in Holliston Crown linen,
and wrapped with dust jackets printed in 2 colors
on 80-pound enamel stock and film laminated
by Edwards Brothers, Inc.;
designed by Diana Gordy;
and published by

THE KENT STATE UNIVERSITY PRESS
KENT, OHIO 44242